GUARDIAN OF SOULS

GUARDIAN OF SOULS

THE SINISTER SPELL OF THE SYDNEY HARBOUR BRIDGE

VANCE A KELLY

Vance A Kelly

Copyright © Vance A Kelly 2022

The right of Vance A Kelly to be identified as the author of this work has been asserted by him in accordance with Copyright Amendment (Moral Rights) Act 2000

All rights reserved. Apart from any use as permitted under the Copyright Act of 1968, no part of this work may be reproduced in any form by electronic or mechanical means, including information storage and retrieval systems, recordings, or transmissions by any means without permission in writing from the publisher, except by a reviewer who may quote brief passages in a review.

All images reproduced from news articles, archives from the National Library of Australia.

Photo of Headstone William J Lewis from Authors collection. Image of Colonel Michael Bruxner – AWM Collection

A Catalogue record for this book is available from the National Library of Australia.

Cover Design by Blackbarn Estate P/L.

blackbarnestate@gmail.com

ISBN 978-0-6456863-0-2 (paperback)

ISBN 978-0-6456863-1-9 (ebook)

First paperback edition December 2022

Contents

Dedication		vii
AUTHORS NOTES		viii
1	BACKGROUND	1
2	THE FIRST TO JUMP	6
3	NO BARRIER TO SUICIDE	20
4	SUICIDE, A SIGN OF THE TIMES	32
5	TIRED OF LIFE - THE FIRST WOMAN	42
6	TEMPORARILY MENTALLY DERANGED	51
7	SUICIDE ETIQUETTE & FENCING	60
8	THE SINISTER SPELL OF THE BRIDGE	69
9	THE WRONG MAN	77
10	DOWN, BUT NOT OUT	87
11	SPRINGBOARD TO DEATH	94
12	1932 - A HELL OF A YEAR	101
13	1933 - A NEW START	113
14	BRIDGE ENVY	122
15	WAR VETERANS, TRAVELLERS & POLICEMEN	130

16	BRIDGE MAYHEM	142
17	WIDOWS OVER THE BRIDGE	152
18	UNREQUITED LOVE	164
19	BARRIER TO SUICIDE	176
20	THE WILD RUSH	188
21	A LIFE WELL LIVED	197
22	BEATING THE NET	210
23	CLOSED FOR BUSINESS	219
24	A NEW LIFE	226

CHAPTER NOTES   233
REFERENCES   255

DEDICATION

To the memory of the Fifty-One.

Author's Notes

As the Sydney Harbour Bridge is often personified in this book, for practical reasons I have used the abbreviation SHB or simply referenced it as the Bridge, the Sydney Bridge and sometimes as she.

Also, not to distract the readers' progress, I have taken the liberty on various quotations from newspaper and historic sources to correct spellings and in some cases knowingly include misspellings to avoid the painful overuse of the literary gesture of (sic). In the case of Chapter 22, (A Life Well Lived) it is a good example of where I have made these corrections only to help the reader enjoy the story. I have also detailed all significant resources, references, citations, and attributions for each chapter and tabled them at the back of this book for easy reference.

Suicide can be a delicate subject for many people, and I have gone to great lengths to show consideration in relation to the individuals mentioned in this book. Not knowing the complete background on each person has meant I have remained as impartial as possible in my opinions and reminded myself continually that there are always two sides to the story.

Apologies for the quality of many of the images as these are the best digital copies made available from newspapers of the time and are free to use, courtesy of the NLA - Trove archives. However, the sketchy old black and white newspaper images help give some authenticity to the era.

This has been a challenging but rewarding story to write and I am extremely grateful to my wife, Carolyn, who has lovingly afforded me her patience, the luxury of time for research, and help make it possible for me to complete this book – Love VK

1

BACKGROUND

'Sydney's Dirty Doorstep'

In 1853, well before commerce and expensive real estate dominated Sydney's waterfront, 4-year-old James Hunter arrived in Sydney with his parents from Scotland on the Windjammer *'Empire'* loaded with 740 tons of coal and 240 passengers. He would later recall as a young boy spending most of his leisure time on the foreshores of Sydney Harbour (Port Jackson), where the water lapped the sands of the bays, where he fished and **'snared seagulls and gathered cockles and mud oysters at will when the tide was low'.** Nearly fifty years later, times had changed, and the once scenic sandy bays of Sydney Harbour described by James Hunter became better known as **'Sydney's Dirty Doorstep'**.

The Harbour had become a bustling, grimy, smelly commercial port surrounded by crumbling wharves, heavily polluted waterways, and overcrowded with vessels of every description. Small fleets of steam tugs were all straining as they towed ships to the docks. Merchant ships from Great Britain, the USA and the Orient were swamped by barges and lighters transferring goods to waiting providores. Coastal steamships incoming with local agricultural products were eager to dock, unload, and then steam out loaded with a fresh load of locally manufactured goods.

The water traffic was often stalled to make way for the larger coal and timber carriers as they slowly navigated their way through the throng of smaller vessels. At the same time, the nearby shipyards were equally laboured, building sea-going merchant ships, while shipwrights and slipways were always kept busy with repairs.

The water's surface, described as darkened with bilge oil, was littered with floating coke ash, half-submerged logs and 'detritus', which is a nice way to describe human and animal waste as well as general debris.

By January 1900, Sydney harbour's dockyards and waterside warehouses had become a home for rats, and the dreaded Bubonic plague touched Sydney. The 'Black Death' as it was known in the 14th century, the same affliction that killed a quarter of Europe's population, first appeared in Sydney on the 19th of January 1900. Arthur Payne, a delivery man for the Central Wharf Company, was the first to be diagnosed. He was quarantined and later released, and luckily, he survived. Spreading from the putrid waterfront precinct of Darling Harbour, the rats had infested the wharves and carried the plague throughout the city. Within eight months, there were 303 cases reported, and 103 people were dead.

In response to the plague, the Sydney Harbour Trust was established and responsible for improving and preserving Sydney's port. With seemingly limitless powers and resources, the Harbour Trust waged war against the plague rats and quickly rat-proofed Circular Quay and Darling Harbour's foreshores while extending clean-up work across all areas of the Harbour. After more than two decades of expensive and exhaustive work by the Harbour Trust, Sydney Harbour and the waterways were revived. Sydney's front doorstep was transformed, and by 1925, Sydney Harbour was considered one of the finest and busiest port facilities in the world.

Whilst the master plan to clean up Sydney Harbour was a huge success, unfortunately, the dark underbelly of Sydney Harbour remained unchanged. Like many popular port cities, Sydney Harbour had a long history of attracting every kind of nefarious activity. At night the Harbour was a massive playground for crime and vice, a mix of opium smugglers, pirates, illegal gambling, murder and a steady measure of harbour tragedies and suicides.

Unfortunately, the Harbour had an attraction to the downhearted and those contemplating suicide, the lure of the calm waters, the night-time tranquillity attracting the soulful, with many using the waters to help end their tiresome journey. Even a simple ferry ride across the waterways of Sydney Harbour was often a setting for suicides. The popular ferry steamers of yesteryear were not just attracting the curious visitor or the daily commuter; they once proved popular among passengers bent on self-destruction, wanting to end their lives by drowning.

One such incident occurred on Saturday, 25 March 1899, when 41-year-old local publican James Ryan took a morning trip to Manly on the ferry steamer *Narrabeen*. James struck up a friendly conversation with a few country visitors who were excited and charmed by the beauty of the Harbour, as well as the friendliness of the locals, when suddenly, and without warning, James Ryan grabbed the port side railing with both hands and vaulted over the side like a gymnast and vanished beneath the swell of water. Naturally, the country visitors had seen enough of what Sydney had to offer, and it wasn't until three days later that the Water Police recovered his body. At the inquest that followed, his wife, Annie Ryan, stated that James had 'suffered from violent pains in the head' and had tried to commit suicide by cutting his throat six months previously.

Another harbour ferry victim was 29-year-old Arthur Newland. He planned his suicide meticulously and even went to the extreme effort of filling his pockets with stones and lead as extra ballast before throwing himself over the side. A brave passenger dived into the water after him, but Arthur sank beneath the water before his rescuer could reach him. Arthur left several notes in a parcel on the ferry seat stating he intended to take his life, as the lady he loved had not returned his affections.

Suicide by drowning was common, and ferries were not the only means of taking that step towards eternity. Waterfront locations from which to make a suicide attempt were in abundance in a huge harbour such as Sydney's. Milsons Point pontoon on the northern side of the Harbour was the scene of a less conventional harbour suicide. On the 6th of April 1916, Sixty-three-year-old James Edward Soden of North Sydney left a tidy pile of his clothing and personal items on Milsons Point Pontoon before taking the unusual step of placing his head inside a large bag that contained a massive stone. Soden then tied the bag securely around his neck, rolled into the water, sank immediately and drowned. Along with his personal effects, the police discovered a few shillings in his pants pockets and a handwritten note which gave details of his name and address and instructions that the few shillings left in his pocket were to be given to his landlord Mr Robert Windsor **'as I owe it to him for board'**.

There was undoubtedly a perilous side to Sydney Harbour, and the tragedy of death around the Harbour never ceased, and over time as the Harbour grew, so did the number of suicides and deaths and whilst Sydney and its Harbour seemed to be thriving, progress and economic demands meant the Harbour was due for another significant transformation.

On the 28th of July 1923, the first sod of dirt was turned, marking the start of the construction of the Sydney Harbour Bridge. Conceived in relatively quiet economic times, its construction fell victim to a worldwide financial disaster (the Great Depression), and not everyone thought kindly of the engineering masterpiece. For many, the Bridge was nothing more than a Sydney folly, and as the construction of the Bridge continued through the tough times of the world's greatest economic depression, the enormous expense of the Bridge offered little economic respite from the harsh realities of growing poverty, long term unemployment, starvation, homelessness, or those simply growing tired and weary of life.

Before the spectacular grand opening of the Sydney Harbour Bridge, the newspapers heralded the fate of the Bridge and predicted it would take on the title of the 'Suicide Bridge'. Sadly, for many citizens of New South Wales, the foretelling would come true and quickly after its completion in March 1932, the Sydney Harbour Bridge became the fashionable location for such an act. The ensuing years witnessed the Bridge take on more suicides and many more detractors. State politicians and local councillors were confounded and resentful that the glorious Sydney Harbour Bridge, Australia's star attraction, was being hijacked by what they described as the demented or mentally unhinged.

Officialdom was stubbornly opposed to preventing bridge suicides and suggested that those feeling suicidal could jump from tall buildings or high cliffs anywhere else other than the beloved Bridge. It was even mockingly suggested that a diving board be installed at a convenient spot and a fee charged for its use. The newly named 'Suicide Bridge' stood centre stage, imposing itself on the city, dwarfing everything around it, standing like a guardian over the city. Its overwhelming presence stunned the senses, and at night with its gleaming lights, the Bridge stood like a dreamlike vision, but for many, it stood like a shadowy giant casting its sinister spell over the city.

Where previously the famous cliffs known as the 'The Gap' or the treacherous cliffs of 'suicide point' at Coogee were the most frequented places to jump, the Sydney Harbour Bridge would prove to be a far more glamorous stepping-off point.

The Sydney Harbour Bridge would one day change the face of Sydney, its Harbour and Australia forever, but unwittingly the Bridge was slightly flawed and provided the perfect setting and the ultimate stage for anyone wishing to leap to their death. The glory days that followed the spectacular grand opening were short-lived, and a dark forgotten chapter in the history of the Sydney Harbour Bridge was to follow.

This is the story of that time.

2

THE FIRST TO JUMP

'A Historic Suicide'

When the Sydney Harbour Bridge celebrated its grand opening on the 19th of March 1932, the Sydney police reported that more than 750,000 people witnessed the spectacle. The newspapers may have exaggerated and claimed there were more than a million, but it was still the largest crowd ever assembled in Sydney. Whatever the actual number was, it was an extraordinary figure given that the population of the Sydney metropolitan area at the start of that year was just over 1.25 million people.

The Sydney Bridge opening was not just a special event that attracted Sydneysiders; crowd numbers were strengthened by thousands of visitors from across the country, our neighbours from New Zealand and well-heeled tourists from England and America, all eager to get a front-row seat on celebration day. So great was the anticipation that a nine-year-old boy named Lennie Gwyther had ridden his chestnut pony named 'Ginger Mick' on a solo journey of 600 miles from the tiny country town of Leongatha in Victoria to participate in the grand event. As he passed through the small towns on his way to Sydney, he was welcomed and cheered on by adoring crowds, his remarkable journey an inspiration to all and a significant sign of a very different time, particularly when a nine-year-old boy could make such an epic journey on his own. The publicity surrounding his marathon ride made him a crowd favourite on opening day, and his story soon became legendary across the land.

The '*S.S Maunganui*', the intercolonial steamship from Auckland, New Zealand, arrived a few days earlier carrying 430 tourists and three stowaways, all excited and keen to witness the Bridge's opening. The ship's Captain, Thomas Bartlett Sewell, skilfully maneuvered the '*S.S Maunganui*' through the heads of Sydney Harbour when suddenly a booming voice from a big American passenger demanded, **'Where's this hyar Bridge.'** When the majestic arc of the Bridge suddenly came into view, the American confounded everyone on board by exclaiming, **'Well, say, that looks just like a coathanger to me.'** The significance of such a reference by the big American was lost in the excitement, but only for a short while, as the name 'coathanger' would later find its place in the Australian vocabulary, and the American received absolutely no credit.

As the '*S.S Maunganui*' navigated its way closer to the Bridge, the tourists marvelled at the grey giant that straddled the shores before them, but while Captain Thomas Sewell stood in awe of the Bridge, unbeknown to him, his regard for the magnificent structure would one day take a tragic turn.

The anticipation of the bridge opening had been building for months, with schools and sporting clubs all preparing for their part in the history-making event. Official postage stamps were commissioned to celebrate the Bridge and countless mementos from ashtrays to glassware and colourful newspaper souvenir supplements all celebrating the occasion. As opening day approached, schoolchildren from across the state had travelled great distances to participate in a walk across the Bridge the day before the official opening. The excited crowd of children wandered along the vast bridge deck, completely unaffected by the poor weather conditions.

Fortunately, the following day, the weather turned around, it was picture-perfect, and a sun-filled sky awaited the official events for the grand opening of the Sydney Harbour Bridge. Leading the day's events was the historical pageant composed of floats depicting New South Wales from the time of Captain Cook's landing, followed by a vast display of primary industries representing wool, grain, dairy fruit, viticulture, and mining. As one newspaper reported, '**it should be explained that 'floats' have no association with the water as many people think is the case. They are vehicles in the pageant, either horse-drawn lorries or motor chassis on which the tableaus are mounted.**'

Once the official opening ceremonies were completed, the Bridge was handed over to the public. With over 300,000 people making the inaugural walk across the Bridge, ambulance officials were overworked and struggled to attend to the casualties among the moving crowds having to treat over 3000 people. Among the crush of the great crowd, 500 people fainted, 300 children were lost, and three people collapsed and died.

A cloudless sky greeted the harbour audience, and the noise of whirring propellers was heard overhead as aircraft performed aerial manoeuvres above the Bridge. Meanwhile, on the water below, the smoking twin funnels of the P.O cruise ship '*Maloja*' traced a course up and down the harbour, leading a flotilla of other cruise liners, coastal steamers, and pleasure boats all heavily adorned in flags and streamers.

As the day progressed, huge crowds inundated the foreshore, with everyone eagerly awaiting an evening of dazzling fireworks and the magnificent Venetian carnival. A spectacle that would transform the harbour into a theatre previously unimagined.

At every possible vantage point, people crowded onto ferry boats, sandwiched themselves on wharves and gathered on rooftops. Spectators on the water's edge keen to secure a more prized view of the carnival stood on wooden fruit boxes they purchased from a small army of enterprising young boys. Everyone was filled with great wonder and excitement by this new colossus. Finally, after eight years of construction and its fair share of controversy, the Bridge stood before the vast audience. Like a giant guardian straddling the northern and southern shores of Sydney Harbour, it dwarfed the surrounding city and the spectacular harbour.

As mainstream television was still another twenty-two years away, the Amalgamated Wireless Company set up a live radio broadcast of the proceedings for millions of Australians and a suitable short-wave reception for audiences in Great Britain, Europe, America, the Far East and New Zealand. Those unable to attend the opening or listen to the broadcast had only to wait for the newspapers the following day when they could share the retelling of the spectacular night-time events. The following highlights from the *Sydney Morning Herald* is a shortened version of an exuberant and other-worldly description of the night-time spectacle.

'**When the fireworks commenced......... it seemed that the forge of Vulcan had been brought to Sydney, from which he struck great showers of sparks. With a hiss and a rear, a line of fire cleared the heavens, seemed to pause reluctantly, and then burst into a thousand sparks, which floated gracefully, like errant stars, above the water...Pseudo diamonds, rubies, emeralds, and amethysts, fit to grace the cloak of a fairy queen, were released with sounds of fire, on their peaceful mission, each declaring the Bridge open for the people of New South Wales.**'

For weeks after the grand opening's success, the Bridge continued to be an enormous public attraction, with thousands of people continuing to pour across the pedestrian footways, all ready to be enthralled by the overwhelming scale of the steel arch and its massive granite pylons. Its dominance over the surrounding city left people stunned. It made the locals swell with pride, and visitors like Professor Ernest Scott, whilst enthralled with what he had seen, remarked, '**The vast steel curve**

that spans the harbour...is a monstrous combination of grace, strength and sheer size.'

Within weeks, a walk across the Sydney Harbour Bridge was a 'must-do' activity. For many locals, an early morning or evening walk across the Bridge had become a healthy pastime, and it wasn't long before the footway became a fashionable weekend promenade. Ladies took the opportunity to wear their finest dress and latest hat, whilst the men would polish their shoes and put on their favourite tie while making a showy walk across the Bridge. It was the perfect location to take in the great harbour sites, perhaps forget about the tough times, and dream of a brighter future, if only for a moment.

Weather permitting, Sunday always proved to draw the biggest crowds. A day of relaxation for most and a holy day when many local churchgoers often visited the prominent precinct of churches nearby, known then as 'Church Hill' just a short walk from the southern approach to the Bridge.

Depending on their denomination, people would attend a service at either St. Philips Anglican, St. Patricks' Catholic or Scots Presbyterian, followed by a lovely walk across the great Bridge. As the crowds ambled across the Bridge, the great flow of pedestrians on the walkways often stalled. People were captivated by the views and would pause and take a moment to gaze over the pedestrian railing to get a bird's eye view of the magnificent harbour and the lively water traffic below.

On Sunday afternoon on 24th April 1932, William James Lewis, a 49-year-old war veteran, was among the steady flow of pedestrians on the eastern footway of the Bridge. He looked at home amongst the well-dressed crowd, cleanly shaven and dressed in his 'Sunday best', a dark grey tweed suit over a white shirt with orange stripes, blue braces, polished lace-up boots and a smart-looking grey felt hat.

Like the enthusiastic sightseers surrounding him, William appeared to be merely taking that casual stroll across the Bridge. Like many other pedestrians, he paused at the centre of the Bridge as if transfixed by the wonderous views surrounding him. William then casually climbed the pedestrian fencing and hoisted himself onto the top handrail. He sat astride and stopped in this position for only a moment as if continuing to admire the view.

A local bricklayer, Joseph Molineaux, from Milson's Point North Sydney, was also walking across the Bridge and noticed William perched on the railing and paused just a few feet away from him. At first, Molineaux thought William was perhaps a workman inspecting the structure. Then quickly, he realized something was seriously wrong. Quick thinking Molineaux then made a rush towards Lewis but as soon as he was within touching distance William Lewis released his hands **'and threw himself sideways as one alights from a horse'** and let himself fall outward and downward, plummeting towards the water 180 feet below.

Molineaux leaned hard up against the railing and watched helplessly as William turned around in the air and finally struck the water below. Suddenly hundreds of nearby witnesses stood silent, gripped with shock. Then all at once, a chorus of screams and shouts broke loose. The few cars that were nearby screeched to a halt, and drivers who witnessed the event leapt from their vehicles. A few men ran to the side of the footway. They craned over the railing next to Molineaux whilst women looked away in horror and disbelief, hoping to erase the scene from their memory. Hundreds of people had just witnessed the first suicide from the Sydney Harbour Bridge.

Dawes Point Wharf, a popular fishing spot, was directly below the Bridge, and local Robert Byrne was quietly enjoying his Sunday fishing when he witnessed the leap by Lewis. He was momentarily stunned as he watched in disbelief as William Lewis plummeted through the air and struck the water. The horrendous impact was like a volcanic eruption of water and formed a massive cloud of spray. Byrne dashed to the nearby Water Police boatshed, located only a short distance from the Wharf. On duty was the Chief of Water Police, Sergeant Charles Percy Bebb.

While Robert Byrne was making his dash to alert Sgt Bebb, Edward Collins of North Sydney had been cruising nearby in his launch. He also witnessed the chilling moment when William Lewis hit the water.

Collins, in his launch, hastily made his way to where William had entered the water and quickly recovered the body which had now floated to the surface. By this time, hundreds of people had gathered to watch from the bridge deck above and a large crowd of curious viewers also started congregating on the shoreline below.

Sgt Charles Bebb, accompanied by police constables Baxter and Burden, were now making a speedy approach in the police launch and pulled up alongside Edward Collin's launch and took charge of William's body. Sgt Bebb then desperately attempted to resuscitate William Lewis in a battle to **'restore animation'** back to his body.

Sadly, all attempts by Bebb to resuscitate William Lewis had failed, and Lewis's lifeless body lay on the deck of the Police launch. Sgt Bebb was left mystified and frustrated in being unable to save Lewis. He was also confused by the absence of any external injuries to Lewis's body. Bebb later learned that when William hit the water, he had landed on the broad of his back, which helped explain the volcanic-like explosion of water on impact. This type of impact also crushed William's ribcage with an estimated force of nearly thirty tons and killed him instantly.

Sgt Charles Percy Bebb had been a marine engineer, and at age 22, he joined the Sydney Police Force in 1908. After completing his probationary training as a constable, he soon joined the Water Police under the leadership of the notably named Sgt William Shakespeare, who, not surprisingly, became a well-known identity on the Sydney Harbour waterways. Twenty years later, in 1928, Sgt Shakespeare died suddenly and shortly after, Charles Bebb became the new Chief Sergeant of the Sydney Water Police.

Bebb was a powerful-looking man, tall and athletic, and he carried a broad physique attributed to many years of competitive swimming. He was a devout family man with a bearing that made people feel safe in his presence. With nearly twenty-five years of dedicated service, he had also earned enormous respect amongst the community and the Sydney Police Force.

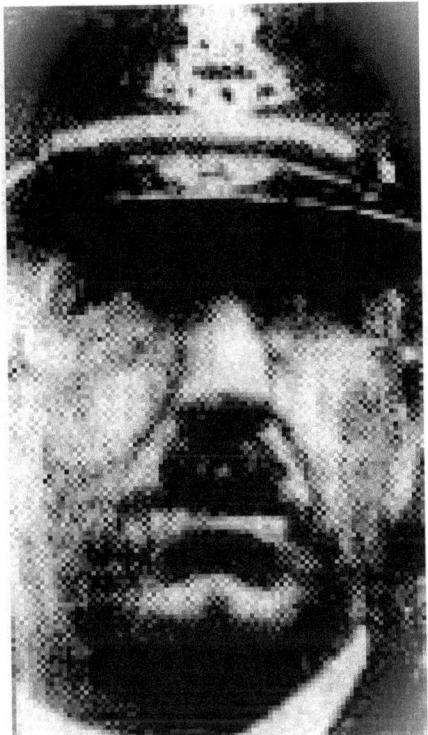

Fig 1. Sgt Charles Percy Lloyd Bebb

When Bebb returned to shore with William Lewis's broken body, Sgt Bebb found nothing to help identify him. William had no money, papers or personal effects found on his person. The only identifying feature was a distinctive tattoo on his right forearm showing two hands clasped around a heart.

William James Lewis now held the unfortunate distinction of being the first person to commit suicide from the Sydney Harbour Bridge. The *Braidwood Advocate* reported the news of William's death as a **'Historic Suicide'**.

The following day was Anzac Day, and unaware of William's identity or veteran status, news of the **'First Bridge Suicide'** described as **'Mans Big Drop to Death'** was on the front page of the popular Sydney newspaper, the *Daily Telegraph*.

Conceivably it was no coincidence that William Lewis decided to jump to his death on the eve of Anzac Day. An important day for all Australians to commemorate, honour and pause to reflect on war veterans past and present, but perhaps Anzac Day was not such a special day for William, but a sad reminder of a tragic time. A time when the war had left him a broken man, a time that had taken the life of his younger brother Frederick on the Somme, maybe Anzac was a day he would rather forget.

William was born in Mile End, London, England and emigrated on his own to Australia in 1907, a single man who never married. In March 1915, he enlisted in the Australian Imperial Forces and was a Private with the 3rd Battalion. When he enlisted, William mentioned his bouts with scarlet fever and Pleurisy, but he was still accepted.

While serving in France in 1918, William was wounded, a shrapnel wound penetrated the left side of his chest. During his time in repatriation, he was diagnosed with a heart condition, a systolic murmur and a kidney condition known as albuminuria (kidney disease).

Suffering from his wounds and considerable poor health, William was discharged permanently and returned to Australia in February 1919. The medical board responsible for assessing war veterans when discharged from service rated William's disability at 30%. This assessment by the board also determined his working capacity in the general labour market and his war pension entitlement.

Albert Lee Hansford, a friend of William's, later confirmed the seriousness of William's health and his state of mind. He gave evidence to the coroner's inquiry stating that William Lewis had a severe heart condition and had continued medical treatment for over ten years. He explained that William was recently discharged from the Prince of Wales Hospital at Randwick. Albert Hansford believed that after numerous operations, the aftereffects on William had depressed him and played upon his mind.

The difficult financial times would have also hampered William's thoughts. Like many injured veterans, William had enormous difficulty maintaining a lifestyle on a lowly war pension and little, if any, prospect of future employment. Given the brutal battles William had faced in the past and the possibility of more painful health battles in the future, his circumstances had become miserable.

Whether his suicide was planned or impulsive, we will never know; however, the eve of Anzac may have triggered his action. Reflecting on the loss of a brother and his wartime ordeals, his health in serious decline and a future not worth considering, William Lewis may have judged suicide from the Bridge a more noble end rather than continuing with an embattled life and the strain of declining health.

By Wednesday, three days after William's suicide, the newspapers officially released his name, and a funeral notice was published the following day. The war repatriation department covered the funeral expenses, and to this day, the Commonwealth War Graves Commission maintains William's war grave at Rookwood Cemetery in Sydney.

After his death, the City Coroner returned a verdict of '**suicide while suffering from the effects of war injuries**'. The *Labor Daily* newspaper, a strong supporter of the working class and the plight of veterans, expressed its deep disappointment at William's death and described the tragedy as '**Just Another War Victim...mind unbalanced by wounds**'.

While the *Daily Telegraph* took the bold step of making it front-page news, newspapers around the country followed through on the story, confident in the knowledge that a tally of suicides would soon follow.

A few days after the historic jump, the *Grafton Daily Examiner* claimed the Bridge would be a structure linking the sad and weary with death, and the new highway of life had been converted to one of death. The Examiner claimed that no one was surprised that the Bridge had attracted the mentally unbalanced to leap to their death.

Five weeks after the Sydney Harbour Bridge's official opening, it looked like the honeymoon period for the Bridge had come to an early end. Many critics had foreseen the tragedy of suicides on the Harbour

Bridge. Newspapers around the country had warned that the Bridge would attract a new wave of suicides and the historic leap by William Lewis had become the 'told-you-so' moment.

Twenty-four hours after William Lewis jumped, a second man jumped at 6.15 pm on Anzac Day, the 25th of April 1932. Like William Lewis, he climbed the trellis fence and onto the railing, then took off his pullover, casually passed it to a woman walking nearby, and said, **'Here, take this; I won't have any use for it now'**. Confused by what was happening, the woman slowly reached out and took the pullover, and then suddenly, the man jumped from the railing. The woman stood screaming in horror as two other men who witnessed the jump rushed to the fence only to see the man strike the water.

The water police were immediately notified and for some hours the police launch searched the area and the nearby foreshores late into the evening. The following morning the Water Police started an extensive search dragging the harbour water with grappling irons, and still, the search failed to find any trace of the body.

Was it possible the man miraculously survived his leap, then struggled to shore and disappeared into the night in a very sore and sorry state? Could it be his body remained lying at the depths of the harbour, or perhaps he was taken by sharks? The *Sun* newspaper later reported that there was 'NO TRACE' of the second bridge victim.

The identity of the man and the outcome remained a mystery. There was no further evidence, and no body was ever recovered. Although there were plausible witness accounts, there would be no official notice of death or suicide without a body.

Overall, the publicity surrounding the William Lewis suicide, and the mystery jumper that followed, was subdued and no doubt much to the disappointment and dismay of the many critics of the Bridge. The month of May looked like the Bridge would be suicide free. Perhaps the touted suicide fad was merely hysteria. Critics of the Bridge may have been left scratching their heads for a while, but it was simply the calm before the storm.

On Sunday afternoon May 29th, amongst the flashy weekend sightseers, Robert Anderson made his way along the pedestrian footway to the centre of the Sydney Harbour Bridge. As he proceeded to climb the fence, he quickly looked around to make sure there were no pedestrians close enough to prevent him from jumping. As he threw himself from the railing, a passing tram full of passengers witnessed his leap from the Bridge.

When Robert left the railing, Customs officials on the government launch below watched as Robert twisted and turned grotesquely through the air but managed to hit the water feet first and sank quickly below the surface.

The customs officials couldn't believe what they witnessed and were even more startled when Robert Anderson miraculously returned to the surface, conscious and started swimming feebly about, seemingly uninjured. The men on the nearby launch then raced towards him, clutched him by the hair, and hauled him on board, whereby he shakily declared that **'he had to do it'** and then added, **'it was a long way down.'**

The launch then made its way to the Government boat shed at Dawes Point where they were met by the Water Police and the central ambulance, which immediately transported him to Sydney Hospital. Not surprisingly, when Robert was admitted to the hospital, his condition was described as critical. He had a fractured spine as well as serious internal injuries and was continually being resuscitated in an attempt to keep him alive.

Robert was 33 years old, a native of Bingara, New South Wales, and was employed as a railway clerk. When he was eighteen, he enlisted and served in the Australian Infantry. Having seen action in the field in France during World War I, he returned when the war ended with some physical scars, being wounded in the foot and having been gassed, which left him suffering from asthma.

In 1924, the war veteran later married Daisy McClelland from Parkes in NSW, and together they settled down to domestic life in the quiet Sydney suburb of Lakemba. At the time of Robert's leap from the Bridge, it was not certain if he and Daisy were still living together, as he advised the police, he had been feeling depressed and his wife was staying with relatives in Parkes. Fortunately, upon hearing the news, Daisy returned to Sydney.

Nearly two weeks after Robert Anderson's leap, news of him surviving the leap and his remarkable recovery in hospital slowly emerged in the newspapers. Laying in a hospital cot with a fractured spine in a quiet ward of Sydney Hospital, Robert, drifted in and out of sleep with his wife Daisy by his bedside. As he drifted in and out of sleep, he held Daisy's hand, and now and again, he looked into her troubled eyes and said softly, **'Don't worry, it'll be all right. It'll be all right.... I'm glad it didn't come off'.**

Daisy's soothing presence calmed him as she spoke softly to him, and he drifted off into a calm sleep. Sometimes he would wake, startled as he relived his experience of jumping off the Bridge. He reflected, staring past the row of hospital beds with fear in his eyes as if he saw that grim expanse of water again. **'It's fine here. I wasn't feeling so good at the time; nerves bad, or something. I had a job with the railways, and I was all right. Just a bit - well, nervy.'**

When Robert Anderson made his jump from the Bridge four weeks after William Lewis, Anderson had no idea that he also made history. There was no mention that he was the first man to survive jumping from the Sydney Harbour Bridge. As notable as it was for the history of the Sydney Harbour Bridge, Robert received little publicity and indeed no fame or fortune for surviving his near-fatal attempt at suicide. Once Robert Anderson recovered from his injuries, he returned home, but Daisy was no longer by his side. He later led a quiet life working and living in Port Kembla, south of Sydney.

He died in 1960, aged 61, and as a returned soldier, he was interred at Wollongong City Memorial Gardens.

The dark chapter in the life of the Sydney Harbour Bridge had begun. Just two months had passed since its grand opening, hailed as the colossus of the southern hemisphere, the golden girl of Sydney Harbour was soon to be making headlines for all the wrong reasons. It was official, Sydney's beloved Bridge would have a new title bestowed upon it, **'The Suicide Bridge'**.

Fig 2. Police Detectives testing the ease of climbing the fence.

3

NO BARRIER TO SUICIDE

'It was a thing to throw oneself from the top of a column, or any high place sufficiently public for the exhibition'

Before war veteran William James Lewis made the 'historic jump' to his death, the building of the SHB was rightly being celebrated as an engineering triumph, a picturesque structure built for utility, and as the Bridge neared completion, *The Sydney Morning Herald* proclaimed the following.

'Gigantic in dimensions and graceful in contour, the main bridge is destined to take its place among the engineering triumphs of the world...the giant structure has been moulded into a veritable poem of symmetry...The arch rib, graceful at the crown... elegant in its strength and simplicity, demonstrates clearly its purpose, taking the eye down to the majestic abutments on each side. So harmonious is the effect that the tremendous size of the structure as a whole is belied by its beauty.'

This grand and poetic description of the Bridge was not without merit; however, amidst all the admiration of this engineering triumph, one crucial design feature had been overlooked. Today anyone familiar with the pedestrian footpath on the Sydney Harbour Bridge or who has taken a walk on the eastern footway may have noticed that the pathway is shrouded on both sides by an arched fencing barrier made of wire mesh and strands of barbed wire.

It may come as a surprise to learn that on completion of the Harbour Bridge, the arched fencing we see today was not part of the original construction. This was a later addition and was completed only after fifty-one people had jumped to their death, countless suicide attempts, and considerable pressure placed on the state government. Originally no safety barrier or netting had been constructed either on the eastern and western pedestrian footways or around the gigantic granite-faced pylons. Absolutely nothing had been considered to prevent a person from simply climbing up and over the pedestrian fence and plummeting into the harbour 180 feet below.

The original pedestrian fencing on both sides of the bridge was approximately 4 ½ feet tall overall, its modest height offering the pedestrian a fabulous uninterrupted view of the harbour and the surrounding city. This structure remains today and was constructed using a riveted flat steel diagonal trellis pattern framed in steel. Unfortunately, the diagonal trellis design was like a ladder and offered a comfortable footing for climbing. A climb that a curious or adventurous child could easily make. Or, as proven by William Lewis, a climb made just as easily by a considerably older war veteran in poor health and standing just 5ft 3 inches tall.

Mounted just a few inches above the top of the framed trellis was a large circular balustrade or railing. Unintentionally, of course, the top of the horizontal framework and the railing mounted above it provided a comfortable grappling point from which a person could hoist themselves up, gain their balance, and then ready themselves for the perfect jumping-off position. An early observation suggested the fence construction was an invitation to suicide, hinting that in the same way an open door to a thief is a temptation to steal, a fence on a bridge built like a ladder is perhaps an invitation to climb and jump.

The day after William Lewis jumped, there was an investigation by police on the pedestrian footway, and a detective demonstrated how easy it was to climb the fence and railing. The exercise was of no surprise to many, but it clearly proved the point; the fence structure was remarkably suicide friendly.

Today with so much emphasis on public health and safety, it seems unthinkable that during the various stages of design and construction of the Sydney Bridge, absolutely no provision had been considered to make it difficult for a pedestrian to climb onto the top railing, take a moment if needed, and then cast themselves wilfully off the Bridge towards certain death.

However, the SHB was not alone in its suicide-friendly architecture. Bridges and tall structures around the world were constructed in the same utilitarian manner for decades, and they often replicated the same design. The Clifton Suspension Bridge, which spans the river Avon in Bristol, England, was constructed nearly seventy years before the SHB, and just like the SHB, its pedestrian fence had similar diagonal style latticework, which provided the would-be suicide with the same series of ladder steps to the top railing which could be easily mounted.

Opened in 1864, the Clifton Bridge remains one of the world's greatest engineering marvels. It was also a colossus and quickly acquired fame throughout the world as England's suicide bridge. The height of the Bridge from the high water was a staggering 245 feet. Anyone who had jumped from this great height had **'either been seriously dashed to pieces against the rocks on the river'** or mutilated on impact with the water. The Australian newspapers regularly covered news of the Clifton Bridge suicides, and instant death was the outcome in every case until July 1885 when 22-year-old Sarah Ann Henley jumped and unbelievably survived. It was said that Sarah wore so many skirts that she parachuted down to the river below, landing in the mud and suffering only bruising to her limbs. What Sarah was actually wearing was a stiffened crinoline fabric petticoat designed to hold out her heavy floor-length skirt. This excessive Victorian fashion of the day formed a balloon-like expanse of her dress, acting like a parachute that slowed her fall.

After sixty suicides from the Clifton Bridge, a horrified local member of parliament submitted plans to erect safety barriers to the pedestrian walkway. By this time, the Bridge had been standing for sixty-eight years. The Clifton Bridge authorities were incredibly proud of their Bridge. They explained that it was one of the world's greatest engineering marvels and that no barrier to prevent people from jumping could ever be erected. Unbelievably, they argued that engineers had determined that any addition to the Bridge would increase its resistance to the wind and therefore cause the so-called engineering marvel to collapse.

Publicly they maintained that their toll collectors were always vigilant and constantly on the watch for what they called the 'suicide look'. They proudly claimed that for every person who committed suicide, they had managed to have stopped at least another fifty. The inspector in charge of the tolls also towed the company line announcing that '**If we turn the Bridge into a birdcage, it would probably fall with the first gale of wind. A screen or a covered fence would act as a sail. Even now you can see the Bridge sinking and heaving when a gale blows...it is like walking on a rolling ship's deck.** The local council office was even less sympathetic towards suicide victims and was reported as saying, '**There are ten suicides off the cliffs for each one on the bridge, it is no use blaming the bridge**'.

On average, the Clifton Bridge had eight deaths per year up to 1998, when barriers were finally installed. The average figure sounds less remarkable but still amounts to 1072 suicides over 134 years. Sadly, the barriers have not entirely prevented suicides from the Clifton Bridge with the average suicide rate only halved since 1998.

Closer to home, the Victoria Bridge (named after Queen Victoria) over the Brisbane River in Queensland was reconstructed as an iron structure and was opened in 1874. Like the SHB, it had a similar pedestrian fence with the same diagonal style trellis that once again made for a convenient step up and over. It had a long history of bridge suicides that continued to make the news almost until the day the Sydney Harbour Bridge had its first suicide.

Notably, it was not only bridges, but tall buildings, cliff faces, tall towers, and monuments around the world that also proved equally attractive to the suicidal, with many of these structures being suicide friendly, all having easy access and few preventive measures in place.

As far back as 1834, a monument to Prince Frederick, Duke of York, the second eldest son of King George III, was erected in London. It is a giant granite column built in the Tuscan style, a copy of the celebrated Trajan's column in Rome. The column rises from a square pedestal or base, and the capital at the top carries what is described as a square balcony or viewing gallery where the bronze statue of the Duke proudly stands on a podium in the centre. The total height of the monument, including the statue, is 137ft 9 in.

On completion of the column and its viewing gallery at the top, it was open to the public for an inspiring view of the surrounding city of London. At 10 o'clock each day, for the price of sixpence, people would enter through the formal entrance at the foot of the monument and then ascend the winding staircase of 168 steps to the narrow viewing platform surrounding the statue at the top. A walk around the platform was accompanied by a guide who pointed out the top sights of London. The paying visitor could then take a moment to gaze upon the wonderous city surroundings. A bare iron fence, just four feet high, was installed around the viewing platform's perimeter, and just like the SHB, it could easily be climbed and was insufficient in stopping a suicide. Sixteen years later, and after many gruesome suicides, it was finally suggested that an iron railing be installed above the fence to prevent other jumpers. Eventually, the platform was 'caged-in', and the monument was later closed to the public.

Decades before the Sydney Harbour Bridge was constructed, Sydney Town had experienced its own suicide crazes and had already established some favoured locations. Whilst Sydney was short on tall monuments, it still had plenty of treacherous coastal cliff faces nearby and several significant bridges that lured many to their death. Pyrmont Bridge and the Northbridge Suspension Bridge were extremely popular locations. Both bridges were modest constructions, but hazardous leaps from both bridges had recorded countless suicide victims in the past.

An ocean cliff face on the South Head peninsula near Watsons Bay, known to all Sydneysiders as 'The Gap', had a massive drop to a rocky outcrop below which was repeatedly smashed by rough swells from the Tasman Sea. Before the construction of the SHB, it was described as the most 'fashionable' suicide spot in Sydney and proved to be the most popular site of them all and remains equally notorious to this day.

Close to Coogee Beach on the northern cliff face was another site known as 'Suicide Point', and like the Gap, it was an easy step off the edge to certain death. Even iconic Bondi Beach had its favoured suicide point, the infamous Ben Buckler Point, another treacherous cliff face that formed the northern tip of the famous Bondi Beach arc. Melbourne also had its preferred locations. For decades, the state government in Victoria was helpless in preventing what was described as 'suicide mania'. The various bridges that crossed the expanse of the Yarra River in Melbourne were frequently used as jumping-off points for suicide.

Historical evidence clearly supported the fact that bridges and tall structures were hot spots for suicide, most of which had fences that could be easily surmounted. Sadly, historical evidence also reveals that suicide prevention was always an afterthought. So why were there no protective barriers built in the first place? The warning signs were there, and why would the Sydney Harbour Bridge be the exception to the risk of suicide attempts?

Perhaps the decision-makers subscribed to the greater-good theory, and therefore the aesthetics of the Bridge design shouldn't be compromised for the sake of a few suicides. Or was it likely, that historical facts surrounding suicides from around the world were considered, and the authorities then factored in the financial balance against the public consequence and determined that they would worry about it only if and when a suicide occurred?

In fairness to the Sydney Harbour Bridge designers, it is reasonable to suggest, as one Sydney newspaper reported, '**Beauty of design is as essential as utility of purpose or economy in construction**'. Therefore, it is likely that the Sydney Bridge designers were only asked to provide fencing considered functional and fit for purpose, similar to proven designs previously used and in keeping with the overall aesthetics of the architectural brief. But the question remains, why copy a trellis framework that encourages people to climb it?

Given the enormous task of building the Bridge and the years dedicated to its construction, and apart from no suicide prevention measures, remarkably, there were only a few minor teething problems after the official opening. During the planning and construction stages of the Bridge, there was much debate over the toll charges, and in simple terms, the big question was, would enough revenue be raised to cover the ongoing bridge costs? Initially, it did not, and as arguments over tolls continued, it seems little attention had been paid to the welfare and working conditions of the toll collectors.

The southern approach to the Bridge was the toll collection point for vehicle traffic, with the toll collectors' stations acting as the separation lanes for the approaching traffic. There were six lanes for traffic and six toll collectors, and whilst traffic on the harbour bridge remained light, there was no centre line painted on the carriageway, and Sydney's motor traffic shared the road with the much slower and sometimes unpredictable horse and cart.

After opening day, eighteen men were appointed as toll collectors, each wearing a uniform like the local tram conductor and shouldering an oversized money pouch. Each man stood at his post stationed like a bookmaker at the horse races, standing on a raised platform behind a semicircular railing with a large sign mounted high above his head on a bar with a single word "TOLL". Within days the toll collectors all complained of receiving electric shocks; static electricity was being generated from vehicles and transmitted to the drivers' hands when they made contact with the toll collector. The simple solution of providing rubber foot mats for the collector prevented the sudden static jolt, and the collector was no longer hesitant in collecting the revenue.

By the start of winter, the Bridge's height and its exposure to what was described as cyclonic winds and rain at an 'uncomfortable slant' would also prove troublesome for the toll collectors. The suffering collector was often seen rubbing his hands and stamping his feet to keep warm, while his flimsy tram conductor uniform was hardly up to the task of protecting him from the extremely wet and frosty conditions. It wasn't long before the Tramway Union approached the newly appointed Minister for Transport and the man in charge of the bridge, Mr Michael F Bruxner, and requested that the Government provide better conditions for the toll collectors by way of warmer uniforms, waterproof boots, and shelter sheds.

Mr Bruxner explained that it had only been four months since the previous standing State Government opened the Bridge. Toll shelters were in the original construction plans, but the proposal was initially considered too costly, and the previous Government scrapped the idea. He also stated that the idea of shelters for the collectors had been considered for some time by the new Government. However, they were still determining traffic control and having difficulty finding suitable protection. Mr Bruxner followed up quickly and responded with the tender process for constructing shelters, and once a design was approved, he pledged construction would be completed within four weeks. Minister Bruxner was good to his word.

Before becoming the state minister for Transport and the Deputy Premier of New South Wales, Michael Bruxner, was a successful grazier and WW I veteran. Born in 1882 in Tabulam, a small rural town on the Clarence River in the far northeast of New South Wales, Bruxner later ran a prosperous stock and station agency and became a leading citizen in the rural region of Tenterfield. When World War I broke out, he enlisted and was a commissioned officer in the pride of the Australian Imperial Forces, the Light Horse Regiment. He was wounded at Gallipoli and later continued serving in the Sinai and Palestine campaigns with the Anzac Mounted Division. Bruxner had an outstanding service record, was decorated with the Distinguished Service Order and the French Legion of Honour and completed his military career as Lieutenant Colonel.

After the war, Bruxner became actively involved in rural or what they called 'country' interests and was encouraged to enter politics. His rawness to politics was offset by his distinguished war record and his passionate patriotism. He soon became a parliamentary member for the Northern Tablelands in 1920 and in 1922, became the Progressive Party's leader, renamed the Country Party in 1925. Bruxner was described as a natural politician, a true leader with an approachable manner. For most of his political life, he would be referred to as 'the Colonel', a style he greatly enjoyed.

The 'Colonel' was an early campaigner against the construction of the Harbour Bridge, and he actively represented the rural citizens who were hotly opposed to the enormous expense of what they described as a fanciful bridge. 'Country Interests', as they were often referred to, considered the Bridge as a symbol of extravagant expenditure that would only benefit city interests. They believed the money could be more usefully disbursed in advancing rural communities and agricultural production.

In 1922 when the Parliamentary Bill was presented for the construction of the SHB, then referred to as the North Shore Bridge, Bruxner voted against the Bill, and like his country supporters, he passionately believed that **'the Bridge was a Sydney requirement and as such should be paid for in most by Sydney'**. He informed parliament that **'If the North Shore bridge is to be built out of the money of the State, I will not support its construction'**.

A decade later, in May 1932, the New South Wales political landscape was abruptly and significantly reshaped, along with the future political path of 'The Colonel' Michael Bruxner. In simple terms, the existing Labour Party Government led by the imposing Jack Thomas

Lang, who officially opened the Bridge, was sacked from his position as Premier of the state of New South Wales.

Jack Lang served as the Premier of New South Wales during much of the construction of the SHB, serving two times from 1925 to 1927 and again from 1930 to 1932. Known simply as 'The Big Fella', Lang was a dynamic and hard-bitten politician, a larger-than-life figure whose stature sent shivers among his political foes.

In his first term as state leader, he was responsible for initiating a good number of social reforms. He introduced pensions for windowed mothers, the child endowment scheme, a mandatory workers' compensation scheme, the abolition of student fees in state-run schools, laws to safeguard the native flora and laws to penalise shipping discharging oil in the Harbour and waterways. The second term in office was not as kind to Jack Lang as his first, but he was dealt a poor hand to reignite his second run. The Great Depression left little in the government purse to chase the level of reforms like his previous tenure.

There is no denying that Lang loved Australia, the State of New South Wales and notably the Sydney Harbour Bridge. His speech at the opening ceremony was nationalistic and unifying. He reminded everyone of the importance of the Federation of Australia in 1901, something the other states of Australia, in particular, Western Australia, were having difficulty reconciling.

On the 19th of March 1932, when Jack Lang formally opened the Sydney Bridge, highly regarded for his oratory ability, he proudly declared, '**The bridge unites people who have similar aims and ideals but are divided by physical and geographical boundaries. It is the fulfilment of a dream entertained by many of our pioneers who have not lived to see its realisation. Just as Sydney has completed this material bridge which will unite her people, so will Australia ultimately perfect a bridge.... a bridge of common understanding, that would serve the whole of the people of our great continent. The bridge will yet be built and will carry**

Australia on to that glorious destination which every man who loves our native country feels is in store for her.'

On 13th May 1932, nearly two months after the opening of the Bridge by Jack Lang, he was dismissed from power. Considered the first constitutional crisis in Australia, the parliament was dissolved, and a caretaker government was called in to run the state. A new caretaker coalition Government was formed, led by Bertram Stevens of the United Australia Party and Michael Bruxner, leader of the Country Party with Stevens appointed as Premier and 'the Colonel', Michael Bruxner, appointed Minister for Transport and Deputy Premier in what was later called the Stevens - Bruxner Government.

Michael Bruxner, the man who once campaigned so vigorously against the construction of the SHB a decade earlier, was now responsible for its administration. No one could have missed the irony in Bruxner's political inheritance of a bridge he never wanted, a bridge that would be a thorn in his side and continue to haunt his early years as Deputy Premier and Transport Minister.

Fig 3. Toll Collectors early morning 21st March 1932

4

SUICIDE, A SIGN OF THE TIMES

'No man can poison himself under sixpence. The bridge leap costs nothing, and you can leave the landlady to pay the gas bill.'

By 1932, suicide had become a familiar affair, an ordinary happening, and people were accustomed to its frequency. People were seemingly unruffled by the news of another suicide by a war veteran, a poverty-stricken mother, or an unemployed labourer.

Throughout the course of previous decades, a series of economic recessions around the world, followed by the Great War and, ultimately, the Great Depression of 1929, had a collective effect on people. The era brought personal pain, financial hardship, and a hardened view of day-to-day living, and suicide had become a sign of the times. However, this was not the only era in history that suicide had become an ordinary happening, and it wasn't the first-time populations had developed an indifference to its occurrence. Historically the ordeal of suicide has plagued humanity for thousands of years.

In ancient times suicide was chronicled by the Greeks, who were quite accustomed to suicide. They held routine tribunals regulating and authorising suicide should the reasons be judged sufficient. When famine threatened their islands in the Aegean Sea, the ancient Greeks passed a law that compelled all adults over the age of sixty to take a dose of poison from the deadly hemlock plant, with the intention that these suicides would then make room for the growing younger generation.

Greek history also told stories of the Leucadian Cliff, a landmark made famous by the suicide of lovers and known for the large crowds that attended to watch 'Lovers Leap'. It was thought those who leapt from the cliff were said to be cured of the passion of love. No doubt the outcome proved fatally correct and permanently cured everything. The ancient Greeks were undoubtedly different, and as Greek law never intervened on matters of the heart, locals later celebrated the lovers in song and verse.

In the Middle Ages, suicide was far less acceptable in the Christian faith. Although there is nowhere in the Bible that states suicide is expressly forbidden, it was propagated as a sin and could result in a person being excommunicated from the Church with no provision for Christian burial and the confiscation of all property belonging to the person who had killed themselves. Fortunately, by the early 20th Century, many Christian churches had softened on the idea that suicide was a sinful act.

The Japanese have an ancient and deeply entrenched culture of suicide, and for many centuries suicide was regarded as a noble act. What the Japanese call an honourable death that would prevent shame upon oneself or family, has continued to shape their cultural tolerance towards suicide. Located just offshore from Tokyo Bay is an active volcano known as Mount Mihara on the small Japanese island of Izu Oshima. The island, once a popular holiday resort for Tokyo residents, suddenly became Japan's most fashionable suicide destination, and news of its popularity had spread to Australia. In 1933, at the peak of its popularity, it was described as a '**suicide place more fatally alluring than Sydney's Gap or Harbour Bridge**'. Within five months, there had been nearly 200 suicide attempts, with more than 40 people successfully throwing themselves into the smoking volcanic crater to a burning death.

Following the line that everything is bigger in the United States of America, but not necessarily better, in 1930, the U.S.A recorded the staggering statistic of between 18,000 and 20,000 suicides annually and an estimated 30,000 attempts at suicides each year. Reports followed that suicide in the United States had become a 'national habit'. In the U.S, the credited Dr Frederick L. Hoffman in his summary of the national suicide record in 1930 published his view stating that suicide had become a **'social problem of the first importance'** and made recommendations for the formation of a national society for suicide prevention, with branches in all cities around the nation. Dr Hoffman was undoubtedly an early pioneer of suicide prevention, and fortunately today, there are numerous suicide prevention organisations and crisis lines that are just a phone call away.

In Great Britain, in 1931, the British Registrar-General's statistical review surprisingly showed the lowest British birth rate on record; this shocked many statisticians, but more disturbing was the highest rate of suicide on record, with 5147 victims.

Not to be left out of the growing statistical evidence of increasing suicide rates, the Police Commissioner of South Australia in 1932 revealed the remarkable finding that South Australia in its past ten years, had 657 people commit suicide, equal to more than one a week. This was not a comfortable number for anyone. Still, a relatively modest figure compared to the German State of Bavaria, which in 1933 alone had recorded a total of 1825 suicides, which was equal to five suicides a day.

The evidence was in and the overwhelming statistics from around the world clearly showed that a modern era of suicide had emerged. The idea of a worldwide suicide epidemic with fashionable destinations from which to commit suicide had become a reality, and bridges around the world were the star attractions.

When it was built in 1912, the Arroyo Seco Bridge in Pasadena, California, was proclaimed the highest concrete bridge in the world and spanned an enormous rocky gorge 175 feet below. Like other significant bridges around the world, suicide from the Pasadena Bridge was so prevalent it was nicknamed the 'Suicide Bridge' nearly twenty years before the Sydney Harbour Bridge would assume the same name. Unfortunately, the Pasadena bridge had a bad reputation before it was completed. As if straight from a Hollywood script, stories circulated that a worker fell to his death during its construction and landed in the wet cement under the bridge, and his body is still entombed to this day.

One attempt at suicide proved more comical than tragic when Henry Breuer wishing to die, drove his car at high speed off the bank of the approach to the Pasadena Bridge. His car fell short of tumbling headlong down the rocky cliff when his car struck a heavy wire fence. A determined Henry then climbed from his car, made his way back up the rocky bank and proceeded onto the bridge footway where he climbed the bridge railing and jumped. After falling only 40 feet, he landed safely in the only remaining tree in the canyon below. He then climbed out of the tree and in complete frustration, gave up in his attempt at suicide. It appeared to Henry that he wasn't meant to die, so he gave up and walked away. The only injury he sustained was a cut lip.

During the Great Depression, the number of deaths from the Pasadena Bridge increased, with over 30 persons having jumped to their deaths since it opened.

In 1929 the local police and the city's chief engineers proposed installing netting 15 feet under the bridge to prevent further deaths, but suicides continued well after. In 1993 a suicide barrier was eventually installed, but it still maintains the unfortunate reputation as the 'suicide bridge'.

Before the Sydney Harbour Bridge was officially opened, there was a well-held public view that the rate of suicide attempts in Sydney would increase, and the bridge would become the new and preferred location for suicide and described by some detractors as the ultimate **'stepping-off point for eternity'**. The previously favoured Sydney location, The Gap at Watsons Bay, was now fenced with barbed wire and watched over by regular police patrols. Ben Buckler Point at Bondi was another popular location; for years it had attracted both murder and suicide and recorded more than thirty suicides between 1920 and 1929. Then in November 1929, the Salvation Army erected an iron signboard at the approach to the Point. The anti-suicide sign said, 'ARE YOU IN TROUBLE? – IF SO, CALL AND SEE THE SALVATION ARMY - THEY MAY BE ABLE TO HELP YOU'.

It would later be claimed that this simple sign had worked and prevented many suicides. Lieut. Colonel Orr of the Salvation Army Anti-Suicide League optimistically stated, **'Since we placed a notice there three years ago, there hasn't been a leap'**. Not everyone was convinced. Had the sign worked or had those contemplating suicide sought an alternative method of suicide?

Just a month before the Sydney Harbour Bridge opened, the *Cessnock Eagle*, a regional newspaper, parodied the anti-suicide organisations, such as the Salvation Army with its fictitious take on suicide. The article from the *Cessnock Eagle* titled 'The Suicide Club' and was written by the 'Optimist'. The tongue-in-cheek article explained that the club had held an important meeting and carried several drastic resolutions. The fictitious president of the club, 'Mr Melancholy', declared to his members that the Gap, the official Sydney site for suicide, was losing its popularity as a **'hop off'** place.

The president noted the obvious, that **'none who had used it had ever complained about it afterwards'**, but when the new Sydney Bridge is opened and in operation, it will alter the future of metropolitan suicides, as well as anyone from country areas who could afford the expense of travelling to the city. 'Mr Melancholy' also stated that **'there was no denying the fact that the world demanded progress. It was evolution and the members of the Suicide Club desired progress too'**. The president moved that all future suicides use the Sydney Harbour Bridge and **'The Gap, from henceforth be discarded.'**

The fictitious 'Mr. Depression' seconded the motion and agreed that the Gap had gone out of fashion, and it was behind the times. In full support, 'Mr. Depression' announced that **'What they wanted was something modern'** and the new bridge **'filled their requirements to such an extent that it was ideal'**.

The fictitious meeting continued, claiming the **'The Bridge was more modern, there was a pride about it and in addition, it provided the suicide club with many facilities that were absent from the Gap. If a member wanted electrocution, it was there. If they desired tram-mangleation it was there, if they desired death through motor traffication, it was there - not to mention water smash-is-ation, if one preferred it...The bridge provided all of these things, free'**. The meeting concluded with the resolutions, **'unanimously adopted, and as a result all official suicides, so far as the club is concerned, will take place on, or from the bridge, after the official opening in March.'** In a satirical approach reminiscent of a Monty Python comedy sketch, the 'Optimist' article in the Cessnock Eagle made its point. In a time with different sensitivities, it wittily and unapologetically predicted the tragic role that awaited the Sydney Bridge.

A few days after the first bridge suicide, the popular Sydney newspaper *Truth*, known as the people's paper, provided its readers with a bold assessment of suicide, headlining that the Bridge will **'NOT'** fascinate suicides and that old-fashioned methods must prevail. The *Truth* declared, **'Felo-de-se (suicide) has its vogues, seasons, and popularities...it even has its sex appeal, for while women prefer to suicide one way, men, as a rule, prefer masculine methods of death'**. The *Truth* said that statistics revealed men prefer a gun or razor whilst women are attracted to drowning or poison. The news article continued with further assessments from an unnamed doctor who had studied the psychology of suicide. The doctor gave a gruesome statistical account of the various forms of hangings, cut throats and poisonings, and said that the bridge would not supersede the old forms of suicide. The doctor claimed the following...

'There is no more likelihood of the bridge becoming the State's most favourite death point than there is a likelihood of deranged people following the example of the Glen Innes grazier who built a stack of timber, set it alight, climbed on top, and shot himself through the brain. He shot himself on his own funeral pyre.' The doctor continued...

'The old-fashioned methods of committing suicide are the most popular. Figures support this argument. They show also that few people have the nerve to throw themselves from high places such as cliffs and bridges. Though many people have gone to their deaths over the Gap at Watson's Bay, police records show that hundreds went to the edge of the precipice, looked down at the jagged, foam-covered rocks, and quailed...

Last year in New South Wales, 225 men and 22 women committed suicide. Sixty-four men died by the gun, but only eight women chose this way out. Forty men cut their throats, but only four women could face the razor's grisly slash...

Gas poisoning, the easiest and cheapest form of committing suicide, was not as popular as many people would imagine. Twenty-five men and nine women died by this means. Some of them placed tubes leading to gas jets in their mouths. Most of them, however, just blocked all apertures, turned on the gas, and laid down to die.

Apparently, men fear the cold embrace of the sea. Last year, seven men and 11 women drowned themselves'.

'No!' said the psychologist 'the bridge will not supersede the older forms of suicide. Its dizzy height and the cold blue waters below will not fascinate the majority of those willing and determined to go out by their own hand.'

The unnamed doctor may have studied the psychology of suicide and statistics, but he may have underestimated the deadly lure of the Harbour Bridge. That men feared the cold embrace of the sea was a bold conclusion, and he may have overlooked the absence of any 'jagged foam-covered rocks' below the bridge. However, the view put forward by the doctor that the bridge would not become the 'State's most favourite death point' would be put to the test, and only time would tell.

There was no doubt murder and suicide were intriguing news stories, and the newspapers provided the curious public with far more detail than we would be comfortable with today. It was not unusual for journalists to employ a particular investigative style of reporting, looking for all the nitty gritty and often including oddities or peculiar twists to engage the reader. In the case of one bridge suicide victim, the newspapers described how the victim's gold cufflink miraculously hung on his bald spot while he floated face down in the water. In another gruesome suicide, the journalist reported how the victim had smashed every bone in his body but astonishingly died still clutching onto his pipe.

While crime and suicide were a popular newspaper script, hopefully, anyone considering self-harm was not an avid reader of this material and managed to avoid the newspapers as they were often merciless and quite comfortable with making a mockery of suicide, often describing the victims as 'irresponsibles', week minded, morbid, demented, or incurables.

The *Lithgow Mercury* even suggested that economics played a role in the method of suicide, and the cheapest choices were the gas oven or the bridge leap. The paper stated that '**Poisons are becoming unpopular among suicides in N.S.W. of late. For February, only four cases were reported, two by cyanide and two by Lysol. The gas oven and the North Shore Bridge are two unfair competitors. No** man can poison, himself under sixpence. The bridge leap costs nothing, and you can leave the landlady to pay the gas bill'.

One news article titled 'A Casual Suicide' described how James Brown, a 50-year-old taxi driver from Bondi, calmly arranged the details of his suicide and politely wrote a letter of apology to the woman owner of his garage. The newspaper gave a detailed account of how James Brown attached a large rubber hose to his taxi's exhaust and passed it through a small hole he had made in the cabin floor. Placing himself inside the taxi, he started the engine, locked all the doors and windows, and laid on the back seat. Two days later, and late in the evening, the garage owner noticed the lights on in her garage and went to investigate, only to discover Brown lying lifeless in the rear of the car.

She notified the police, and as soon as they arrived, they forced open the taxi door. Brown had been dead for some time and had pinned his penciled letter of apology to the front seat of the car. The letter read as follows…

'Sorry if you have to burst the door to get in, but I had to fasten it inside as I did not want to be disturbed while taking my sleeping draught(drink). The police will see you get compensation when the cab is sold. If you are not use to 'stiffs', there is a little whisky in the bottle, it is good and will steady your nerves'.

James Brown left a letter that was described as calmly polite, and in the face of tragedy, he found some light-hearted advice for his landlady. This was just another sign of the times, a tough and unpitying time when it was fine to make a mockery of suicide and not surprisingly, a stiff drink was offered as a simple solution for steadying the nerves.

Fig. 4 Notice erected by the Salvation Army at Ben Buckler cliffs

5

TIRED OF LIFE - THE FIRST WOMAN

There is a stage in human existence when hunger and hardship, coupled with hopelessness, make death appear a happy release.'

After the 'Great War' of 1914-1918, the world faced a slow and painful economic recovery, only to be met by a mighty plunge into financial ruin with the collapse of the American stock market in October 1929. Known as the Great Depression, an economic wave of disaster had spread globally, and as each year progressed, so did the depth of the financial crisis. Daily life, for many people, had become cruel and unforgiving. For many, it was a tormenting life of physical and mental hardship, starvation, unemployment, financial ruin, physical illness, or mental distress.

The possibility of being poverty stricken and trying to live with an uncertain future was a fear that some people couldn't deal with. Only five days before the opening of the Sydney Harbour Bridge, 38-year-old William James Power jumped to his death from a suspension bridge in Hornsby, a suburb north of Sydney. William was dismissed from his job at the railway department only weeks before, and a note addressed to his wife was found in his pocket, which read: **'Goodbye, there is nothing but poverty before us'**. The hopelessness of William's circumstances was not uncommon, and many people were destined for poverty no matter how hard they tried to fight against it; described as threadbare living, most people battled on, but everyone had a different breaking point and overwhelming fear was often the main driver behind their fragility.

By 1932 the devastating effects of the economic crisis had reached their peak in Australia. Unemployment across the nation had jumped to 32%., the second-highest unemployment rate in the world. The number of unemployed in New South Wales had reached 125,000, and the number of men, women, and children living on food relief was nearly 500,000, a total equalling a fifth of the state's population. Long lines of defeated-looking unemployed men waiting on Post Office steps where jobs were advertised were a common sight, all of them waiting for any work opportunity or the chance to apply. It was reported that when one Sydney company advertised at the Post Office for a night watchman, there were over 500 applicants.

The cities had seen an increase in begging, families hawking their wares were commonplace, and evictions and bankruptcy rates were at an all-time high. Across Australia, increasing numbers of impoverished and homeless people sought refuge wherever possible.

In Sydney, James Richardson and his wife and son were evicted from a cottage in Railway Parade Granville. Richardson then erected a tent for his family on nearby Margaret Street and stored his furniture and belongings under a tarpaulin beside it. A few days later, the police ordered James to move his tent. Richardson and his family carried all their belongings to a nearby vacant block of land. They again erected their tent and took a stand against moving anywhere until they could find a house.

In Victoria, the Minister for Public Works, Mr J P Jones, whilst driving from Warrnambool to his office in Melbourne, found a mother and her two children asleep on the side of the road. He discovered they had no home and had walked over 140 miles searching for work. The mother and her children had been without food or shelter for days. Accompanied by the mother and her two children, Mr Jones continued his journey to Melbourne, where he found them shelter and no doubt a hearty meal. Feeding the people had become a national crisis. In Melbourne, they established the Anti-Starvation Crusade, and in Sydney, the Sydney City Mission set up bread and soup lines.

The Federal Government introduced assistance programs such as the 'Sustenance' program, which came in the form of food coupons, which became known simply as the 'susso'. For the unemployed to qualify in New South Wales, the relief program or 'susso' required the person to register at the Labour Exchange. An individual had to make a declaration that they had been unemployed for more than fourteen days and state they had no financial means of supporting themselves. They then had to wait another seven days to receive food coupons, when the coupons were exchanged for bread, meat, and essential groceries at designated shops. Each fortnight after that, the recipient had to restate their declaration to continue receiving support. Reduced to receiving charity, thousands of men joined the coupon queues, desperate to place food on the table. Leaving their dignity at home, it took an extremely robust man to join the susso queue each fortnight. Never knowing how long it would last, it was a demoralising and overwhelming situation for many families.

51-year-old Francis Edward Thompson, a labourer from Manly, was on the 'susso' and was no stranger to 'tuff times'. Francis had a tough beginning as a child, a wayward teenager, a runaway at fourteen, and living and sleeping on the streets of Sydney. His parents were of good character and encouraged him to return home. Still, eventually, he was detained by the authorities, and under the recommendation of his mother, Emily, he was placed in a reform school. Francis spent his teenage years on the ex-Naval Ship *'Sobraon'*. On this converted naval ship, wayward and neglected boys were taught elementary education, nautical and industrial skills in the hope that they would leave better prepared for the adult world.

By the time Francis was 23, his life had changed dramatically when he married Ethel Barden, and together they settled down and started a family. In 1914 when World War broke out across Europe, Francis immediately enlisted with the 1st Battalion, Australian Imperial Forces. Now 35 years old, married and with five children, Francis, perhaps lured by the monetary incentives, felt compelled to join the AIF and fight for the mother country. Francis's war service was cut short when he was medically discharged almost as soon as he arrived in Egypt. His war record is unclear as to the circumstances surrounding his discharge, and he returned to Australia in February 1915. On his return, he returned to his old job as a labourer and family life with Ethel and his children, and as the years passed, they had three more children to add to their already large family.

On the morning of Friday, 10th June 1932, Francis made his way from his home in Manly to the State Labour Exchange at Circular Quay located a short distance from the Harbour Bridge. Francis planned to join the long line of unemployed and hand in his unemployment declaration at the Exchange office, and then wait another seven days for his food coupons. But Francis didn't get that far; his journey was suddenly diverted by what was later described as the deadly lure of the bridge.

Around midday, several pedestrians on the bridge witnessed Francis quickly climb onto the handrailing between the 4th and 5th spans on the city side of the bridge and, without hesitation he took an almighty leap into the air. The shocked witnesses watched in disbelief as Francis turned over and over, his arms and legs waving helplessly in the air, and then in the last few seconds, he braced himself in the foetal position before hitting the water. At the same time, Customs officials Fred Peterson and Tom O'Connell were passing beneath the bridge on board their Customs launch and watched helplessly as Francis hurtled towards them and struck the water only metres away from the launch, the force so powerful, water sprayed over the vessel and the officers on board.

Peterson and O'Connell quickly dragged Francis on board the launch and discovered that he had sustained horrendous head injuries but was still hanging onto life. They immediately made their way to the Water Police boat shed nearby, where an awaiting ambulance wagon quickly took Francis to the Sydney Hospital. On arriving at the Hospital, Dr Beattie, the on-duty doctor, rushed to meet the ambulance wagon outside. Thompson's body remained motionless on a stretcher. Dr Beattie and ambulance officers worked feverishly to revive him, but their desperate fight proved hopeless. Francis was pronounced dead on a stretcher inside the wagon.

During the investigation into Francis's death, the police confirmed that when they recovered his body from the harbour, they found a letter in his pocket addressed to the labour exchange manager. It appeared Francis intended to visit one of the food relief offices earlier in the day, but his course was diverted.

The Coroner, Mr Edward Erskine May, later returned an 'open verdict' on the death of Francis Thompson. He considered that Francis might have had every intention of throwing himself from the bridge but changed his mind at the last minute and fell into the water below. It was a strange verdict, considering the witness accounts but perhaps this was a compassionate decision to protect the family through a difficult time and from any stigma attached to suicide. Whatever the verdict, Francis was clearly in a distressed state of mind, and perhaps like suicide victim William Power, the fear of nothing but poverty before him was too much to carry.

Two weeks after Francis Thompson made his fatal leap, a young woman 'tired of life' followed the same ruinous path along the Sydney Harbour Bridge. At around 11.00 o'clock, the morning of June 24th, 1932, James Thompson, Tom Mace and Lyall Clarke, mechanics from Walsh Bay, were working on erecting barricades at the southern approach of the bridge to prevent sightseers from climbing the great arch. In the distance, they observed a woman wearing a black dress and blue sweater climbing the trellis near the eighth span on the western side of the bridge. Too far away and unable to alert anybody to prevent the troubling scene that was unfolding before them, the men stood powerless. They watched helplessly as 24-year-old Alberta Joyce Ellks continued to climb to the top railing and then took a leap into space. The men watched in disbelief as the horrifying scene played out before them. The high winds carried Alberta's body outwards from the bridge, turning her body twice in the air until she hit the water feet first and then, as witnesses described, 'she sank like a stone'.

Anxiously the workman scanned the water waiting for any sign of life. For what seemed like an eternity, Alberta's body finally rose to the surface and floated on top of the water, facing upwards. Not far away in his boat was Thomas Atkinson, a harbour 'waterman' who noticed a huge splash in the water. Completely unaware of what had occurred, Atkinson rowed towards the area and was shocked to see Alberta's body floating on the surface. He rowed immediately to her assistance, plucked her from the water, and discovered that she was still alive but barely conscious. Atkinson then rowed furiously through the water and managed to get her to the Water Police boat sheds. He was met by Sgt Day and Constable Jordan, two of Sydney Water Police's most capable officers.

When Sgt George Day joined the Water Police in 1915, his reputation on the waterways of Sydney preceded him. Day was once an Australian championship rower and an extremely popular competitor on the Parramatta River racing circuit in the days when gambling on sculling races proved as popular as horse racing. It wasn't long after starting as a constable, under the guidance of Sgt William Shakespeare, George Day was pulling people from the water of Sydney Harbour. Then in November 1927, when the ferry 'Greycliffe' sank in the Harbour, taking with it forty lives, George Day was responsible for rescuing eleven people and rightly received an award from
The Royal Humane Society of Australasia.

Fig. 5 Sgt George Frederick Day

28-year-old constable Walter 'Wal' Jordan was also a champion rower. A strapping young man described as 6ft with broad shoulders. His formidable size and sporting prowess extended from football and rugby to amateur wrestling and tennis, and with his tree-trunk arms, he was easily feared by criminals.

Like most of the men in the water police, they were conditioned to the job of rowing boats and retrieving bodies from the harbour, either found floating on the surface, trapped under wharves, and sometimes mutilated by the blades of propellers from passing steamers. It had always been an unsavoury occupation, and Sgt Day and Const. Jordan, were comfortable with the task, however, Alberta Ellks was their first Harbour Bridge suicide jump, a new encounter that would test their nerve.

As soon as Day and Jordan managed to get Alberta ashore, they were relieved to see that she was alive and conscious but suffering from shock. While they comforted her, she quietly explained that she had been in good health but was depressed. She then told them her name and that she lived at King Street Newtown. It wasn't long before the ambulance arrived and prepared Alberta for the drive to the hospital. At one point, to the amazement of the ambulance men, she suddenly sat bolt upright on the stretcher, her body stiffened, and then she quietly laid back down. The ambulance then made a desperate drive to Sydney Hospital, where Doctors and ambulance officers were astounded to discover that she had no broken bones and no outward signs of injury, landing feet first, perhaps saving her from more significant injuries at the time.

The following day it was reported that Alberta had survived her fall, but after a few desperate hours in the hospital, she died from a severe cerebral concussion. Before succumbing to her injuries, she had little to say, and in her final moments of despair, she had time to tell the ambulance officers that she was '**tired of life**'.

Ambulance officers and hospital staff were disheartened to see a young soul of just 24 years of age, worn out and with no fight left in her young body. Alberta died leaving behind her husband Rupert, a commercial traveller, and her two children, four-year-old son Raymond Edward Ellks and baby daughter Helen Cecelia who was just eight weeks old.

On July 1st, the inquest into Alberta's death was concluded, and the Coroner returned a verdict of suicide while '**temporarily deranged**'. The inquest revealed that although Alberta was in good physical health, she suffered from severe depression. The Coroner also heard evidence from her husband Rupert, who stated that '**she wanted to die**' and that Alberta had previously attempted suicide. Rupert Ellks also stated that after the birth of their baby, his wife became depressed and had previously attempted suicide on two other occasions and only a week before her death, she had returned from an institution where she received treatment.

Alberta's husband Rupert Ellks remarried just four months after her death, and shortly after, tragedy struck again when daughter Helen died soon after from severe gastroenteritis; she was just six months old. There may have been more behind the story leading up to the day Alberta took her own life, and it will remain a mystery; however, it is evident that Alberta was suffering from postpartum depression or more often referred to as postnatal depression. Even today, the causes of this depression are not entirely understood. However, it is a condition strongly considered detrimental to the well-being of women after childbirth.

Today these moments of deep depression and variability of the mind brought on after childbirth affect one in seven women and are well recognised within the public health sector, and indications that someone may be struggling with postnatal depression today are no different to the same signs a hundred years ago or even centuries earlier. Some of the more common signs include feeling inadequate and a failure as a mother, a sense of hopelessness about the future, feeling exhausted, empty, sad, and teary, feeling guilty, ashamed, or worthless, feeling anxious or panicky, having trouble sleeping, worrying excessively about their baby, and feeling scared of being alone or going out. In some cases, women may experience thoughts about leaving their families or worry that their partner may leave them. They could also have ideas about self-harm or harming their partner or baby.

24-year-old Alberta Joyce Ellks had the unfortunate distinction of being the first woman to jump from the Sydney Harbour Bridge; alas, others would follow, and the Sydney Harbour Bridge would become the stepping-off point for women with similar stories to Alberta.

6

TEMPORARILY MENTALLY DERANGED

'Bereft of all hope, a state of mind quite sufficient of itself to produce insanity'

On July 15th John Cameron a member of the Royal Australian Artillery was making his way to the Gunners Barracks at Mosman. Whilst walking on the western footway of the Bridge, he noticed an overcoat and some belongings left against the pedestrian fencing. Cameron checked one of the overcoat pockets and found a note which read, **'I, G Jenkins, commercial traveller, intend to take my life. I am suffering from heart and nerve trouble as a result of war injuries.'** These were the last words written by 48-year-old Gabriel George Jenkins, and based on the limited information, it appeared that Gabriel Jenkins jumped from the bridge, but there were no witnesses to the event.

The following morning Sgt Frazer Foott, along with a helping hand from Customs officials, made an extensive search beneath the bridge but failed to find any signs to confirm that Gabriel plunged to his death. Further investigations by the police also revealed that on the day Gabriel jumped, he was served with a summons to appear in the Central Police Court the following day to answer charges of fraud.

When Gabriel failed to appear before the court, the Magistrate was informed that Gabriel Jenkins had jumped from the Bridge, but at this stage, Gabriel's body had not been recovered, and there were no witnesses to his jump. The prosecution against Gabriel claimed they were not satisfied that Gabriel Jenkins was, in fact, dead, and the Magistrate issued a summons for his arrest on allegations that he defrauded a gentleman by the name of Thomas David Laney of £5s.

The prosecution had planted seeds of doubt, and even the police were unsure if Gabriel had jumped from the Bridge, but eleven days later, Gabriel's severely decomposed body was found floating under the No.4 wharf at Circular Quay. It was reported that several other notes were found in Gabriel's belongings, all intimating his intention to commit suicide.

Naturally, Gabriel's reason for taking his life will remain a mystery; however, he was not just a commercial traveller and war veteran who had fallen on hard times as first thought; his story is more intriguing.

Gabriel Jenkins was born in 1885 in Kyneton, Victoria. He was a qualified schoolteacher and a Captain of cadet training, having been certified by the highly regarded Duntroon Military Academy. As Captain and Area officer, he was involved in the instruction of military cadets and the compulsory training of future commissioned officers in Geelong, Victoria. After training and preparing many young men for service in the Australian Imperial Forces and seeing them embark for the battlefields of Europe, Gabriel also enlisted in the AIF in 1918 as a commissioned Lieutenant with the General Education Service Unit and embarked for England.

The war just ended as Gabriel arrived in England, and his service was cut short, and he returned to Australia in 1919, and his occupation as a schoolteacher in Geelong. A few years later, perhaps tired of teaching and disenchanted by the war effort, he sought a change, and he moved to St Kilda, an inner seaside suburb of Melbourne and took up a new trade as a merchant. Eventually, he made his way to Sydney. It is not known precisely what brought Gabriel to settle in Sydney, but he never returned to teaching and remained a bachelor.

A week after Gabriel's body was recovered from the harbour, a coronial enquiry into his death was held, and a few more intriguing details came to light. However, like many suicide enquiries, it only raised more questions than answers. His older brother Alexander from Victoria was present at the enquiry. He stated that Gabriel was quite distressed by the recent death of his mother and suffered from war injuries which Gabriel also said on his note.

However, on close examination of Gabriel's war record, it clearly shows he served in the General Education Services unit and was not involved in any active service in the field of battle, having arrived in England three days after the signing of the armistice. Also, his medical record on discharge from the AIF confirms he had no disabilities and noted that his heart and lungs were clear, followed by the statement from the medical officer, 'feels well'.

The question remained as to why Gabriel took his own life. He was far from financially ruined, having a significant amount of money in his bank account, and he certainly had sufficient funds to look after his fraud allegation of 5£s. The only significant clue was his note, where he mentioned he was suffering from heart and 'nerve trouble'. Robert Anderson, the first bridge jump survivor, lived to explain to his wife Daisy that his nerves were also bad at the time. **'I wasn't feeling so good at the time. Nerves bad, or something. I had a job with the railways, and I was all right. Just a bit —well, nervy.'**

What was described by doctors at the time as a person suffering from 'nerve trouble' or a 'nervous condition' was the equivalent of what today is often diagnosed as a generalised anxiety disorder. Without the correct diagnosis or medication, it is a debilitating disorder that involves persistent worry and fear of everyday situations. The fear can intensify and cause an increase in heart rate and other symptoms such as sweating, trembling, nervousness and a sense of impending danger that can lead to severe panic attacks and sometimes even self-harm. It seems highly likely that Gabriel suffered from this serious illness for some time and never revealed the full extent of his condition to anyone before his death except his brother Alexander. Gabriel may have also been considering suicide for some time as curiously he prepared his will only three months before his death, leaving his estate to the value of £232's to his brother Alexander.

The Coroner concluded that Gabriel Jenkins died from the effects of injuries received, having cast himself from the Sydney Harbour Bridge to the water below, '**while temporarily mentally deranged**'. Struggling with his mental health, Gabriel may have been at breaking point; the recent loss of his mother and the humiliation of going to court for fraud may have triggered an overwhelming panic attack, severe enough to cause a deranged state of mind that led to his tragic jump from the bridge. This is speculation, of course, but a simple explanation, and not surprising based on a few clues and similar circumstances faced by other suicides.

Shortly after Gabriel Jenkins jumped from the bridge, another bridge fatality had worry '**pray on his mind**', and with so much to live for, he was overwhelmed by the prospect of losing everything. On Friday morning, July 22nd, the same bridge workers who witnessed Alberta Ellks leap to her death only a month earlier were stunned once again to watch in the distance as 44-year-old William 'Jack' Chandler prepared himself to perform the same deadly stunt as Alberta.

The four Walsh Island workmen, James Thompson, Lyall Clarke, Tom Mace, and Fred Platt, were still working on the barricades on the arch at the southern approach to the Bridge when they saw a man climb over the rail on the eastern pedestrian walk. At first, they thought he was possibly a bridge workman, and they watched as the man hesitated for a few moments. But to their disbelief, he unexpectedly let go of his hold and jumped out of the decking. The four men once again could only watch from afar as William Chandler, a heavily built man, hurtled towards the water. He slammed into the water '**with a crash** like the report from a gun, missing a small rowing boat by only a few feet.

The man in the nearby rowing boat, Mr John Arthur Immer, who then rescued Chandler from the water, gave his graphic account of the event. '**I was rowing towards Circular Quay, directly under the sixth span of the southern side, when I saw the man hurtling downwards, with his arms and legs spread out.** For the moment it appeared to me that he would strike my boat, but he struck the water flat about four yards off...The splash was terrific, and my boat threatened to capsize. After disappearing below the surface, the man floated upwards within my reach. He was unconscious and groaning, and his clothes, with the exception of his singlet and collar and tie, had been swept off his body. I grabbed him by the shoulders and held him so until a 'Stannards Brothers' launch came, about five minutes later.'

Immer and Hedley Hearne, the motor driver from the Stannards launch, held onto Chandler until the Water Police launch reached the scene. Lifting him aboard the Police launch, the police took him to the Government boatshed where the Central District Ambulance was waiting. William Chandler drifted in and out of consciousness and was unable to talk but groaned in agony as he was placed in the ambulance. He was barely conscious by the time he reached Sydney Hospital, and unfortunately, William Chandler died an hour and a half later. After witnessing the suicides of William Chandler and Alberta Ellks, bridge worker James Thompson declared, '**Friday is certainly the unlucky day on the Bridge.**'

William Chandler was born in Kent, England and was an errand boy when he was just 13 years old and in his late teens, worked as a Postman. In his mid-twenties, he travelled to Australia and was employed as a timber worker. A hard-working man by nature and keen to make a good life for himself, he met and married Leonora Moore in Sydney in 1915. William eventually became a Lineman, the occupational term used for those who set the large wooden poles and strung the high voltage power lines between them, an occupation considered one of the most dangerous in the world. The Lineman faced the frightening statistic of approximately one in three linemen being electrocuted and killed on the job.

This high-risk work was well-paid, however, during the Great Depression, continuous work for the Lineman was difficult to find, and it wasn't long before William joined the ranks of the unemployed. A circumstance that William found challenging to live with and a personal struggle that would eventually overwhelm him. William was not in any immediate financial crisis, having property and substantial money both in savings and bonds. He worked hard, took great pride in what he achieved, and established a secure life for Leonora and himself.

As a Lineman, William was considered fearless and hard-working, but having never been unemployed, he was in unfamiliar territory, and his future was suddenly uncertain. William Chandler, a proud man, was plagued by the most common of human fears, failure, and the frightening thought of losing everything he had ever worked for. Overwhelmed by this prospect, William left home early in the morning of that tragic day. Dressed in a fine blue suit, a tie, and a new pair of tan shoes, he made his way to the Sydney Harbour Bridge and left a final message in a handwritten note to his wife, which read, '**Forgive me for what I am contemplating, there is no other way.**' His loving wife stated at his inquest that '**her husband had worried when he became unemployed and had allowed this to pray on his mind**'.

Leonora was devoted to her husband and remained in the home they bought together until her death in 1952. At the time of writing, their small cottage at Charles Street Leichhardt in Sydney still stands today. William Chandler's final few words reveal a heartbreaking story. A story not too different from many other hard-working, devoted husbands and family men who took their own lives during difficult times.

The day following William Chandler's leap from the Bridge, Sgt Bebb recovered another body floating in the harbour near Kirribilli

Point. The body was that of Bernard Cummins, a 37-year-old Customs clerk who was reliable, hard-working and highly regarded by his employer. Bernard was reported missing by his wife, Bernice, two weeks earlier. She explained to the police that she had been ill, and Bernard had gone out and bought her a pair of slippers. '**Here's a present, darling**,' he said. He then left for work and later rang a family friend, Mrs Groghan, who lived near his flat in Womerah Avenue, Darlinghurst, and asked if she could take care of his wife until he returned as he was detained at work and would not be home until late. However, Bernard never returned home. At first, it was thought Bernard Cummins was another bridge suicide. When Sgt Bebb recovered his body from the water, he found a sealed envelope in Bernard's trouser pocket. Inside the envelope was a message addressed to his wife. Scrawled on a brown piece of paper and signed 'Bernie', it read '**Dear Bernice, forgive and forget me. It's my head and I am afraid**'.

Further investigations revealed that Bernie drowned, and there were no injuries consistent with a fall from the bridge. It was also discovered that Bernie had been unwell for some time and received specialist help for his memory loss, depression, and severe head pains. Seemingly overwhelmed by his state of health, Bernie ended his life, the Coroner stating he died from '**asphyxiation from drowning caused by immersing himself in the waters of Port Jackson while temporarily mentally deranged**'.

While opinion still circulated 'that no sane man, woman, boy or girl will attempt self-destruction', it is interesting to note that the Sydney City Coroners' preferred the phrase 'temporarily mentally deranged'. At the same time, 'temporary insanity' was still a favourite with the Coroners in England. Perhaps the New South Wales courts were more sympathetic in an already insensitive time. But whatever the phrasing, the verdict still highlighted the momentary vulnerability and frailty of the human mind when subjected to overwhelming fear, distress, and anxiety.

Shockingly, the human cost of the tuff times was not just being played out in harbour tragedies. The past few months had been particularly disturbing, with the Sydney newspapers reporting that an appalling wave of crime had gripped New South Wales. The *Truth* newspaper highlighted that 'Murders, assaults on women, train wreckings, burglaries, factory thefts, bag snatchings, sex outrages, motor thefts, business frauds, and pilferings were providing the police with an anxious time.'

The *Truth* continued with a staggering summary of deaths that highlighted the extraordinary level of crime reaching across the state of New South Wales, with men, women, and infants all victims of a most difficult and ruinous time. A couple were slaughtered and buried in shallow graves in Holdsworthy. A wealthy Sydney solicitor was murdered in his sleep while his wife was battered and close to death. A 55-year-old man was brutally murdered with an axe at an unemployment camp near Sutherland railway station. The mutilated body of a baby was found near the harbour foreshores, the third such crime in as many months. A married woman was killed by her secret lover at Erskineville. A well-known farmer at Glen Innes was shot dead at his farmyard. A man was shot dead by a woman with whom he formerly lived outside the children's court.

The daughter of a wealthy businessman died after taking a strychnine-laced laxative powder in her home at Cremorne. A Ryde resident was shot dead after attempting to steal cabbages from a nearby vegetable grower. At Mosman, a man killed his wife and daughter and then committed suicide. A man was stabbed to death by his wife in his home at Five Dock. A woman and her maid were murdered at Cooma, and their slayer committed suicide.

If the overwhelming crime wave was not enough, there was more bad news for the people of New South Wales to wrestle with when the basic wage was officially reduced in August 1932. The state weekly wage of 4 pounds 2 shillings had been reduced to 3 pounds 10 shillings a week. But even with a reduction in the basic salary, the employed were still grateful to be employed. In a peculiar twist, it placed an even higher value on being one of the employed, as the employed still considered themselves the lucky ones.

Walsh Island workers, who saw a man jump from the bridge to-day.—Left to right: Messrs. L. Clarke, Tom Mare, James Thompson, Fred Platt.

Fig 6.

7

SUICIDE ETIQUETTE & FENCING

'Prevent irresponsibles making it a stepping-off point for Eternity'

A few weeks after the suicide of Alberta Ellks, the *Perth Mirror*, possibly the Harbour Bridges' harshest critic, published its view on the Sydney Bridge.

The article on page one of the *Perth Mirror* titled 'Suicide Bridge? - Sydney's Fear' read as follows. '**An agitation has been raised for adequate steps to be taken at once to prevent the Harbour Bridge from acquiring a reputation similar to that enjoyed by the Gap. It is suggested some simple and inexpensive addition to the sidewalks could be devised to prevent irresponsibles making it a stepping-off point for Eternity. One idea is that two or three strands of barbed wire be placed on either side. This would not be costly.**'

Surprisingly, the views expressed by the Perth newspaper triggered a wave of interest and suggestions that the bridge needed to be fenced. The reference to a simple solution such as a few strands of barbed wire, was perhaps more tongue in cheek, a further niggling from a sibling state. However, the fact remained that the problem of suicides from the Sydney Harbour Bridge was going to continue if a covering more substantial than a few strands of barbed wire was not added to the footway.

This was not the first time that the subject of fencing had been raised; the earliest suggestion regarding fencing the footway of the SHB had been presented to the State Government in 1930, two years before the bridge was completed. A delegation arranged by Colonel Orr of the Salvation Army and Reverend George Cowie, convenor of the Social Service Committee of the Presbyterian Church, lobbied the Government to provide safeguards against possible suicide attempts. The delegation was largely ignored and informed by the State Government that '**The footways are as safe as those of other large bridges in the world, and it is not deemed necessary to provide special safeguards.**' The subject of fencing suffered an authoritative silencing, and it wasn't until the 6th bridge suicide occurred in August 1932 that the need for fencing became more compelling.

On August 3rd, 1932, 43-year-old William Bray, unable to find employment for many years, feeling overwhelmed by his lonely and impoverished life, made his way along the pedestrian footway to the centre of the bridge where he stopped, took off his hat and gazed out over the harbour. William then placed a note inside the hat, left it on the footway, and proceeded to climb over the bridge railing.

Charles Broughton of Parramatta was about 160 ft away from Bray when he noticed what was happening. Without hesitation, Broughton shouted to Bray, '**Come back you'll fall**' and for a moment, caught his attention. Bray turned towards Broughton, outstretched his arm, pointed to the hat on the path, and yelled back at him. Unable to hear what Bray was yelling, Broughton then made a desperate run towards him but was too late. Broughton was transfixed as he watched helplessly as Bray turned in the air, plunging face-first into the water and was killed instantly. His body was soon recovered by Sgt Day of the Water Police, with the newspapers reporting that Bray was found floating face down in the water and by some means, a gold sleeve link had become detached from Bray's shirt cuff and '**was balanced on a tiny bald spot on the back of the unfortunate man's head**'.

William planned his jump from the bridge and felt it was courteous to leave a note to assist the police with their investigations. As he prepared for his jump, it seems likely that at the last moment, he noticed Charles Broughton and yelled to him about his hat, which contained the note, making sure that Broughton would recover his hat and pass it on to the police. Later at the Coronial inquiry, police presented the note that William Bray left in his hat as evidence. The note was addressed to the police and declared the following.

'**Urgent – I've just gone over the Bridge - this is to certify that I was working for the N.S.W Railway till I got my foot and ankle smashed up at Albury in April 1929. They paid me compensation (£500) in a lump sum, which is all gone now, and I do not see anything else for it now, but to do away with myself rather than beg or starve. I have been sleeping anywhere these last few nights. I have no friends or relations in Australia.**' William Bray gave his address as '**Here there and everywhere**'

In his final moments, William Bray demonstrated a form of what was described as 'suicide etiquette', a term used back in 1912 when the Yarra River Bridge suicides in Melbourne were going through yet another suicide epidemic. The Adelaide *Daily Herald* covered the epidemic, and, in the article, 'Etiquette of Suicide' explained that there was a 'certain regard' for someone whose suicide was courteous, clean, and tidy as opposed to someone who left a public mess or inconvenienced others.

The article highlighted the case of a man who took poison to end his unhappy life and left a note which included his reason for using poison, stating it was a clean method and made no mess. The article also described how a Quaker girl cut her throat over a 'pale to avoid making a mess'. It's not likely the Sydney Bridge Suicides inconvenienced others, as suggested by the *Herald*. And there was certainly no mess or any evidence that the victims were given a 'certain regard' for their courteous actions, but curiously, there were many cases where the Sydney Harbour Bridge victims displayed an apparent favour for ceremony or etiquette.

In most cases, the bridge victims made their way to the same spot on the bridge, the centre of the bridge, which more often than not was the customary station on the walkaway and later described by the press as the usual 'jumping off point'. Some showed a preparation for suicide which often involved a specific dress code, with some victims making a point of dressing up as if attending a special occasion. A suit and tie, polished shoes and a hat for men, a more fashionable hat for women, a colourful dress, gloves, a favoured coat or handbag, or even a bouquet were all part of the custom in preparation for the final journey. Curiously many victims then removed some of their fine clothes, as if placing an even greater value on them than their own life, folding them carefully and then placing them neatly on the spot from where they jumped. And then, as a final gesture, they often left behind a note containing their parting words and, every so often, a few vital clues to their despair. These intriguing courtesies were executed with calm, correctness, and a purpose right to the end.

The handwritten note was perhaps the most critical part of the etiquette of suicide and a vital piece of information for police investigations and anyone related or connected to the suicide victim. Like William Chandler, who left a heartfelt note asking for his wife's forgiveness or William Bray, who left a note addressed to the police attesting to his actions, these were actions of people who had prepared themselves for the end.

William Bray was officially the 6th suicide from the Bridge and the newly appointed City Coroner, Mr Herbert Howell Farrington, presided over the inquiry into his death. After spending six years as a Police Magistrate in the Mudgee and Lithgow districts of New South Wales, Herbert Farrington had established a fine reputation as a sound arbitrator who had won 'the respect of litigants, counsel and police'. He would soon prove to be one of the most effectual Coroners during the most difficult of times.

At the conclusion of William Bray's inquest, Coroner Farrington returned a verdict of suicide from '**injuries and immersion willfully caused by casting himself from the Sydney Harbour Bridge**'. It wasn't long before this phrasing from the new Coroner would become a familiar expression for bridge suicides. The same week of the coronial inquiry into the death of William Bray, there were six more suicide verdicts passed by Coroner Farrington. One particular inquiry was the case of 42-year-old Mrs Murial Walsh, who drowned after casting herself over the side of the ferry *Kiandra* and into the harbour. She left behind some clothing and a suicide note to her husband, which was carefully pinned to her handbag. The Murial Walsh case not only exhibited 'suicide etiquette' but was a timely reminder that ferry suicides continued, and not all deaths on the harbour were bridge suicides.

Shortly after William Bray jumped, the Sydney *Daily Telegraph* published a plea to the Government to act, a call to action, claiming that the Government was shirking responsibility and had a duty '**to save unfortunate people from themselves**' and suggested '**that the Transport Department should do something to make these mad acts impossible**'. The *Daily Telegraph* noted how previous suggestions had been dismissed and taken lightly by the Government '**but the time has arrived for action**'.

The retiring City Coroner, Mr Edward May, on his departure from his esteemed position, also commented on the bridge suicides and declared, '**I am quite satisfied that the Bridge is a lure to death.**' and agreed with suggestions that a guard should be erected along the footway railings. Mr May went further to explain that '**The Gap once attracted suicides but there were, on an average, only three or four fatal cases a year, most of those, who intended jumping over being stopped by police. If it is impracticable to erect a guard along the footway, then the only way to stop these** unfortunate, people from plunging to death is to have police on guard.' Unfortunately, the only response from the Government was from the Minister for Transport, Mr Bruxner, who simply said, 'the responsibility was for the police'.

Meanwhile, the Sydney newspapers were not so quickly silenced on the call for fencing. Over the following weeks and months, they strengthened their appeal by publishing shared concerns from the public. One headline from the Sydney *Daily Telegraph* declared 'RAISE THE WALL' followed by a statement from an unnamed Macquarie Street doctor 'I can only suggest that the wall be raised without the symmetry of the Bridge being impaired, or else a wide lacing of barbed wire along the wall,' said the Macquarie Street doctor. 'If the Bridge becomes any more aligned in the minds of the people with suicide, it will be a bad day for this city, and for a population unstrung by troubled times.'

In a letter to the Sydney *Sun* newspaper, Mr B D Sweetland expressed his concern that not even Dr Bradfield, the Government Engineer and master builder of the bridge, said he had no idea of any means by which suicides could be prevented from leaping from the Bridge. Mr Sweetland continued, 'Let it not be said by future historians that at this period of our history there existed no one of mind inventive enough to cope with this evil. I respectfully suggest an arch or half-arch of wire netting - foot-square mesh - erected on stanchions or davits fastened to the parapet, and covering the footway, extending the length of the bridge.' Mr Sweetland evidently had an engineering background and a vision that offered a far better solution than strands of barbed wire, and it wasn't long before there were other like-minded calls for fencing and netting of the footway.

Local resident F. S Burnell from Cremorne, in a letter to the Editor of the *Sydney Morning Herald* suggested an alternative solution. 'Sir....

For persons of suicidal tendencies, the Harbour Bridge evidently holds an irresistible attraction. The municipal authorities of Rome were faced with precisely the same problem a few years ago, when a section of the 1700-year-old wall of the city, enclosing the famous Pincian Gardens, became a favourite resort for suicides, who leaped off it to the roadway, sixty feet or so below. To discourage this practice, a strong wire netting, of sufficient width, was extended, not horizontally, but at an upward tilt, between iron stanchions, projecting from the wall...

Burnell continued, 'Suicide is usually the result of a sudden impulse, prompted by opportunity. To leap off the wall into the net, crawl to the edge of the net, and drop deliberately into space, calls for a cold-blooded determination rarely found in combination with this particular form of psychosis. May I suggest that similar measures would prove equally effective in Sydney?'

The increasing publicity surrounding the Bridge suicides also prompted various public statements from the Salvation Army and some of Sydney's prominent clergymen. Colonel Carpenter of the Salvation Army made his appeal that the Army would favour any move to prevent people from using the Bridge to commit suicide. The Salvation Army had not considered any structural form of safeguard but stated that the Salvation Army had erected a notice at 'The Gap' inviting those in distress to call in at the Salvation Army headquarters. Col. Carpenter stated, ' **Only today, a mother burdened with worries went to 'The Gap' to throw herself over. She saw our notice and called on us. After receiving spiritual help, she was diverted from her purpose.**'

Reverend F. H McGowan stated that regarding suicides, '**The Bridge seems to have an attraction in this regard, covering it might reduce the danger**' and fellow clergyman, Reverend F. W Reece of

Mosman, thought having a more watchful eye on the bridge with extra Police patrol was the answer. Reverend George Cowie from the Fullerton Memorial Church in Surry Hills, a charitable man who cared for many of the disadvantaged in Sydney, was an early campaigner for fencing the bridge as far back as 1930. As was his way, he took a hands-on approach and had written a letter to Mr Reginald Weaver, the secretary for Public Works and Minister for Health, asking to meet a delegation with suggestions for fencing. Rev. Cowie had gone down this route before and failed to inspire any interest from the authorities. Unfortunately, his attempt failed again, and not a single reply from the government departments to meet and address the problem was forthcoming. '**Officialdom**', as the *Daily Telegraph* explained, '**will not go out of its way to prevent the beautiful structure from acquiring the name of 'Suicide Bridge'.**

While Sydney's prominent clergyman and charitable organisations expressed their concerns and were in favour of anything that would help reduce the possibility of people taking their own lives, local councils shared a far less positive view and continued to treat the matter lightly. The Lord Mayor of Sydney, Samuel Walder, gave the impression that it was not much to worry about, declaring '**every city had a spot favoured by suicides**' and that it would take a regiment of police to prevent such suicides. And a wishful thinking Mayor of North Sydney, Alderman Hubert Primrose, suggested that the Harbour Bridge suicides were simply a phase. Primrose claimed, '**the Bridge suicide phase would pass, as did the old-time craze that people had of throwing themselves under trams and trains.**'

It seemed that it was still early days for trying to prevent bridge suicides; the numbers were low, with only six victims, and it appeared anyone in a position to make something happen was not that interested.

While there was a sudden flurry of calls to fence the bridge, all seemingly ignored, a bridge tragedy of a different kind had caught everyone off guard. On the evening of the 5th of August 1932, Constables

Clifford Bush, aged 26 and Joseph McCunn, aged 23, were struck by a fast-moving car near the centre of the bridge. The constables were regulating traffic when the car crashed into them, hurling them into the air, and both constables died from their injuries. The force of the impact was so severe the radiator of the car was forced back into the engine, the bonnet dented and twisted, the front lights broken, the windscreen shattered, and the front bumper was completely torn off. Naturally, the news surrounding the tragedy was intensive, and the Sydney Bridge was again in the public spotlight.

During the inquest that followed, the outcome was full of surprises when the key witness was exposed for attempting to blackmail the driver of the vehicle. Despite the extensive damage to the car, there was no supporting evidence that the driver was speeding or driving recklessly. It was concluded that the lighting on the bridge was poor after being reduced by one-third to save expense. On that particular evening, this alone contributed to the accident, with the driver unable to see the police constables in the middle of the roadway. The driver was later acquitted, and the bridge lighting was restored to its original brilliance. The shocking police tragedy on the bridge placed another target on the back of the bridge, and there was now a sense that the Sydney Harbour Bridge was becoming significantly more sinister.

8

THE SINISTER SPELL OF THE BRIDGE

'Morbid fancy today plays round the Bridge as a stage for suicide. To the disordered mind, the majestic arch over the deep and silent water becomes a theatre of sublime tragedy.'

By September, just six months after the opening of the Bridge, it was becoming increasingly clear that the fascination over the grand grey structure had shifted from a romantic architectural form to a 'stage for suicide', a bridge as sinister and as notorious as 'The Gap'. The *Truth* newspaper in Sydney keenly followed the events of the bridge suicides and frequently commented on the 'uncanny spell' of the Harbour bridge, often describing its **'Grim Lure'** as a magnet, drawing in both the happy and the harassed. The newspaper's reputation for melodramatic reporting had assumed the bridge a sinister character.

Unfortunately, the negative publicity surrounding the run of bridge suicides had brought it to the attention of anyone with the slightest inclination toward suicide, and there was an alarming increase in the number of failed attempts to jump from the bridge. Just as reports of **'Another Bridge Suicide'** made the news, stories of **'Struggles on**

the Bridge' were also making headlines, and it wasn't long before the public played a crucial role in saving lives. The passing taxi driver, the tradesman working on the bridge, ordinary folk on their way home from work, and everyday users of the bridge, were now more alert to suspicious behaviour as suddenly everybody on the bridge seemed to be a potential suicide.

On a single evening, a railway employee returning home from his night shift on his regular route along the bridge ran to the aid of a young man screaming for help. The young man's girlfriend had attempted to jump, but during the ordeal, she fainted and was lying unconscious on the footway. A lovers' quarrel had been the cause for her sudden attempt at suicide. Only a few hours later, an older woman was found at the centre of the bridge, slumped on the railing, her head resting on her arms and weeping bitterly. She was noticed by a passerby and a bridge employee, who both came and comforted the lady. She explained to them that she was deeply distressed and worried over her domestic situation. She made no claims about wanting to commit suicide, but clearly, the time and place were ominous.

While many suicide attempts were often thwarted, they were a simple testimony to the various hardships people faced. Even the youth of the day found everyday life difficult, with family circumstances sometimes overwhelming them.

Mr Ken Weeks, the son of a well-known city hotelkeeper, after missing the last train at the end of a long workday, was making his way home on foot at 1.00 am. On his way across the bridge, Ken spotted an 18-year-old youth taking off his clothes and placing them in a pile on the footway. The youth then suddenly spotted Ken and made a rush for the railing. Ken Weeks sprinted towards the youth and made a desperate lunge and whilst suspending himself over the railing grabbed the youth and held onto him by the wrist. Ken yelled for help as he held onto the youth who swivelled perilously in the air. It wasn't long before another man came to assist, both men pulling the youth back across the railing and onto the footway. Collapsing to the ground exhausted and distraught, the youth declared to his heroic rescuers, **'I've been downtrodden all my life, and I've had trouble at home.'**

Late in the evening on the 26th of September 1932, Robert Millard was making his way home in Jeffrey Street, North Sydney, when he noticed a young man ahead of him starting to climb the railing. Millard made a dash towards him and managed to grab hold of the youth, who had only a single hand left clinging to the railing. Both men struggled, fighting against each other with superhuman effort, one trying desperately to perform a rescue while the other was just as desperate to jump to his death. Fortunately, Millard, a man of strong build, overpowered the young man, ultimately knocking him breathless with a blow to the stomach and then dragging him back over the railing to safety.

Millard stated, **'the youth dropped like a log and was violently ill.'** With the determined youth finally subdued, another pedestrian arrived on the scene. Millard asked the pedestrian to watch over the youth while he ran to telephone the police. When Milliard returned, the youth was alone, evidently, the other pedestrian didn't want to be involved and made his escape. Robert Millard then handed him to the police for questioning.

Still distressed and feeling regretful, the young 18-year-old revealed that he had been unemployed for some time. He had just managed to get a job and spent his entire first wage on alcohol. The youth confessed to police it was the first time he tasted **'strong liquor'** and was too afraid to go home. Under the influence of alcohol and struggling with anxiety, his choices that night were reduced to either an uncertain suffering at home or committing suicide. The brave rescuer Robert Millard later explained that, ironically, he'd sent a letter to his brother just the day before, telling his brother he always kept a sharp lookout on the pedestrian footways while on his daily walk across the bridge, but he never saw anything suspicious.

On another occasion, a young 22-year-old woman had just lost her baby, her husband had left her, and she was determined to end her own life. The young woman caught a taxi at 1 am and asked him to stop on the bridge. The taxi driver, who was naturally suspicious of her behaviour, watched as she left the taxi and immediately made her way to the tramway fence and started to climb over the railing. The taxi driver then jumped from his car and made a fearless dash towards the young woman as she looked determined to continue her journey towards a fatal leap. As he grabbed her, she became hysterical and shouted, '**let me go over, let me jump and end it all. I have lost my baby and my husband has dumped me. Let me jump over and be at peace with little Patsy.**' The Taxi driver comforted the woman until the police arrived, and the deeply distressed woman was remanded in custody and held for treatment and observation at what was known as the 'Reception House' at Darlinghurst.

The 'Reception House' was originally appointed by the New South Wales government as the 'Lunatic Reception House', and in the case of attempted suicides, it provided a place for temporary detention and, if required, treatment for up to fourteen days in preference to sending them directly to goal or admission to an asylum for the insane. The primary purpose of detention for anyone attempting suicide was to observe and help establish if they were insane.

Another city taxi driver, William Turner, received a fare from a passenger who said he wanted to be driven over the bridge. William was halfway across when the passenger asked if William could pull up. William believing the man was like many other tourists and interested in taking in the view, did what he asked. Suddenly the passenger sprang from the car and made a run for the railings. William quickly realised the man was not just another tourist and raced after him and managed to catch hold of him just as he started climbing the trellis work. '**Let me go!**' '**Let me go!**' he shouted, '**I want to go over, right or wrong!**' William restrained the hysterical man long enough for the patrolling police to arrive on the scene, take charge of the situation, and deliver him to the Reception House.

Jean Susie Boulton was just 17 years old, described as a 'vivacious' young girl, and 'decidedly pretty' with golden hair. 'Susie' as she was best known, was from a wealthy family and lived at home with her widowed mother, Laura, and her older sister Margie in the harbour heights suburb of Bellevue Hill. Susie seemingly didn't have a care in the world. She had a comfortable life, the newspapers noting that she was rich and cultured and even had a car of her own. There was little doubt that Susie was a high achiever. She attended the Science faculty at university and was an accomplished musician and painter. Her study schedule had been intense, and she passed her chemistry exams with first-class honours. On her school break, she was preparing to equal her performance in the forthcoming examinations.

On the morning of September 8th 1932, Susie decided to take a break from her usual study routine and planned to have a long lunch in the city and do a spot of shopping. Dressed in her favourite woollen dress and a fine knitted jumper, she left home in her usual high spirits and happily told her mother she was spending the day in the city. On her way to lunch, Susie was inexplicably sidetracked, and as the *Truth* newspaper spookily described it, she **'mysteriously succumbed to the curiously sinister spell of the Bridge'**.

At around midday, Susie was standing at the Sydney end of the Harbour bridge and proceeded to climb up the grille of the pedestrian railing. The only witness, Mr Arthur Sheen of Willoughby, saw Susie sitting astride the top railing; she took a moment and then, taking one glance at the water below, Susie lunged sideways into the open space and spun perilously to the depths below, turning over and over until she hit the water. As Susie spiralled to the water below, Mr E Nissen, a superintendent with the Timber Merchants' Association, was aboard the launch *'Satsma'* and was only fifty metres from where Susie entered the water. Also nearby were Mr Downey and Mr Wittman of the Harbour Trust on another launch approaching the bridge when the huge splash in the water also attracted them. Both launches rushed towards Susie who had now floated to the surface.

Mr Nissen on the *'Satsma'* reached Susie first and dragged her aboard. The Harbour Trust launch then arrived, and the crew quickly assisted by taking her aboard their vessel and then rushed her to the nearby Water Police station at Dawes Point. A small crowd had gathered and witnessed Susie's motionless body being carried ashore. Her left arm and side were terribly swollen, her face was cut, and her eyes were blackened and swollen shut.

Sgt Bebb and constable Bent of the Water Police were on the scene and were concerned by her facial injuries believing she may have struck something in the water as her wounds were not consistent with others who had made the massive plunge. Sgt Bebb immediately wrapped her in thick blankets and applied hot water bottles. Only recently had Sgt Bebb's team installed an emergency kit for such a scenario. It included a large number of blankets, water bottles and a large kettle continually on the boil. The kit appeared extremely basic, but it was sufficient until the central ambulance arrived.

As the crowd watched over her, Susie remained unconscious, and the anxious spectators knew she was not expected to live. She was then transported to Sydney Hospital, where doctors and nurses described her condition as grave. She had a fractured skull and fractures to her left arm and wrist, and her nerves were severely shocked making it challenging to determine the full extent of her injuries. Whilst the situation looked grim for young Susie, the doctors gave her a fighting chance with a special team of nurses and doctors who staged a night-long vigil, maintaining a determined effort to save her life.

By this time, the Police had identified Susie after recovering her white handbag, which she had left on the bridge. It contained her motor licence, £5 in notes and silver, and several expensive vanity cases. A reporter from the Sydney *Sun* newspaper had been on hand during the discovery of Susie's handbag. He immediately made his way to the home address shown on her licence and called on the unsuspecting family. After hearing the tragic news and fearing the worse, her mother, Laura and her sister Margie made their way to Sydney Hospital and Susie's bedside.

Late that evening, Susie regained consciousness. Suddenly noticing her painfully injured body, she struggled to ask what had happened to her. Her mother and sister were mystified and unable to explain the truth, as Susie had no recollection of the day's events. To prevent further distress, her family and friends thought it best not to refer to her experience and explained to her that she had been knocked down by a car.

The staff of nurses at the hospital maintained constant care over Susie's condition, and the acting medical superintendent attended to her every five minutes. Susie continued to improve, and four days later, the 'decidedly pretty' girl, who was given little chance of survival, was showing signs of making a full recovery. It took several more weeks before Susie could show any sign of her former vivacious spirit, but with ample means to afford the best specialist treatment and only partial paralysis of her left arm and a weakened eyelid, she eventually made a complete recovery.

She was eventually told the truth about the cause of her injuries, but she maintained she had no recollection of a single event on the dark day she took the plunge off the bridge. The fact that Susie had no memory from that day was a condition later explained by psychiatrists as **'amnestic fugue'**, a rare disorder whereby a person performs actions whilst in a trance-like state. It usually involves the person taking unplanned trips or wandering and often taking on a dual personality. The psychiatrists were not puzzled by her case and described Susie as a wide-awake sleepwalker who left her home, went into town, and journeyed to the bridge. Although considered extremely rare, this condition is thought to be brought on by a pattern of extreme worry or anxiety, a fatigue from over-study and mounting into a fear of failure and possibly self-harm.

Once the truth that surrounded the cause of Susie's injuries was revealed, it must have been an incredible experience for Susie to understand, but without a single memory of her actions, it was also an experience she was unable to share. Susie Boulton was the first woman to jump from the Sydney Harbour Bridge and survive, and surprisingly her jump was never proclaimed as such. It made sense that she could not make her account public, as she had no memory of the event, but following her remarkable recovery, Susie Boulton was interviewed by the *Truth* and gratefully declared…'**I have a good deal to be thankful for, I have my life and I will soon have my good health. I have my mother and my friends, and I have the splendid goodwill of those dear doctors and nurses who have done so much and are still doing so much to help me.**'

As was the case for all suicide attempts, including that of Susie Boulton, it was still a criminal offence to attempt suicide (until 1983, when it was finally abolished), but anyone who failed in the attempt, no matter what the reason, had their day in court to explain their actions. Many cases were sad and desperate, and the court often could not ignore the effect of harsh punishment on someone already struggling with life. In most cases, the offender would plead guilty with the promise of never attempting to do it again. The courts were generally lenient, and the person was either admonished and discharged or ordered by the magistrate to enter a bond and in particular, keep the peace towards him or herself for a period of time set by the court.

Although the act of attempted suicide appears somewhat inconsistent with criminal activity, it was still a crime in 'common law', and the court appearance often worked in preventing the offender from ever attempting the act again. Unfortunately, this was not quite the case for 37-year-old Margaret Martin, who, in an unsuccessful attempt to throw herself from the bridge in May 1933, was released from the Reception House after extensive observation and then had her day in court. Just five days after her release, the *Labor Daily* reported the following news, '**Took Life in Second Attempt - Failed on Bridge but Gassed Herself – Pathetic Case.**' Margaret did indeed gas herself, only to be found dead in the laundry by her daughter.

9

THE WRONG MAN

'Jumping over the Harbour Bridge is easily explained. The height and atmosphere are fascinating, and it is handy, but the main reason is simply that someone else has done it.'

After the great war ended in 1918, the returning war veteran had been high on the list of suicide rates, and most of the public sympathised with their struggles. But as time passed, the ageing, wounded and sometimes forgotten war veterans were gradually sidelined by the economic and political unrest around the world. By 1932 when William Lewis made his historical suicide leap from the bridge, the public was hardly surprised to hear he was a war veteran. The world had suddenly become crowded with a suffering society, and war veterans like William Lewis shared in the social and economic crisis just like everyone else. As one news journalist aptly described, '**The pencil of time had traced lines in their faces. It had whitened their hair, and the passage of years had taken the old buoyancy from their step. They were men older than their years, battered also in the economic war that followed the war of shells**'.

For many war veterans, the repatriation process had run its course, and the veteran was soon unable to survive on his diminishing war pension and desperately sought employment. Employment for war veterans had always been difficult, but during the depression years, unemployment numbers swelled, and work opportunities for the ageing veteran were nearly impossible. Up against a seemingly endless choice of healthy young men just as desperate for work, the veterans' chance of finding employment was next to none. With the strong possibility of his declining health and some certainty that it was not likely to improve, the veteran was already disadvantaged.

Even Australia's most celebrated war heroes were not safe against the difficulties of the Great Depression. Honoured with the highest military distinction, the Victoria Cross, and loved by all Australians, Albert Jacka's last fight was his greatest. In extremely poor health from his war injuries, his fight against the economic depression was desperate, and despite all his efforts, he died in circumstances that left his widow and child with only the ordinary pension of £2 '2 a week.

Hugo Throssell, the first Western Australian to be honoured with the Victoria Cross, also found life difficult after the war. He had seen the suffering of war, and his outspoken view on politics and his stance on the futility of war had altered the public's view of the national war hero. His very public political opinions badly damaged his employment prospects, and he fell deeply into financial debt, and sadly on November 19, 1933, Hugo Throssell VC took his life. The war veteran was aware of his circumstances, he had seen many things in his time, and the war experience had changed his view of the world, but he could have never imagined that many years after the Great War, his life back home would become so desperate.

William James Connoley was one such veteran who faced this bewildering and harsh reality. William was not only a war veteran but was 60 years of age and, unfortunately, considered an old man. William was 43 years old when he volunteered to join the Australian Imperial Forces in September 1915. He stated he was born in Carlton, Victoria, and his occupation was a greengrocer. He fudged his age so he would not be excluded for being too old to enlist and stated he was 38 years old and was made a private with the 3rd Battalion. While serving in

France, he was wounded by shell shrapnel which struck him in the face, and he was hospitalised. William had fully recovered from his wounds within a few weeks, and eager to rejoin his unit, he continued to serve until the war ended in November 1918.

After the war, William returned home and tried to return to the life he had before the war and re-established himself in the only trade he knew, a greengrocer or barrow-man as they were known in the day. The barrow-man would buy wholesale fruit and vegetables direct from the growers, and with a council permit and a suitable site, he would park his wagon and hawk his produce to the passing customers. Some vendors occupied fixed stands in prime locations while others trundled their barrows in and out of the traffic, looking only for temporary sites.

Before the war, there was a strong community of street stalls and market sellers all sharing in the trade, however after the war, times had changed, and by the early 1930s, the worsening economic depression had made competition for permits and sites difficult, and barrow markets began springing up all over Sydney streets. Unlicenced hawkers were now vying for the same territory as the licenced hawkers, so the city council imposed limits and held ballots to help control the increase in men turning to self-employment as barrow men to earn an income.

Often unable to secure a site and a permit through the city council, William's prospects for the future were severely compromised. At 60 years of age, William was no longer the strong young man he was before the war. Although toughened by years of hard work, he was not up to the daily task of slogging the city streets with a heavy barrow trying to sell whatever fruit and veg he could manage. Without a permanent site to conduct the only trade he had known for over forty years; it was obvious to William he was not likely to find an alternative living. This was the final straw for William, and on Monday, September 19, a downcast William Connoley wilfully cast himself from the Sydney Harbour Bridge.

On the same day, the Sydney *Sun* newspaper reported news of William's leap, describing him as an old man who climbed over the railing on the western side of the bridge near the city, balancing on the railing for a moment, and then leapt out. William struck the water feet first and slowly came to the surface, at which time the crew on the Sydney tugboat *Bondi* spotted him in the water and rushed to his aid. William appeared conscious, and the crew on board threw a hook over the side, managed to catch on to William's clothing, and held him up above the water until a nearby customs launch pulled alongside and pulled him on board.

After reaching the government boatsheds nearby, the central district ambulance then rushed him to Sydney Hospital. William remained conscious and appeared to be suffering from signs of shock and immersion and had a small cut on his back. They also found that he was carrying his military discharge papers in his coat pocket. At first, it appeared William had not sustained any severe injuries, but on closer examination, he had neck and spinal injuries and was suffering from shock; two hours later, he quietly passed away. Just before William died, he managed to reveal to the police that he jumped from the bridge because he was disappointed in the day takings of his fruit barrow, a seemingly simple explanation, but one the police knew masked a more tragic background.

At William's inquest, Frederick Briggs, who lived at the same address as William and had known him for some years, provided additional information about William's state of mind before his death. Fred stated that William was worried and deeply despondent **'because he had failed to secure a suitable site in the ballot for barrow positions.'** Like many war veterans, particularly an ageing veteran, William was exhausted by the daily struggle to survive. Finding it hugely challenging to make ends meet whilst physically battling to maintain the only trade he knew in an overcrowded marketplace; it is not difficult to recognise William's tragic decision to end his life.

A few days after the William Connoley inquest, the popular Sydney sporting newspaper *Arrow* commented on the growing number of bridge suicides. It published its startling view on suicide, contending that jumping from the bridge had become a fashionable method and people were copying others. The newspaper made the following surprising claims.

'In most things there are fashions, and suicide is no exception. Today it is the Harbor Bridge, yesterday the Gap, and thousands of years ago, a cup of deadly potion. Many people, for some unknown reason, choose most violent deaths, such as jumping under trains, or jumping from great heights to rocks below. This is certainly sudden death, but ghastly. Some prefer to leap into water...Other fashions in suicide are shooting and severing an artery, and both these are fairly common...

The craze, for that's what it sometimes is, for jumping over the Harbour Bridge is easily explained. The height and atmosphere are fascinating, and it is handy, but the main reason is simply that someone else has done it. It is evident through the years that suicides are not original. They just copy what someone else has done.'

If the *Arrow* news article was an accurate gauge of the public view of suicide, everyday Australians were certainly fascinated but were also dispassionate about suicide. Today, the *Arrow* newspaper and many other newspaper commentaries on the bridge suicides would be condemned for their cold and often unsympathetic views on suicide, but in stark contrast to today, Australians were once renowned for being more robust individuals, known as straight talkers, who were extremely comfortable with frankness, and preferred truthfulness over pretext.

William Connoley's death struck a different chord with the Sydney *Sun* newspaper, and the *Sun* also reported its concern for the growing number of suicides and stepped up its campaign for a safer bridge. It declared the Bridge a '**Suicide Menace**' and highlighted '**At any time, someone jumping from the bridge may fall on a boat and kill or seriously injure passengers. At the most, it would cost £30,000 to erect a substantial steel framework with a stout covering of** steel net over the walk. But a barrier sloping inwards from the top of the outer rail, and so constructed that it would not offer a foothold, would prove just as effective and would cost not more than £15,000.

The following day the Sun newspaper made another case for fencing the bridge and printed the following article, headlined, 'THE BRIDGE TO ETERNITY'

"Unless we want our Harbour Bridge to acquire the name of 'Suicide Bridge' or some other such grim sobriquet, it might be worthwhile for the authorities to consider a cheap means of preventing feeble-minded or distraught people from jumping from the rail. Barbed wire is not very expensive. Within the six months....nine people have jumped into the harbour from its deck, more than ever gone over the Gap in a year, and more than were killed by accident in the five years building of the bridge and approaches. Is it not time some consideration was given to this unhappy state of affairs?'

The *Sun* followed with the response from the government minister responsible, Transport Minister, Mr Michael Bruxner. Mr Bruxner was quoted as saying that he felt the expense of netting the Bridge against suicides was not justified, particularly as it would be difficult to '**encase the structure**' to prevent a determined person from jumping. The minister also announced that he responded to the Legislative Assembly following investigations on the practicability of protecting the footwalks of the SHB. He announced that the cost of erecting four miles of protective fencing would be high, an estimate of £30,000 and as '**far as he could ascertain, no similar structure in the world had been ordered to prevent suicides.**' Bruxner concluded that '**the consensus of opinion of those with whom he had discussed the matter was that the less made about the occurrences, the less there would be of the continuance of them.**'

Minister Bruxner rightly and wrongly believed that if everyone just stopped talking about it, it would all just go away, and remarkably he was not alone in his opinion. The *Daily Telegraph* also made a 'Plea for Protection' to fence the bridge, accusing the government ministers' of their complacent attitude and declining to accept their responsibility, particularly Mr Bruxner. It appeared that all efforts made by the Sydney newspapers were once again easily brushed aside, and then a few days later, and not surprisingly, there was another bridge jump.

At 8.00 am on Saturday, September 24, Mr J B Reynolds, a harbour customs official, was walking to the Government boatsheds along Hickson roadway, which stretches beneath the eastern footway approach to the SHB and approximately 90 metres away from the southern bridge pylons. Reynolds was hurrying to duty on board the customs launch '*Mariposa*', and as he made his way along the roadway, he heard a swishing sound followed by an awful thud close behind him. He momentarily cringed and then turned around to see what he described as a '**ghastly mess**'. Reynolds couldn't believe what had just happened, and as he struggled to compose himself, he realised how close he had come to being killed by the man who had just jumped from the bridge and struck the asphalt pavement only a few feet behind him.

When the police arrived, they determined that the victim had landed on his head, that his face had been crushed and mutilated beyond recognition, and that nearly every bone in his body had been broken. The central ambulance took the body to the morgue, and the Sydney city police started their investigations. Firstly, they searched his clothing and noticed the name J C Jones marked on the victim's shirt, followed by the maker's name. The police followed this slender clue only to discover that the original owner Mr J C Jones from Potts Point, had died two years prior. A police constable miraculously thought he recognised the mutilated man and thought he was an old tally clerk who he had seen working at the wharves. He then enquired at the shipping offices, but nothing came from this.

The following morning, a man calling himself Leslie Lionel Dunlop, who lived at the city night refuge in Kent Street Sydney, was sitting with two other diners at a café and read the newspaper account of the bridge tragedy. He apparently remembered an old friend and workmate who he believed matched the description in the paper. Strangely the report in the paper stated that the man's face had been crushed and mutilated beyond recognition. Despite this critical fact, Dunlop went straight to the police, and after seeing the body in the morgue, he identified the body as George Williams. Dunlop claimed he knew Williams and stated he was unemployed and was down and out, but he never heard him express any desire to end his life. Dunlop's evidence was noted as purely formal, and there was nothing on the body besides a bunch of keys. The only other evidence submitted was a coat found on the railing on the footway, which contained a small bottle of Chlorodyne in the breast pocket. After having formal identification, the police task was considered complete.

By Monday, news circulated that the man who jumped from the bridge was George Williams, age 57, an unemployed labourer from Papakura, New Zealand. He had no fixed place of abode and had been residing at a soup kitchen in Kent Street, Sydney. By the following Friday, September 30, the acting Coroner, Mr Atkinson, recorded a verdict of suicide in the case of George Williams, and he was buried in a pauper's grave at Rookwood Cemetery, west of Sydney. George Williams was the eighth person to suicide from the Sydney Harbour Bridge, or so everyone thought.

A fortnight after George Williams was buried, enquiries began about the whereabouts of William Lehane, a retired cane cutter from Queensland who was reported missing. He was 57 years old, unmarried and had been in ill health for some time, but over the years, he had saved enough money enabling him to live in retirement in Sydney. Lehane would often visit his brother Pearce Lehane who also lived in Sydney. It was known that William often left his lodgings for weeks at a time and usually stayed with his brother Pearce and his failure to return to his own boarding house after September 24 initially didn't raise any concerns. It was only when Lehane's brother called at the boarding house weeks later that the disappearance of William Lehane was discovered.

Shortly before William Lehane disappeared, he made the following remarks to his brother and sister-in-law... '**I do not know why people throw themselves over the bridge into the water, they might linger on in agony for months. If I wanted to commit suicide, I would throw myself over onto the concrete below and make a proper job of it.**'

Lehane had a considerable sum of money to his credit at the Commonwealth Bank, and given his unexplained absence, his relatives believed that he was dead and were considering the question of the administration of his estate. The question that naturally had arisen was whether there had been a mistake in identification in relation to the case of George Williams, who plummeted to the pavement on September 24.

The family engaged the services of well-known city Solicitors Garratt, Christie and Barnes, who made efforts to collect evidence to determine that Williams and Lehane were one and the same man. The solicitors had to prove beyond a reasonable doubt not only that the dead man was not George Williams but also that it was William Lehane. A witness from the lodging house had come forward and confirmed they had seen Lehane leave his lodgings at 7.00 am and head towards the city on the morning of September 24. The witness also described the clothing he was wearing, which tallied with the clothes on what was believed to be worn by George Williams. It was also confirmed that William was taking Chlorodyne, a medical sedative. Further inquiries in New Zealand showed that George Williams was unknown in the small town of Papakura, but a woman in Wellington forwarded a photograph of her missing husband for identification. The woman in Wellington was also given a description of the deceased, but she declared it did not match any details of her husband.

Over a year later, the Attorney-General was asked to reopen the coronial inquiry into the death of George Williams, but he refused permission unless Leslie Lionel Dunlop came forward to assist further or the misplaced bunch of keys found on the body were recovered. Then it would be necessary for an application to probate court to swear William Lehane. A legal tangle continued, and eventually, on December 14, 1933, the family had their day in the Equity Court to hear a ruling by the acting Chief Justice, Sir John Harvey. The Chief Justice found that the investigative work by the police and the ruling by the acting coroner was careless and hasty and '**that it appeared strange that the clothing of the dead man of which the Police Department had charge, should have been destroyed so soon after the tragedy. It was also strange that certain keys handed to the Public Trustee could not be produced.**'

The Chief Justice was also critical of the fact that the body was identified by Leslie Dunlop, a man whose word was accepted by the police without any verification of his credentials or any further investigation. The Chief Justice concluded that the evidence provided by solicitors Garratt, Christie and Barnes had proven that the body was that of William Lehane and no one else and overturned the findings of Coroner Atkinson and even questioned if George Williams or '**any such person ever existed.**'

William's sizeable estate worth £732 was settled a month later, in January 1934, but no changes or reburial arrangements for his final resting place were made. Even with a generous amount of money left behind after his death, William Lehane shares an unmarked plot with five unfortunate others in the paupers' section of Rookwood Cemetery. The original burial record of George Williams was later adjusted to read William Lehane on November 9, 1934.

10

DOWN, BUT NOT OUT

'The history of this economic upset will show it has not been mastered by codes and cabals but by feminine courage.'

It is often assumed that men suffered most during the Great Depression, and it is their story that is so often told. However, the effects of the Depression on women and the families they desperately sheltered were exhausting and equally damaging to their well-being, and their plight during these difficult times is often forgotten.

Women faced the mental stress attached to being a good housewife, a nurturing mother, a dutiful wife, or all these obligations combined, so it was not unusual for a woman to be consumed with despair if she felt she was neglecting any of these responsibilities. A young mother had little time to wallow as she staved off poverty and hunger, by her very nature, will wrestle with any obstacle for her family to survive. For newlyweds or new mothers, they relied on the unity of other women, and often a street community would form a bond. Women helped each other while the husband was out seeking work or doing his own kind of bonding at the pub. Often women would become the innocent victims of abusive husbands or abandoned by their husbands on the promise of finding work in the country and sending money home. As time passed, no money was forthcoming, and the husband never returned.

While local councils and unions joined forces to establish unemployment camps for men, women's associations were doing exemplary work in relieving distress among widows and deserted wives. A Country Help Committee was formed in Sydney in 1931. Its purpose was to assist out-of-work and destitute girls to obtain work in country districts. The committee was trying to bridge the gap between the out-of-work city girl and the overworked countrywoman. The committee's work was admirable, with no fees or big salaries promised, as a good home was more important to girls who had been out of work for a long time.

Often the authorities were sympathetic to those on the brink of complete despair and sought assistance or gave a helping hand, as was the case for Mrs Moffitt of Bondi. Mrs Moffitt's husband had deserted her some time ago, and she had no food in the house and had little left in the way of furniture or possessions as they had all been sold to pay rent and clothe her four young children aged between 3 and 14 years old. When Police Inspector Robson and Sgt Morrison visited Mrs Moffitt's home in Bondi, they arrived intending to have to make an eviction, but once they entered the house, they discovered her tragic circumstances and quickly changed their plans.

Inspector Robson immediately purchased meat and food for Mrs Moffitt and her starving family. Sgt Morrison then arranged a collection of money among his colleagues and friends and arranged for the removal of the few remaining possessions and made plans for the Moffitt family to move to a new home where they could be cared for.

The harsh circumstances could not break some women, and although sometimes treated like forgotten citizens, some stood defiant. One such case was of an impoverished woman living in a 'Bag Humpy', a simple tent-like shelter made from disused jute sacks. After attempts by the local health inspector and a Council order to have her removed from the gaze of locals, the defiant but proud woman sent a letter of protest to the Council. Addressing her letter from '**Down and Out Flats**', the woman wrote: —

'**I am not going to sleep under the gum leaves for you or any member of your council. I won't leave. Your order is decidedly impudent. I have no means of paying rent. I am on the dole, with no money or anything else, and no relatives, and I have the permission of the owner to stay on this land.**

'**I have lost everything and have had my furniture taken from me...I am not always going to be down and out, but people like you would keep a person down**'.

After receiving the letter, the local Council changed their mind and allowed her to stay in her bag humpy for three more months. The lady from 'Down and Out Flats' was not going down without a fight; she was a robust and steadfast woman who miraculously maintained her sense of dignity and a fantastic sense of wit through it all.

Being destitute or penniless often led to people taking unusual steps in the hope of changing their situation, as is the extraordinary account of the lady who dug up her entire backyard looking for a hoard of buried coins. Mrs Mitchell, with her two-year-old son and unemployed husband, had recently moved into the home of the late Mrs Amy Grimshaw. It was thought that the departed Mrs Grimshaw was destitute and died penniless. However, a year later, it was discovered that this was far from the truth.

The late Mrs Grimshaw had in fact left a will with a sizeable estate. Two bank books showing a balance of £500 and more than £100 had been found in the house by police when she died. Then there was speculation that the eccentric lady had buried 1000 pieces of gold in her backyard. Wild speculation or not, hearing this news made little difference to the new tenant Mrs Mitchell as she intended to find the buried treasure. While Mrs Mitchell's unemployed husband went out each day looking for work, she dug furiously with a heavy mattock, slowly digging up every square inch of her yard until there was nothing left to turn over. It was never revealed if Mrs Mitchell was successful in her treasure-hunting attempt. However, the lure of 1000 pieces of gold sovereigns buried in the backyard would certainly prompt a search at any time or place.

As robust and devoted as many women were, it didn't always work out well in desperate times. Often the harbour bridge and the harbour waterways were scenes of many disastrous outcomes, as was the case for 53-year-old Ethel Hull, who on the 2nd of October, suffering from depression and poor health, made her way from her sister's harbourside home at Blues Point down to the shoreline of the harbour. Still in her nightwear, she plunged into the water and drowned; her body was recovered two days later by the Water Police.

A week later, a young woman with her 10-month-old baby attempted to throw herself and her child off the bridge. Fortunately, the police were close by and prevented her from taking such a drastic measure. Distressed and appearing completely broken, the woman declared to the police that she was greatly worried and decided to end her life. Even without the entire disclosure of her situation, the young woman's case was not unusual, as it was estimated that in the 100 years prior to 1934, 1.5 million people had committed suicide, and one-fifth (300,000) of that number was represented by women.

The Harbour Bridge suicides would highlight the desperate plight of many women during a difficult time, and of the fifty-one Sydney Harbour Bridge suicides that took place between March 1932 and February 1934, thirteen of the victims were women, and each of them had a heart-rending story to tell.

Ethel Rosalind Lee was 33 years old and had been in ill health since the birth of her child. Suffering from all the symptoms relating to postnatal depression, Ethel could not rid herself of her torment. On Saturday, October 15th, 1932, Ethel went shopping at her local shops in Brighton Le Sands with her husband Francis and their seven-month-old baby.

Ethel appeared cheerful and gave the baby to her husband while she went into a nearby butcher shop. She then came out and asked her husband to wait a while as she went to another shop farther along the street. Her husband patiently waited, but after a time, Ethel didn't return. In a panic, her husband desperately searched the neighbourhood, but it wasn't long before her husband realised something more serious had occurred. Ethel's husband was deeply concerned and quickly reported her missing to the local police and advised them she had recently suffered from a nervous breakdown and had been in ill health since the birth of their child.

No one could have imagined that Ethel secretly slipped away from her husband and child and made her way directly to Sydney Harbour Bridge; however, several hours later, news from Sgt Slaney of the Water Police to the Brighton Le Sands Police confirmed Mr Lee's worst fear. Ethel had indeed made the journey from Brighton Le Sands to the bridge, climbed the fence and jumped from the railing at the centre of the bridge. Constables McCloghry and Bent of the Water Police were patrolling the harbour waters shortly after 1.00 pm and were shocked when they saw Ethel topple from the bridge above. The constables described her fall, which **'looked like a doll tumbling in mid-air.'** They could only watch in disbelief as Ethel struck the water with a terrific explosion.

The two constables immediately raced to her aid, and within minutes she was hauled aboard the police launch. As they pulled Ethel aboard, the police detected her lips were moving as if trying to speak, but Ethel suddenly slumped in constable Bent's arms. The police launch then sent a siren signal to the Water Police depot nearby, where ambulance officers and Sgt Bebb were anxiously waiting. They desperately applied artificial respiration for fifteen minutes, but Ethel died from her injuries before she reached the shore. Eyewitnesses to Ethel's jump, Mary Delaney of Balmain, and her aunt were about 250ft away from Ethel and saw her climb up and over the fence and quickly disappear before they even had time to call out to her. The two women were so overcome with emotion they were unable to provide coherent statements to the police, and both were on the verge of collapse. Before jumping, Ethel left her handbag containing her bank book and identification on the footbridge. After his desperate efforts to find his wife, five hours later, Francis Lee returned home only to be met by the police, who informed him of the distressing news about his Ethel. Francis was later taken to the city morgue, where he identified the broken body of his wife.

Just six days after Ethel Lee's tragic death, 25-year-old Jessie Mary Couch, under immense feelings of unworthiness and suffering from depression, also jumped from the Sydney Harbour Bridge. On October 21st, 1932, witnesses on the bridge had seen Jessie standing by the railing. They noticed she was especially well dressed and wore a lovely white beret and fashionable horn-rimmed glasses. Nearby pedestrians watched in dismay as Jessie suddenly scrambled up the trellis fence and onto the railing. She hesitated for a moment and then hurled herself outward.

Jessie's body plunged into the water below and was rapidly carried away by the strong current taking her some distance from the bridge. A witness on the waterfront had seen Jessie hurtling through the air and immediately notified the nearby Water Police. Sgt Bebb immediately set out in the Police launch, raced to the scene, and found Jessie's lifeless body floating near Kirribilli about 650 feet from where she hit the water. Jessie had suffered terrible injuries and most likely died on impact. The *Daily Telegraph* highlighted the curiosity that 'despite the great drop', Jessie's fashionable glasses were still on when police found her body.

Three weeks earlier, whilst walking across the bridge with her young son Kevin, Jessie confessed to her husband that she had contemplated jumping, but she said, **'her nerve had failed her.'** The presence of her young son perhaps checked the impulse to jump. Her husband, Anthony Gerard Couch, had been aware of her nervous condition for nearly three years, but after hearing of this incident, Jessie sought medical help. She consulted her local doctor and a Macquarie Street specialist, who stated Jessie had 'delusions of unworthiness'. It was recommended that Jessie go to a hospital, and she agreed. The specialist also mentioned, **'she is not to be regarded as severely**

affected.' Tragically for Jessie and her family, this conclusion from the specialist was inaccurate.

We will never discover the exactness of Jessie's illness. A young woman overwhelmed by feelings of unworthiness brought on by a postnatal condition or a recurrence of the troubling nervous condition she had years earlier, or perhaps it was the tragic effects of both. Only three weeks earlier, the young mother had resisted the impulse to jump from the bridge, but unfortunately, medical help didn't make a timely breakthrough, and she was lured back once again to the 'suicide bridge'.

The same week the City Coroner held the enquiry into the death of Jessie Couch, there were also six more suicide hearings, which included two hangings, one strychnine poisoning, one gas poisoning and two self-inflicted 'cutting of the throat'. While there were undoubtedly reasonable explanations as to why people committed suicide, there were also various theories on the methods adopted by the victims, but most theories on the methods adopted fall short of the mark, with one suggestion that women preferred poison as it entailed no disfigurement. There is no evidence to support this theory as a jump from Sydney Harbour Bridge often left the face, and the body disfigured, and there was ample evidence of cases where women had used gruesome methods with little regard for how they looked after the event. Only a few weeks before Jessie Couch took the 'high jump' as it was sometimes crudely referred to, 52-year-old Agnes Murphy of Maroubra, suffering from depression and worry, cut her throat with a large carving knife, a wedding gift from her brother, and she died in a pool of blood in the laundry.

11

SPRINGBOARD TO DEATH

The best preventive, of course, would be a return to prosperity, for most of the victims seek death as a relief from worry'.

When the Sydney *Daily Telegraph* reported on the death of Jessie Couch, the newspaper also revealed that whilst the Bridge 'had no special precautions' to prevent people from jumping, there was a mathematical expectation that an unguarded Sydney Harbour Bridge would produce a fatal leap every sixteen days, and therefore **'twenty-two persons may be expected to throw themselves over the bridge within the next year'**.

In other words, at the end of every fortnight, give or take a few days, it became an arithmetical certainty that another desperate man or woman would thus find death. The newspapers were making every effort to generate interest in fencing the bridge, and the disturbing prediction by the *Daily Telegraph*, if taken seriously, should have been enough to rouse interest from the authorities. However, 'officialdom' was far from convinced that it was necessary to take any action at all.

Most of the local city councillors and politicians continued to treat the matter exceptionally lightly.

The Lord Mayor of Sydney, Samuel Walder, had previously offered nothing to the fencing discussion and was preoccupied with his many worthwhile charitable responsibilities as well as preparing for retirement and receiving his knighthood. He dismissed the problem as being too difficult and that it should be a matter for the police. Meanwhile, North Sydney Council held a meeting to discuss the bridge suicides where their views were mixed and somewhat surprising.

North Sydney Alderman Mr F Hardy, who was genuinely concerned, noted that the bridge had initially only one patrolman at each entrance to the bridge and suggested that police regulating pedestrian traffic in the city could be better engaged on the bridge and stationed at regular intervals along the bridge as had been done on the Brooklyn Bridge in New York. The Mayor of North Sydney, Alderman Hubert Primrose, stated that the Government was already considering the matter and would no doubt find a way out. Primrose thought the suggestion was a waste of time and stuck by his initial belief that bridge suicides were a phase that would pass, and it was not the Council's problem.

Further council discussions revealed further indifference to the problem when solicitor and elected Alderman David Blair Grant Hunter astonishingly suggested that the **'Council should use the weapon of ridicule. A springboard, he said, could be placed at some convenient spot, with a notice directing the attention of the public to its position, and indicating a charge of a shilling a head for those wishing to use it'.**

The comment from Alderman David Hunter was not only a clear example of his character, but his mockery of the situation was a significant indication of the lack of compassion 'officialdom' had for the bridge victims and the circumstances that brought them to their despair.

On October 29th, a few days after the council meeting and the crude suggestion of charging suicides a fee to springboard to their death, Alfred John Stannard, a 50-year-old unemployed labourer from

Balmain, made his fatal leap. No one witnessed Alfred jump, but a lone fisherman on the waterfront at Dawes Point noticed a massive splash in the water and suspected it may have been a suicide from the bridge above. He instantly ran to the nearby water police shed and notified Sgt Bebb.

At the same time, the crew onboard a boat beneath the bridge noticed a body floating in the water and thinking it was one of their crew, yelled, 'man overboard'. As they made their approach to recover the crewman, they were shocked to discover the broken body of Alfred Stannard. Shortly after, Sgt Bebb and Constable Elliott arrived on the scene and recovered the body, quickly pulling it onto the police launch 'Osiris'. Constable Elliott steered the police launch back to the boat shed while Sgt Bebb tried desperately to resuscitate Alfred, in the slim hope there was some slight trace of life left in his body. Unfortunately, his efforts were in vain. Soon after the central ambulance arrived, the body was taken to the Sydney hospital and afterwards to the morgue, where Alfred's brother-in-law made a formal identification. The police also recovered from Alfred's waistcoat pocket £1 and a shilling, and an Unemployed Workers' Union card, which bore his name and, ironically, the inscription 'The Right to Live'.

A few days later, the Coroner's inquiry revealed that Alfred had been one of the long-term unemployed, his wife of thirty years, Margaret, confirming that he had been unable to find work for over three years and had grown despondent. The same day, the *Labor Daily* reported further on Alfred's death and following on from the inscription on Alfred's Union card, the headlines read, 'RIGHT TO LIVE – DENIED HIM - New Name to Bridge Death Roll'.

After Alfred's death, the *Daily Telegraph* made another appeal for fencing and a brief update on the lack of action taken by Minister Bruxner. Once again, the Minister for Transport, Mr Bruxner was questioned about netting the footway as several offers had been made to the Government by companies willing to contract for the work. It was revealed that Mr Bruxner had not officially presented the question of protecting the footway Bridge to his Cabinet Ministers as he stated much earlier. Mr Bruxner stated that he had only 'unofficially' approached his colleague's regarding the fencing and was met with such an indifferent reception that he did not press the matter further.

Meanwhile, the enthusiastic and persistent North Sydney Councillor, Alderman F Hardy, called for another council meeting. Despite the baffling opposition from other councillors, Alderman Hardy remained determined to help prevent bridge suicides. Hardy joined forces with North Sydney's municipal engineer Mr Alexander Buckham and prepared a report on installing additional fencing, including an estimate of the cost at £4000. Mr Buckham's report suggested arching over the footway with a heavy-gauge steel wire, electrically welded, with fabric galvanised and painted, carried over and secured to 'T' section ribs. A suitable material, curved to a five-foot radius, would be practically invisible from a distance.

Mr Buckham concluded in his report, **'If one life per annum could be saved by adopting such a safeguard at reasonable cost, the responsibility is so urgent that the work should be put in hand at once, especially since the footways could not be policed against suicides except for an annual sum greatly in excess of the capital expenditure mentioned'.**

With the understanding that no one wanted the bridge's aesthetic altered, Ald. Hardy made special mention that the arched fencing proposed by engineer Buckham would not blemish the beauty of the bridge and should be presented to the State Ministers for consideration as soon as possible. Ald. Hardy was met with strong opposition from Ald. David 'springboard' Hunter and his followers, who argued against the recommendations, with Ald. Hunter stated that the North Sydney Council was not in charge of the bridge and felt it was **'presumptuous to consult their engineer on a matter which did not specially concern the council'**. Fortunately, the 'Buckham' recommendation from Ald. Hardy went to a vote, and it was decided by seven votes to six in favour of sending a copy of the engineer's report and sketch plan to the Minister for Local Government. This was a small but significant victory for Ald. Hardy.

Except for a sympathetic Alderman Hardy and his like-minded colleagues, it was disappointing that many public officials had offered questionable opinions and little in the way of any helpful solutions. For the early campaigners to 'fence the bridge', it must have been frustrating and discouraging. All efforts by the newspapers, the public, the church, and the passionate work of Alderman Hardy, ultimately fell on deaf ears and failed to garner any support for a prompt solution by the Government. This early campaign to fence the bridge seemed hopeless, and astonishingly nothing more was done.

Fig 7. Alderman David Blair Hunter

A few days after the North Sydney Council finished debating whether to put forward the fencing proposal, 63-year-old Daniel Hogan, an unemployed miner, hurled himself off the bridge. When Daniel took his walk across the Harbour Bridge on Saturday morning the 26th of November 1932, he stopped at the southern end, scrambled up the fence and onto the railing where he balanced, and yelled at the oncoming pedestrians, **'I'm going to end it all'**. Roland Hulme was close by when he heard the call from Daniel and made a run towards him, while two more witnesses, Max Murray and William Sutcliffe, also made a desperate dash for Daniel, but the men were unable to reach him in time. They could only watch as he plummeted to the water below, tumbling over a dozen times and striking the water face down.

When Daniel reappeared on the surface, the captain of a nearby Lane Cove ferry, the *'Lady Scott'* stopped and recovered the body from the water and discovered that his coat and trousers had been shredded by the impact and almost completely ripped from his body. There was little doubt that Daniel died on impact.

Daniel Hogan arrived in Australia from Dublin, Ireland in 1891, and with his brother Patrick, they worked as miners in Western Australia for many years. When his mining days ended, he moved to Sydney, and at the age of forty-four, he enlisted for duty in the Australian Imperial Forces in 1917. His age may have had some bearing on his application, but he was immediately discharged as medically unfit, suffering from defective eyesight in his right eye, a condition from his mining days and severe eczema of his right leg.

It is not known what Daniel did for so many years after his effort to join the AIF, but as a miner, he was not afraid of hard work and may have drifted from job to job and scratched out a reasonable living as a labourer. But then, as he aged, he lost his right eye, and work opportunities diminished year after year. Daniel was unemployed for many years before he perished, but he somehow managed to fight his way through the depression years. He lived a solitary existence, a lonely figure, living in boarding houses and managing his best on the meagre amount from his invalid pension. He joined the ranks of many in the same desperate situation, and one day he decided he would end it all.

Daniel Hogan was the 12th bridge victim, who, apart from a few meal tickets from a city café found in the pocket of his shredded clothes, died lonely and penniless, with nothing but the clothes and shoes he wore on the day he jumped from the bridge.

1932 had proven to be a turbulent year, a year that many would rather forget, but it was hard to ignore the run of tragedies surrounding the SHB since its opening just eight months earlier. The SHB had been the stepping-off point for twelve suicides, and with the certainty of more to follow, the title of 'Suicide Bridge' was now firmly implanted in the public's mind.

12

1932 - A HELL OF A YEAR

'Please plant me with as little fuss as possible.'

Throughout history, many great bridges around the world shared the title of 'Suicide Bridge', great bridges such as the Pasadena Bridge in California, USA or the Clifton Bridge in Bristol, England, and some more notable than others like the Golden Gate Bridge in San Francisco, California, USA. Built five years after the Sydney Harbour Bridge, the Golden Gate Bridge was running similar numbers of bridge suicides to the SHB. By 1995, with no improved fencing since its opening, the official death toll on the Golden Gate Bridge was edging close to 1000. In an attempt to discourage what authorities described as 'record breakers', they halted the official count at 997.

Whilst the Sydney Harbour Bridge never had to worry about 'record breakers' at this stage in its early history, as far as the newspapers were concerned, the Harbour Bridge, with an average of one suicide every fortnight, had earned its title of 'Suicide Bridge', an image far from what its creators had ever envisaged.

When the Sydney Bridge was opened, Dr John C Bradfield, the Chief Engineer of the Harbour Bridge, was asked about the possibility of bridge suicides; his view was upbeat and unusually romantic. Described as big-brained, level-headed, and an untiring thinker and worker, Dr Bradfield explained, **'Who on earth could suicide from the Bridge at night in the face of such a romantic scene — city lights, a sparkling harbour stretching down to the Heads; glamorous views of the upper bays, with their ships and ferries shimmering along the waters?'** Bradfield stated, **'It will be impossible for people to fall into the harbour. There will be shoulder-high railings on each side of the footways, and if people have the nerve to climb these and jump 170 feet into the harbour, they will be intent on committing suicide anywhere.'**

Bradfield, considered the 'father of the bridge', confidently concluded by saying... **'I think the Bridge will lend itself more to romance and as a place for girls to pop the question during Leap Year.'** Dr Bradfield was naturally extraordinarily proud and passionate about the bridge. He worked tirelessly for decades for its construction. He was optimistic and in love with his dream and thought of romance on the bridge rather than suicide. Fortunately, his awkward phrasing of 'Leap Year' was never used again.

1932 had been an eventful year for Australians. Acclaimed journalist and author Gerald Stone devoted an entire book detailing the year's turbulent events, titled '1932 - A Hell of a Year.' Stone highlighted the vulnerability of the Australian economy and the political upheavals and described the year **'as the year that changed a nation'**. The year started poorly with the death of Australia's horse racing hero, the thoroughbred 'Phar Lap' on April 5th, 1932, only a few weeks after the bridge opening. As news of the horse's death filtered through to the race-loving Australians, the nation slowly went into mourning. The country also lost some greatly admired and inspirational Australians, war hero Albert Jacka VC, MC & Bar, and Edith Cowan OBE.

Lance Corporal Albert Jacka was the first Australian to be decorated with the Victoria Cross, the highest decoration for gallantry 'in the face of the enemy' during the First World War, receiving the medal for his actions at Gallipoli. Albert later served on the Western Front, was twice further decorated for his bravery, and received the Military Cross and Bar. He never fully recovered from his wartime wounds and died at age 39. The public was shocked by his death, and an estimated six thousand people attended his funeral.

Edith Cowan, Australia's first female parliamentarian, also passed away. Edith was a crucial figure in the women's suffrage movement and a leading advocate for public education and the rights of children and single mothers. During a single term in parliament, Edith secured the passage of her private members' bills which extended women's rights, married or single, to enter professions and changed the inheritance rights for women. It is also significant to note that Edith Cowan's legacy is still celebrated on Australia's 50-dollar banknote as well as the Edith Cowan University in Western Australia.

1932 was also considered the toughest year of the Great Depression, the 'tuff times' had reached close to breaking point for many Australians. With the loss of inspirational heroes, unemployment at a record high of 32%, wage cuts, and no signs of economic relief, the only good news for most Australians usually arrived in the form of sporting achievements.

The Australian's love of sport had been embraced as a national virtue, a lasting passion that has never wavered. The forthcoming cricket test series between Australia and England over the Christmas holiday offered Australian sports fans a welcome distraction from the harsh realities of daily life and the possibility of no more news stories about hardship or bridge suicides.

Unfortunately for the Sydney Water Police, a respite from such troubling times was not part of the job description, and tragedy on Sydney Harbour never seemed far away. On the first day of December, Sgt Bebb and Constable Moses had the murky task of removing a dead woman's body from the mud upriver at Lane Cove. How she ended up deeply embedded in the mud was a mystery, but it was clear to police that she had not jumped from the Sydney Bridge. It was later determined that the woman was Mrs Penelope Cameron, 48, of Orange NSW. Penelope had been suffering from a nervous condition for over two years and was still grieving her mother's death when she suddenly decided to take her own life. Although Penelope Cameron's death was not a Bridge suicide, it was a clear reminder for the Water Police that the possibility of a bridge jump or harbour tragedy of some kind was always just around the corner, and they didn't have to wait too long.

On the morning of December 6th, 50-year-old Augustus Gallen took his last walk, a final journey along the Harbour Bridge footway. It was 8.50 am, morning rush hour, when water traffic below was at its heaviest, with harbour ferries and launches making their familiar crisscross patterns across the harbour. When Augustus reached the centre of the bridge, he climbed over the pedestrian railing and, in clear sight of hundreds of ferry passengers below, sprang from the railing. As soon as he hit the water below, the crew onboard the motor launch 'Scyla' witnessed the jump and sounded four blasts of its horn to alert the water police. Two nearby passenger ferries and another launch, the 'Estelle', also sounded the alarm and headed towards the spot where Augustus entered the water.

Captain Colwell of the launch 'Scyla' managed to get to Augustus first and dragged him on board. The force of the impact had stripped most of his clothes from his lifeless body. The police launch arrived shortly after and confirmed that Augustus had died instantly on impact. The police had little information on Augustus and initially thought the man's identity was a Mr A Over, as the police discovered a Storeman's Union ticket bearing his name in the coat pocket. On further investigation, it turned out that Mr Over was the brother-in-law of Augustus and had given Augustus the Union ticket to help him find employment. Mr Over told the police he was concerned about his brother-in-law, who had been 'worried by employment for some time' and 'had a bad war wound in the hip'.

Augustus Gallen had a troubled life from his early years as a teenager through to his early adult years, spending most of those years on the dodgy side of Sydney's streets. Having left a disruptive home at sixteen, Augustus and his younger brother Maurice were living on the streets of inner-city Sydney as petty criminals. For twelve years, under various assumed names, Augustus had a long list of convictions ranging from simple vagrancy, indecent language, drunkenness, and disorderly conduct, and then graduating to assault, robbery, and assaulting police on two separate occasions. In total, Augustus had been in Darlinghurst Gaol on thirteen different occasions.

At 36 years of age, in March 1917, Augustus joined the Australian Imperial Forces and was made a Private in the 3rd Battalion. By this stage of the war, the grim casualty reports from overseas didn't paint a helpful picture for someone considering volunteering. Still, it offered what many Australian volunteers were sold on, which was a good pay packet.

At the same time, Augustus's youngest brother William was already serving on the Western Front. Unfortunately, he was later one of the fatal casualties listed in the newspaper, dying from multiple wounds sustained in action in France in May 1918. Not surprisingly, from the time Augustus started at the Army training camp at Liverpool Sydney, he battled with authority, his war record citing his consistently poor behaviour, which continued throughout his service in England and France. However, Augustus did spend a short time in the field of action in France and was wounded by shrapnel, from which he recovered. Augustus continued his defiance of military discipline and ultimately received a court martial as well as a 'Service No Longer Required' notice. This had disastrous implications for Augustus as it meant he forfeited any war gratuity and was not entitled to his war medals. Augustus went to war, perhaps desperate to start a new life, but his personality didn't fit what was expected from him. He returned to Australia in 1919 with nothing to show except shrapnel wounds, the loss of a brother and bitter memories.

Life after the war for Augustus was possibly no better than the days of his rebellious youth. For over a decade, he drifted from labouring job to labouring job, and finally, during the depression years, he joined the ranks of the long-term unemployed. Carrying a nagging war injury and burdened by joblessness, every day was a long day for Augustus. With little or nothing to look forward to, he could only reflect on a flawed life and many bad memories from which he ultimately sought to escape. One newspaper described Augustus Gallen as "UNLUCKY THIRTEEN" as he was the thirteenth bridge fatality.

Late in the evening, at around 11.00 pm, the same day that Augustus jumped to his death, a local watchmaker and jeweller, Mr Alois Luigi Furrer, was crossing the bridge on his way home in nearby Kirribilli. As he approached the centre of the bridge, he discovered a lady's handbag and hat lying on the footway. He inspected the bag and found 2 shillings, 7 pence, a pair of spectacles and a sheet of paper on which had the name Annie Morel and an address, 23 Edinburgh Road Willoughby, written in pencil. At that lonely hour of the night, fearing the worse and highly suspicious of what had taken place, Mr Furrer quickly made his way to the George-street North Police Station, who then immediately alerted the Water Police. Following the news, Sgt Jack Slaney and junior constable Elliott immediately set out in the police launch and searched the dark waters below the bridge. Slaney and his junior constable scanned the water continuously with lanterns and electric torches and at 5 o'clock the following morning, Annie Morel's body was discovered, floating in Sydney Cove about two hundred yards from the Bridge.

Evidence at the coronial inquiry revealed that 39-year-old Annie Morel had been in poor physical and mental health for a long time. Annie was an invalid pensioner with an abscessed leg and, unfortunately described as mentally deficient. Annie had lived with her mother Mary for many years, suffering from what her mother described as 'nerve trouble'. Annie Morel was the 14th suicide from the bridge and not the last invalid pensioner or mentally troubled person to seek death to relieve their worry and pain.

Four days later, on the 10th of December, Arthur Ernest Russell, 49, from Randwick, also described as an invalid pensioner, jumped from the pedestrian railing. Whether it was planned or in a state of panic, Arthur didn't jump into the water from the centre of the bridge like those before him. Horrifyingly Arthur plummeted to the solid pavement on Hickson Road below and died instantly on impact. Eye-witnesses to the distressing scene informed the police that they saw a man sitting on the top rail of the southern approach to the bridge. As concerned pedestrians approached him, he stood up quickly, balanced himself for a few seconds and then jumped into the open space below.

William Patrick Doherty of Pymble was one of the pedestrians who made a desperate run towards Arthur but was too late and could only watch as Arthur struck the road surface headfirst. Arthur died instantly; his body described as being 'shockingly mutilated'. When taking his body back to the morgue, it was noted by police that nearly every bone in his body had been broken, but inexplicably the pair of glasses in his pocket remained completely intact. At the Coroner's hearing, it was revealed that Arthur was suffering from an incurable disease. He had been seeing some of the leading doctors of the time, including the highly regarded Sydney orthopaedic surgeon Dr Max Herz. His widow Mary also explained that Arthur's condition could not be cured, and his health would continue to deteriorate with time.

While most newspapers continued rolling out the same headline, 'Another Jump from the Bridge' or 'Another Bridge Suicide', the Sydney *Labor Daily* went a step further, claiming the bridge was now known as the 'Bridge of Death'. With the third death within a week and the bridge title now elevated to the 'Bridge of Death', the newspapers once again pressured the Deputy Premier and Transport Minister, Mr Bruxner, about fencing the bridge. The following article, championed by the Editor Mr Delamore McCay, appeared in the Sydney *Sun* newspaper.

'No Guard, Says Bruxner - Following the latest Bridge suicide, the Deputy-Premier and Minister for Transport (Mr Bruxner) was asked again whether the Government would consider the

advisability of netting the Bridge railings so as to prevent people jumping off.'

'I think more good would be done by giving these unfortunate happenings less publicity than by fencing the Bridge,' said the Minister. 'Psychologists say that the undue advertising of this sort of thing leads weak-minded people to take the same course. I think myself that if the papers refrained from making these tragedies a matter for sensational headings, suicides over the Bridge would cease.'

'Even if the Bridge were fenced,' continued Mr Bruxner, 'there are other bridges in Sydney; there is the Gap, and miles of high cliffs. No special precautions have been taken to make it impossible for people to jump from these places, and it would, in fact, be impracticable.'

'There is no bridge in the world where anything has been done to prevent suicides, such as the suggested netting or fencing.'

'To stop people falling to the roadway at the Bridge approaches it; would further be necessary to protect the parapets, and, even so, there are many high buildings in Sydney'.

Minister Bruxner had always been a straight talker and was not afraid to tell it how it was. His frankness today would be overwhelmed with complaints from the PC brigade and his political opponents. But Australians were more robust individuals back then, and personal sensitivities were outweighed by more important issues such as poverty, employment, having food on the table and a simple roof over the family's head. The Minister believed that everyone was living through hard times and that the cushioning of the truth was not in anyone's interest. He firmly believed that the newspapers should leave the bridge suicides out of the headlines and that the **'suicides over the bridge would cease'**.

Naturally, the editor for the *Sun*, Delamore McCay, had the final say, stating, '**It is obvious that, at least, if the mention of the tragedies were conveniently suppressed, the Minister would not be irked by questions on the subject**'.

Mr Bruxner's view that less publicity alone may prevent fewer suicides was perhaps a lightweight argument, but his main adversary always seemed to be poor timing, and as poor timing would have it, four days later, there was another suicide, and the day after that, yet another.

On December 14th, the headline from the South Australian *Advertiser* reported the '**Fatal Lure of the Sydney Bridge**' had claimed yet another victim. Norman McCrae Gair was 28 years old, a young Scottish coal miner who had been unemployed for over 18 months. It was noon, and just like many bridge jumps before him, the young man made his way along the footway to the ill-fated spot at the centre of the bridge. Norman had prepared himself for this day and followed many of the etiquettes displayed by other bridge suicides. He took off his hat, folded his coat which contained a handwritten note stating his intention to end his life and then placed the items neatly on the footpath. Workers on the Harbour Trust dredge were stationed directly below the bridge and watched helplessly as Norman hurtled through the air and plunged into the water. They quickly set off in the tender to see if they could recover him from the water, hopefully alive. When the men managed to pull Norman onto the boat, they discovered that most of the clothes had been ripped from his body, but he appeared to have only a few bruises. The dredge workers were hopeful that he was still alive, but Norman was killed instantly when he struck the water. It wasn't long before Sgt Bebb of the Water Police arrived and took charge of Norman's body. Norman Gair was the fourth bridge suicide within nine days, a worrying tally for authorities, but the tenth day would add another victim to what was to become known as the 'Red Roll'.

The following morning, on his daily route to work, George McDonald was walking across the Harbour Bridge when he witnessed a well-dressed man walking briskly in the same direction ahead of him. Then, suddenly and without faltering, the well-dressed man, like a gymnast, vaulted the railing, hurled himself outward, and plummeted to the water below. George rushed to the railing to watch as the man narrowly missed several launches below.

One of the launches was carrying waterside workers, (wharfies) who all witnessed the man plummet into the water. They quickly made a dash to pluck him from the water, only to discover he was killed on impact. They then transported the body to the Water Police shed, where Sgt George Day took charge. Sgt Day immediately searched the body for identification. He discovered just a few pence in his pants pockets but was shocked to find a note in his vest pocket that simply read, **'Name, Charles Diamond, born in England, 1892. No relations in Australia. Please plant me with as little fuss as possible.'**

The matter of fact like note left by Charles Diamond was a clear indication that he intended to take his own life. As far as he was concerned, this was all the information he wanted to share with the authorities, and he was pretty specific about his funeral arrangements. Further investigations by the police uncovered no additional information on Charles Diamond, if, in fact, that was his real name, as they were unable to confirm his identity. Charles Diamond's final wish that he be buried with as little fuss as possible was fulfilled. His body was later buried in an unmarked grave in the pauper's section of Rookwood Cemetery, not far from bridge victim William Lehane who was erroneously buried as George Williams a few months earlier.

With five bridge suicides within ten days, the frequency of suicides was now becoming an obvious concern, but surprisingly even after Transport Minister Mr Bruxner had been quizzed on the seriousness of the suicides, little interest or effort had been shown to either slow or prevent any further suicide attempts. It appeared that quite a few more suicides would have to occur before political minds could be changed.

The day after Charles Diamond jumped from the bridge, even the Australian Communist Party publication known as the *Workers Weekly* protested the flurry of bridge suicides and blamed capitalism for the problem.

'The capitalist Press and other lackies are agitating for the wiring in of the bridge, in order to prevent people throwing themselves off it. The question of removing the cause, capitalism, is not raised. All they want is that the unemployed go somewhere else and die, where they are not exposed to the public eye. The Bridge and the suicides typify capitalism. The Bridge is a triumph of science and engineering, yet the only use it is to these whom capitalism has deprived of any hope in the future is a place to die.'

The Salvation Army Anti-Suicide Bureau was naturally far less political and believed there was no harm in trying a more straightforward solution. As the authorities were doing nothing helpful, the Salvation Army again suggested placing a simple sign like the sign they put at Ben Buckler Point at Bondi. They proposed the signs be placed at the entry points to the pedestrian walkways. Lieut. Col. Orr of the Salvation Army placed his recommendation directly before Minister Bruxner, claiming it would reduce the number of suicides from the Harbour Bridge. Orr also suggested that the long-term continuation of patrolling the bridge was impractical, and he favoured the erection of an inclined barrier above the existing railing to obstruct the would-be suicide.

The 'Fatal Lure' of the Sydney Harbour Bridge was hard to ignore, but timing is everything. Customarily the end of the year is the worst time of year for any chance of success with political bargaining or negotiations, so it was doubtful the anti-suicide sign suggestion ever came up again. Meanwhile, the much-anticipated distraction of cricket over the Christmas period was a far more conspicuous pastime for most Australians. But even the friendly game of cricket turned nasty with the introduction of the English team's bodyline tactics. The December test match series played across the country between England and Australia, was a demonstration of the English employing the speedball from the bowler aimed at the opposing batsman's body. This became known as the infamous 'Bodyline' tactic, designed mainly to target the great Australian batsman and sporting hero Don Bradman.

In the final week of 1932, in addition to the bridge suicides of Norman Gair and Charles Diamond, the Coroner heard evidence surrounding the death of Nora Agnes Sparre, 63, who was found dead with her head in the gas stove at her home. She was just one of four similar gas poisonings within the same week. Also adding to the suicide tally was Harry Atkinson, 31, unemployed and living in the 'Peoples Palace' in Sydney and 70-year-old Frenchman Fernand Aengenheyster, both victims of self-inflicted gunshots.

It had indeed been a hell of a year, and judging by the increased rate of suicides, perhaps many troubled souls didn't want to see out another year.

13

1933 - A NEW START

Thrown at the worst end of life's wheel.'

It was a new year, and if sporting success was used to gauge the mood of a country, then Australia and its people were getting off to a poor start. As was hoped, the cricket season created much to distract the public from the events of 1932, but the English team went on to win the series four games to one. The success of the 'Bodyline' tactic employed by the English team was described by the sport-loving Australians as a menace to the game's best interests. Angered by the English team's unsportsmanlike conduct, the Australian newspapers reported that it was likely to upset the friendly relations between Australia and England. Otherwise, daily life remained unchanged, the new year offered nothing new, and the effects of the Great Depression showed no signs of shifting.

As for the Sydney Harbour Bridge, now firmly established as Australia's 'Suicide Bridge', with no fencing in place and the likelihood of nothing being done to prevent bridge jumps, the Sydney Water Police stationed below stood ready for another year of suicides. Disappointingly they didn't have to wait too long, as on January 6th, Sgt Frazer

Foott of the Water Police recovered the body of Mary Mee Hing in Lavender Bay, a small bay only a short distance northwest of the bridge.

Mary Ann Ahearn was born in Melbourne, Victoria, in 1871. In 1905, at age 34, she married George Mee Hing, a Chinese storekeeper. In an era of particularly conservative views, Mary's parents objected to the marriage and turned their back on their daughter.

George Hing had been a successful storekeeper in Gundagai, and his business prospered, with Mary and George becoming well-known figures in the region. Her husband sold his business interests many years later, and together they travelled to his homeland. On their arrival in China, they met with George's parents, who also objected to their union and wanted nothing to do with Mary. Her husband distanced himself from her and feeling rejected and with nowhere to turn, Mary returned to Sydney alone.

A few months passed, and Mary returned to China to try and reclaim her marriage, only to find that her husband was no longer interested in any relationship with her and that he had married a young Chinese girl.

Completely heartbroken, Mary returned to Australia and resided in a boarding house in George St, in the Haymarket area of Sydney. While trying to establish a new life back in Sydney, Mary made a desperate final attempt to reconcile with her family but unfortunately failed. Her parents once again wanted nothing more to do with her. Mary quickly descended into depression and started spending her life savings mostly on alcohol. Her landlady Kathleen Scuri described Mary's circumstances as becoming sadly desperate, and her drinking had escalated '**to drown her great sorrow**'.

In the early evening of January 5th, Mary, dressed in an overcoat, carrying her handbag and hat, made her way to the centre of the Harbour Bridge. North Sydney resident Mrs Bond and her three children were also on the bridge that evening admiring the twinkling lights and the splendour of the surrounding harbour when Mary Mee Hing hurried past her in the opposite direction. Suddenly one of her children screamed that a woman was jumping over the bridge. Mrs Bond turned to see Mary clambering up the side of the trellis fencing. She quickly sheltered her children from the distressing view and started shouting for help.

A young male steward from the visiting Cruise Liner *'Oronsay'*, also out for an evening stroll, was nearby and heard the cry for help. He raced towards Mary as she scrambled up to the railing top. She made ready to drop when remarkably, the young man managed to grasp her. Slowly he managed to drag her back when suddenly she started struggling and clawing at him. Mary began screaming for him to let her go.

As the young man was determined to maintain his grip, Mary was equally desperate in her struggle to escape and managed to work herself free from her coat. The young steward then tried to get a firmer hold of her. The fierce battle continued until her dress started to tear, and then in a final attempt, Mary thrust her weight outwards, viciously wrenched herself from his grip, and plummeted to the water below.

Mary died heartbroken and penniless. Her landlady, Kathleen Scuri, described Mary Mee Hing as a proud woman who chose death rather than accepting any offer of food and shelter. The police later commented that Mary Mee Hing had been '**thrown at the worst end of life's wheel**'.

It was just the start of the new year, and it looked like the bridge suicides would continue the same course as the previous year. On the evening of Saturday, January 14th, bridge pedestrian Edward Galvin found a wallet and a pair of crutches left on the footpath near the centre of the Bridge. No one saw anyone disappear over the railing, but two fishermen under the bridge heard something hit the water and saw a large spray of water close by. They could only assume someone had fallen from the bridge, so they alerted the police. Sgt Slaney immediately set out and patrolled the harbour, but the darkness of the night hampered the search. News travelled fast when it came to bridge suicides, and that same evening newspaper reports of '**Cripple Disappears on Sydney Bridge**' made the headline.

It wasn't until the following morning that Sgt Slaney finally discovered the body of 33-year-old Horace Royal Lock close to McMahons Point. The police found a note in Horace's trouser pocket, which helped identify him and stated his intention to take his life.

Horace 'Roy' Lock was married and living at Hermitage Rd, Ryde. He worked as an insurance agent after his leg was amputated following an accident when working at a timber yard in Balmain only two years earlier. His health was never the same after the accident, and he received regular nursing treatment.

A few weeks before Horace jumped, he had an unfortunate run of bad luck when he was robbed of £18 and shortly after, he received a court summons notice for recovering his accrued medical fees. Things were not going well for Horace, and it is not difficult to draw assumptions as to his state of mind or understand the reasoning behind his suicide.

Even with the headlines that followed the death of Horace Lock, it was surprising that nothing was raised about the fact that a 'one-legged man' described as a 'cripple' could easily climb the bridge fence and jump to his death. Many may have overlooked it, but the disturbing headlines caught the attention of one man, Senator Arthur George Rae.

Commonwealth Senator Arthur George Rae was a diminutive man, who had been many things in his life, a bush worker, a shearer, a fruit grower, a journalist, trade unionist, party official, a peace activist and finally a politician who was unremitting in his political beliefs throughout his long life. He was described as 'honest, forthright, combative and provocative...a man of humour and humanity, capable of being both entertaining and infuriating.'

Senator Rae certainly had a colourful resume and was an unlikely advocate for fencing the bridge, but this often-passionate spokesman for the working man was one, if not the only, high-profile federal politician who raised genuine concerns over the Bridge suicides.

He made his views public in the Sydney *Labor Daily*, calling for safety first and expressing his disgust about the absence of attempts to prevent the would-be suicide. Senator Rae made a sound and compelling argument and stated the following....

'The appalling list of suicides from the Harbour Bridge is fast earning that noble structure the name of 'Suicide Bridge'. To my mind it is a scandal that no attempt is being made by the State Government to prevent a continuance of these awful tragedies.

It is argued by many that if would-be-suicides were denied the opportunity they would accomplish their desires by other means or in other places, but this argument, born either of levity or callousness is not justified by facts.

All, or, at any rate, nearly all, would-be-suicides are mentally unbalanced, due either to serious ill-health or to intolerable despondency arising from unbearable misfortune. Auto-suggestion and other causes combine to lead these victims of real or in some cases, imaginary evils to commit suicide, and there are many cases on record of persons who have made abortive attempts at self-destruction, who have recovered their mental balance and never repeated the attempt.

To raise questions of constructional difficulty or cost, is the height of absurdity, as curved iron stanchions of moderate strength arched over the footways from side to side and covered with similar wire-netting to that used for safety fences along many of our highways, would make leaping from the Bridge impossible and the cost would not be great.

Leaving the controversial side of this matter aside, I would ask:

Would any private landowner be permitted to give the public free access to land bordered by a precipice without erecting a safety fence along the danger-line? If not, why should the

Government commit or perpetuate conditions for which the private citizen would be criminally liable?

Finally, I would stress the danger to the general public by permitting these opportunities for suicide to continue. Barges, launches, and vessels of all descriptions are continually passing under the Harbour Bridge. Several of those who have made the fatal leap have plunged into the water dangerously near to passing boats. Nothing is more certain than that sooner or later someone in his fall will crash into a vessel beneath with appalling results…Surely this consideration alone! should furnish abundant reasons for demanding that immediate action should be taken to stop the growing roll of Bridge tragedies.'

Senator Arthur Rae described the situation perfectly; he matched the fencing suggestions raised by concerned citizens and engineer Buckham from North Sydney Council and highlighted the dangers to the public. After calling out the 'callous' and irresponsible approach from the elected officials, it was only natural the heavyweight politician was ignored. And unfortunately, his efforts didn't make a shred of difference. Perhaps the local authorities thought that just like the bridge suicides, Senator Arthur Rae might go away.

A week after Senator Rae made his unsuccessful attempt to influence the state parliamentarians, there was yet another suicide from the bridge. On the evening of January 26th, George William Bailey, a 44-year-old machinist and wireworker, jumped from the Bridge. Several pedestrians on the bridge at the time were not close enough to prevent George from jumping and watched as he plummeted, struck the water, and disappeared. The Water Police were alerted and set out in the launch 'Osiris' and combed the foreshores, but his body was not recovered until the next day, two hundred yards from the southern end of Garden Island.

When the Water Police recovered the body, they identified George immediately as he left a letter to his wife and two children in his trouser pocket. Under the Coroner's instruction, the letter's contents were never made public, but his wife explained at the inquest that George had suffered from poor health and depression and was constantly worried about his job. The perfect recipe for tragedy.

George Bailey was the 20th Bridge Suicide, and it looked like the calculated target from the *Daily Telegraph* of a bridge suicide each fortnight had been reached. This was not a welcomed milestone, but it became a measure of what was to follow.

While the newspapers were still reporting on the death of George Bailey, two nights later, Senator Rae's concerns almost became a reality when on the night of January 28th, the next suicide victim nearly landed on Sgt Slaney's police launch.

Whilst on their regular patrol circling the waters below the bridge, Sgt Slaney and constable Alan Noldart witnessed William Heskett leap from the bridge directly above them. They had no time to change course and watched anxiously as Heskett somersaulted through the air and thundered into the water only a few feet from their launch.

When his body reappeared on the surface, Sgt Slaney and Noldart quickly dragged his body from the water and discovered that William was still alive but was missing a leg. By the manner of his dress, and with some relief, Sgt Slaney quickly established that William's left leg had been amputated below the knee. Two amputees within a fortnight must have been perplexing for Slaney and Noldart, and the fact that he nearly crashed onto the police launch reminded them of the real danger from above. However, the threat from above was not quite over when a reckless pedestrian on the bridge threw William Heskett's crutches over the railing, hurtling to the water below, again just missing the police launch.

While Sgt Slaney made his way to the shoreline with the broken body of William Heskett, he held onto some slim hope that William may survive his plunge into the harbour. Once they reached the police depot, Sgt Slaney and constable Noldart watched as William was transferred to the awaiting ambulance, both men hoping only for the best for William, but he died on his way to the hospital.

William Donald Heskett was born in Cumbria, England, in 1879. His father, also named William, was a prosperous land agent and surveyor and, with his wife Elizabeth, provided their children with a quality education and a privileged household maintained by servants and housemaids.

In 1905 at the age of twenty-four, William joined the Scots Guards, one of the five Foot Guards regiments of the British Army. Later in 1912, he emigrated to Australia. Shortly after he arrived, he started work as a labourer and took on one of the time's most physical and dangerous occupations as a timberman.

In 1916 while he was felling trees on a farming property in the tiny country town of Reidsdale, New South Wales, William was seriously injured and had his left leg amputated.

William had no family connections in Australia, his younger brother Arthur was a successful Civil engineer in Chile and his younger sister Ethel had married a Cambridge University man who had fought in the South African wars. William's mother died in 1927, and his father died in 1929, leaving a large estate in trust to the family. Money never seemed to be a problem as William received a monthly sum from the family estate, but unfortunately, the £30 a month he received only fueled his growing addiction to drink.

One newspaper reported that William was a 'Remittance man', historically a reference usually used for someone from a wealthy family who was unwanted or underachieving and banished to a distant British colony. They were then sent regular remittances or 'upkeep money' for them never to return home. It is uncertain if this was correct in William's case; however, if there was any truth to the report, William might have wrestled with the torment of family rejection. The tragedy of losing his leg would have only added to his struggles, and the combination of these circumstances could explain his downhill slide and his dependency on alcohol.

His drinking problem became so grave he travelled to Melbourne and voluntarily admitted himself to an asylum known as the Lara Inebriate Retreat, commonly known today as a rehab clinic. On two occasions over three years, William tried desperately to break his addiction to alcohol, and each time after many months in rehab, he discharged himself in the hope of starting a new life. As the years passed, William gained some work as a clerk, but he could not stop his alcohol dependence, and by all accounts, before his death, he became what they called a 'regular resident' at a well-known George Street wine saloon in Sydney. At age 53, lonely and consumed by an excess of alcohol, William Heskett decided to take his own life. He was later buried at the Church of England Cemetery, Botany and left his remaining estate of £115 to his sister Ethel back in England.

14

BRIDGE ENVY

'Our Bridge'

Carl Phillips was a young American, a fireman onboard the A.M.S *'Monterey'* and eager to make a name for himself. He made the audacious wager of five US dollars with a friend that he would dive from the Harbour Bridge. Thinking it was just a simple matter of making the proper arrangements with authorities, he contacted the police and requested permission to make the daring dive. He was quoted as saying… **'Say, pal,'**… **'I want to dive off that little ole bridge of yours!'** The police, unsure if it was a prank or a desperate suicide victim, replied, **'You want to commit suicide?'** … 'No', said the bold young American **'Nothing doing in the suicide line. I just want to dive, that's all.'** Phillips was told firmly by the police that the dive would not be permitted, and if he attempted to make such a dive, he would find himself in trouble. It was also pointed out to him that there was such a charge as attempted suicide. **'Okay with me,'** said Phillips. **'I'm not looking for trouble.'**

Perhaps Phillips should have been charged with being a public nuisance, as the police took this seriously and decided to make sure that he made no attempts at the high dive. The Water Police were quickly despatched and boarded the *'Monterey'* and interviewed Phillips. The young fireman said, '**he had wanted to make a name for himself, but he had given up the idea.**' To make doubly sure, Sgt Bebb kept watch over the *'Monterey'*, and the police patrol on the bridge was warned about Phillips.

The following day when the papers published the story of Carl Phillip's roguish endeavour, on February 10th, poultry farmer John Richardson returned home in the afternoon after obtaining the dole for the first time in his life. John was 44 years old and had recently lost all his money investing in a failed poultry farm. For a moment, John and his wife Caroline were excited with the groceries they had received for his dole coupons. John then left the groceries on the kitchen table, and appearing overcome, he rushed out of the house. In a panic, Caroline yelled to him, '**where are you going John?**', but he didn't look back and was soon out of sight.

John didn't return home that evening; instead, at 9.00 pm, he jumped from the Sydney Harbour Bridge and was killed instantly. At the inquest, the city coroner expressed the view that John Richardson had become despondent over the loss of his life savings in the poultry farm and returned a verdict of suicide.

Only a few days after the death of John Richardson, deaths on Sydney Harbour seemed to be picking up pace, and suicide from Sydney ferries were still proving to be a popular alternative to the great height of the bridge or the coastal cliffs. 60-year-old George Thomas Hegarty drowned when he fell into the harbour from the Manly Ferry. Passengers and deckhands on board witnessed Hegarty fall into the water and, at first, believed it to be an accident. However, doubts were raised when Hegarty's body was recovered from the icy water, and a search of his clothing seeking his identity revealed he was carrying his last will and testament, leaving his estate to the Salvation Army.

On the 17[th of] March 1933 and just a few days before the first birthday of the SHB, there was yet another suicide from the bridge; in fact, the 23rd suicide victim within twelve months. The fatality was 35-year-old Thomas Francis McDonald, a single man employed as a timekeeper with the Sydney Harbour Trust and stationed on Goat Island, located a short distance west of Sydney Harbour Bridge. At the time, the island had been converted to a shipyard and was used by the Harbour Trust to repair Trust vessels. Only a few people witnessed Thomas jump from the bridge, but his jump caught the attention of hundreds of ferry passengers and people on the nearby waterfront as they all witnessed a great column of spray that shot up as Thomas hit the water.

A ferry stopped to recover the body and started to manoeuvre towards Thomas, but he was picked up by two men working beneath the bridge in a rowing boat. As the men recovered Thomas from the water, the men discovered his body was in a shocking state, with most of his bones broken and his ribs crushed in. Although the men were shocked by what they had seen, it was no surprise that Thomas was killed instantly when he hit the water.

Two days later, the Sydney Harbour Bridge reached its first birthday. It had only been a year since Sydney was overwhelmed with the greatest crowds the city had ever seen, but as the heaviness of the depression era dragged on, and with the bridge acquiring the new title of 'Suicide Bridge', it seemed there was little about the grey giant worth celebrating. The first birthday slipped by almost unnoticed and with no public fanfare.

Naturally, the Sydney newspapers noted the significant anniversary, but the news coverage was less compelling than the prideful and poetic broadcasting of opening day. The *Sun* newspaper quipped, starting with **'much water had flowed under the bridge'** in the past year. Water traffic had been lightened, a population shift to the North was made easier, and it had reduced travel times for many Sydneysiders and the mere mention that **'it had given some score of poor souls an easy way to kindly oblivion'**. The *Sun* explained that except for a 'score of poor souls' it didn't seem that the Sydney Harbour Bridge had such a bad year, with 28 million people having crossed the bridge, including the return trip. This comprised 13 million travelling by train, 7 million by tram, 7.3 million by road vehicles, including horses and carts and 1.5 million on foot.

The *Daily Telegraph* headlined its celebration article, 'Tomorrow Is Our Bridges Birthday, by F. V COLEMAN'. The article by F.V Coleman started with some uninspiring engineering facts such as wind resistance and traffic pressure deflection, the revenue raised, and capital cost reductions, all indicating that overall, the life of the Bridge was in great shape.

Coleman then reported that the authorities had given the bridge a tick of approval, stating, '**The engineers who built it may feel content. It is reported to have behaved during the year exactly as they foresaw...Beyond a touch of paint here and there on the steel, and a pot of tar here and there on the roadway, no repairs have been necessary.**'

Coleman noted the significant number of pedestrians using the bridge and mentioned that some '**unhappy souls did not finish the journey**', but keeping the mood upbeat, reminded readers that by a miracle, two cases who leapt over the bridge survived, and a baby was born while the expectant mother waited in traffic at the toll collection point. Towards the end of the article, F.V Coleman couldn't help but be a little poetic, and with an added touch of romance, finished the celebration article by saying... '**Such has been the first year of the Bridge's life, a year notable for two discoveries. The first was made by the city's lovers, who have turned the footways into a delightful evening promenade. The second was made by the city's pigeons, who have found romantic nesting-places in the steelwork, whence they look down at the lovers in the moonlight.**' F.V Coleman was excited by the Bridge celebrating its birthday and calling it '**Our Bridge**', a patriotic sentiment, which disappointingly was not a sentiment shared by the other states of Australia.

It's hard to imagine today that anyone would criticize the SHB, especially an Australian; however, during the early years in the life of the bridge, it had many critics, and most of the criticism came from the surrounding states of Australia. There was understandable criticism from country New South Wales residents who felt funding a bridge during the harsh times was a waste of money, but what could only be described as Bridge Envy, the newspapers in the surrounding states, including Tasmania, often used criticism of the SHB as a weapon to cast judgement on the people of Sydney and New South Wales.

On the bridge's opening day, the Queensland Newspaper, the *Evening News*, took the opportunity to express its thoughts on the people of Sydney by remarking... '**that the bridge would have been built sooner or later is a certainty. When an idea like this takes root with a people so accustomed to getting what they are after, as are Sydney people, there is only one ending, and that is for them to get it.**' The South Australian newspaper the *News* also took a swipe at the bridge and the people of NSW, firstly mentioning the fact the bridge was conceived in healthy economic times and then pointing out that the bridge had many '**conveniences**' as a subject for '**prideful conversation**', and as a '**jumping-off place**' for people who wish to commit suicide.

The *News* continued, '**Unfortunately the bridge was a project altogether too magnificent for a city of Sydney's size and importance.**' And added... '**If Sydney or New South Wales, had said to itself, before the bridge became too cherished an obsession, 'If a man buys a twelve-guinea suit when he can afford only a six-guinea one, he will soon find himself in trouble.**'

The power of hindsight would be a wonderful tool, but the South Australia newspaper could hardly condemn the bridge or the people of Sydney after South Australia's grand construction of Adelaide Station, also conceived in healthier economic times, almost bankrupted the state. For many people, building these grand structures was often viewed as an optimistic sign, a new beginning, 'a sign that at least something was being done'.

The magnificent Adelaide Railway station and other grand architectural structures, such as the Melbourne Shrine and the Sydney Anzac Memorial, were all great projects under construction during the Bridge building years. All these ambitious schemes employed hundreds, if not thousands of people across the country and indeed had a positive economic and social outcome for many families during the desperate years. But the Sydney Bridge was considered different to these other splendid creations and was often viewed with spite and resentment.

Western Australia, the largest geographic state in Australia, believed itself to be more suited as a sovereign state, even going as far as calling itself *Westralia*. Wanting nothing to do with the other states, it was running a serious campaign for secession from the Commonwealth, and every opportunity was seized to criticise the other states to help bolster the campaign. The *Sunday Times* in Perth, *Westralia*, was unrestrained in its criticism and certainly had nothing nice to say, commenting...

'The Sydney Bridge is a colossus; it literally straddles the harbour and has eclipsed it. It is claimed that it is the longest span in the world, but that is queried. Certainly, another bridge is to be built in America to put the boast out of court. The Sydney structure was conceived in pure vanity and is held up as something more national than even Henry Lawson. Recently a man, tired of life under the depression, threw himself off the bridge into the harbour...it will be known as the Bridge of Sighs...for all time.'

The various states of Australia had long been rivals, particularly New South Wales and Victoria, who often bumped heads over which state was better. To this day, both states still wrangle with one another but have since been joined in the tussle for supremacy by Queensland, which believes it is now the better state. In 1910, Scotsman John

Foster Fraser, a highly regarded journalist from Great Britain and a pioneering travel author published his worldwide adventures candidly and with a fantastic vision. In his book, *'Australia – The Making of a Nation'*, he noted the rivalry among the Australian states and explained it perfectly...**'In my journeys, I heard too much talk about State advancement and too little about Australia's advancement'.**

'The ordinary Australian, if the question was put to him, would insist that there is a national sentiment...talk to such a man, and, although he will begin with phrases about what a very magnificent country Australia is, it is only a few minutes before he is enthusiastic about his own state and is making disparaging comments upon the other States.'

More than a century later, this rivalry between states still exists, with many commentators believing it to be a healthy competitive spirit. In contrast, others consider it a pointless division of the populace and a hindrance to the development of a nation. But the fault-finding between the states has raged on for so long it has become both a social and political sport, and Australians love their sport, so it is unlikely that this so-called healthy rivalry will be restrained. Whether it was bridge vanity as claimed by the Perth *Sunday Times* or bridge envy shared by jealous neighbours, there was certainly no doubt that the bridge was a more helpful weapon for criticism than a symbol of unity or national pride.

Attempts to use the SHB as a symbol or metaphor for unifying the nation were a sentiment shared by only a few. The former state Premier, the 'Big Fella' Jack Lang, previously tried with his patriotic and unifying speech when opening the Bridge, but as his political standing had become tenuous, his speech fell on many a deaf ear. But Australian writer and poet Minnie Filson shared the same passion and sentiment as Jack Lang when also, on opening day, the *Sydney Morning Herald* published her splendid poem titled 'Sydney Harbour Bridge'. Her poem, which personified the Bridge, used the final stanza to express her heartfelt wish that the bridge may teach men the power of strength through unity.

> As I think how in one great stride
> I've spanned a chasm, deep and wide,
> This thought comes swift to the heart of me;
> That I might teach men perhaps to see
> The power of strength through unity;
> Thus more than a bridge of steel would be.
>
> - Minnie Filson -

15

WAR VETERANS, TRAVELLERS & POLICEMEN

'As dead as Julius Caesar'

Lewis Dyson was a war veteran and not alone in having the dream of a good life. Many veterans returning home after the war shared his dream only to discover that everyday life at home was another battle they had to face. Before the war, Lewis was a skilled engineer and draughtsman. Originally from Yorkshire, England he was living and working in the country town of Leeton in New South Wales as an engineer involved with the government's irrigation works programs. In 1914 he enlisted with the Australian Imperial Forces, and with talk of the war being short, he was confident of a quick return and married his sweetheart Effie Stewart just a few weeks before embarking for the war.

Lewis had the distinction of being a 'dawn lander' at Gallipoli with the 1st Field Company Engineers from New South Wales, and while in the trenches at Gallipoli, he had dreams of returning home from war and wrote letters to his close friends in Leeton telling how he looked forward to enjoying the **'times to come after the war'**.

On the 9th day at Gallipoli, Lewis was wounded in the leg by a gunshot and explained what occurred. **'I was shot while getting a box of biscuits along with another chap up to our men who were working a few yards behind the firing line. Three of us started to climb the hill with it, but one was shot, and his leg broken, and we nearly suffered a like fate in taking him down. On leaving us, one of his stretcher-bearers was killed. Afterwards, we lay behind a bank and looked at the box, which was being fired at, under the impression that someone was behind it. We had a smoke and finally decided that as the company had nothing to eat that day, excuses would not be accepted. We got it away all right and were resting in the bush when we noticed bullets were hitting the bush, so we pushed on to find the safest way to the top while my partner took cover. I went down, and somebody got me into a dugout and patched me up.'**

Lewis had a lucky escape, was hospitalised, later returned to Gallipoli, and served until the evacuation. His company was then sent to the Western Front in France, where he remained until July 1918, when he finally succumbed to nervous exhaustion and was medically discharged. After his distinguished war service, Lewis returned to Leeton and tried to take up the life he had before the war. Evidence suggests that settling back into everyday life was more difficult than he expected, and his time back in Leeton was short-lived. He was soon separated from his wife Effie and with no other family in Australia, he explored work opportunities around the world, visiting China, New Zealand, and America before returning and finally settling in Sydney.

Now 50 years old and having been unemployed for over 18 months with only the occasional work as a labourer, Lewis joined the growing number of destitute men, and was getting by with the assistance of charitable organisations and residing at what was known as Canon

Hammond House in Darlinghurst. During the depression, Arch Deacon Robert Hammond, an evangelist, and temperance crusader, established inner city refuges where men could get a bed, a shave, and a hot meal. These refuges became known as 'Hammond Hotels', and today, this charitable legacy has continued in the form of aged care and is well known throughout Australia as Hammondcare.

On the evening of March 24, 1933, Lewis Dyson decided to take his life and jumped from the southern pylon of the Sydney Harbour Bridge to the unforgiving ground below, a jump from which he knew he could not survive. At around 11 pm that evening, a pedestrian, Mr S Kilner, whilst walking along the footpath beneath the bridge, discovered the body shockingly disfigured and face down, lying on a grassy bank at the foot of the pylon.

The following day on hearing the tragic news, his good friend of fourteen years, Selwyn Mort, identified the body of Lewis at the city morgue. Selwyn stated at the Coronial inquiry that he had seen him the morning before he jumped and noted that Lewis appeared entirely rational but also had no reason to believe that Lewis had met foul play. We will never know how troubled and unwell Lewis must have been prior to 'willfully casting himself from the bridge', and sadly, the good times after the war that Lewis Dyson wrote home about in 1915 never eventuated.

In the weeks following the death of Lewis Dyson, preparations were being made for the inaugural Sydney Festival week, including the Venetian carnival on the Harbour, described as a carnival that would 'out-Venice' Venice itself. A celebration of lights and fireworks reminiscent of the Bridge's grand opening, but not part of the first Birthday anniversary of the bridge that passed relatively unnoticed only a few weeks before. The festival was inaugurated **'to cultivate a national buoyancy of spirit and sense of civic and national pride.'** The new Lord Mayor of Sydney, Richard C Hogan, stated he intended to make the carnival an annual event, his vision perhaps the forerunner to the Sydney City festival enjoyed today.

The Venetian carnival was the talk of the town, reminiscent of the excitement surrounding the opening of the bridge. Once again, the newspapers generated an enthusiastic and colourful description of the upcoming event to entice everyone's imagination.

'With a breeze from the Harbour blowing, and the Southern Cross on high, all Sydney and its visitors will flock on the evening of Saturday April 8, to vantage points on bridge and land and vessel to see the illuminations and fireworks and to hear the music, inseparable from Venetian carnivals. Venice, with its Bridge of Sighs, its Gran' Canale, its Laguna Morte, and its Lido, is beautiful, but the Venetian Carnival on Sydney Harbour will 'out- Venice' Venice itself. A naval band will delight the ear from the pontoon in Farm Cove, strains from mandolin and ukulele and mouth organ of course, will spread over the face of the water. The sky will be lit by gyrating, curvetting, bursting, flooding, and spreading shells, by asteroids and starbursts, cracker bags, roman candles and fire balloons; and every vessel in the harbour will be a centre of beauty and joy. In a setting such as the world-famous Harbour of Sydney, the scene should be unforgettable and will be a magnificent climax to a week of dances and sport.'

While preparations for the festival were being made, there was also great excitement on the harbour on 'All Fools Day', better known today as April's fool's day, but it was not quite the spectacle of a Venetian carnival. The first day of April is traditionally set aside for some practical joke playing, and pranksters celebrated the day with a joke against the Sydney Water police. Passengers crossing the harbour on the early morning ferries were startled to see a man floating in the harbour with his face appearing to be slashed and a dagger sticking in the man's chest. The water police naturally rushed to the scene and discovered the body was a well-made dummy looking like a bloodied corpse with the neck and head splashed with red paint and a large dagger protruding from the chest. The harbour hoax caused quite a stir among the ferry passengers and perhaps was a relief for the police to find it was just a prank.

Meanwhile, the inaugural Sydney Festival proved to be a great success. Described simply as a joyous time, with people from all over New South Wales and interstate visitors joining in and enjoying the festivities. The Bondi Beach festival, theatre events, sporting fixtures, beauty competitions, fancy balls and, of course, the Venetian Carnival all attracted large crowds.

As the month continued, activity on the harbour and the bridge remained relatively calm, with the Water Police attending to a yacht stolen by a pair of fifteen-year-old boys, a boat fire, a collision between a steamer and a trawler, and the usual collisions between sailing boats and ferries. With the run of bridge suicides skirting the average of one a fortnight, it seemed improbable, but April remained a suicide-free month and remarkably, not a single attempt had been reported. This sudden change gave cause to think that perhaps the suicide craze had reached its peak. Had it been just a fashionable suicide craze as once described, not likely; this was Sydney Harbour, a harbour that was always full of surprises, and no one knew this better than Sgt Frazer Foott.

Sgt Foott joined the police in 1906 and was already a water police veteran of over 25 years when the bridge opened, and at 47 years of age, he was one of the oldest members of the water police. On May 2, Sgt Foott received a report of a body in the water at Athol Bay near the zoological gardens. Foott recovered the body of Gladstone William Eyre, 71, a well-known artist of North Sydney. Investigations revealed that Gladstone suffered from insomnia and had left his home early the previous morning. Foott was doubtful that Gladstone was a Bridge suicide as his body showed no usual signs or injuries consistent with other bridge jumps. Ultimately the Coroner's report that followed confirmed Sgt Foott's theory, and there was no absolute proof that Gladstone had cast himself from the bridge.

Still, the relative calm over the waters of Sydney Harbour continued for quite a while, but any thoughts that Sydney had seen the end of bridge jumps were eventually dismissed. Almost seven weeks had passed since the death of veteran Lewis Dyson, and unfortunately, on May 13, 38-year-old Ambrose Thomas became bridge suicide victim number twenty-five. Ambrose was what was known in the day as a commercial traveller (or salesman), an occupation during the depression that was demanding and often unrewarding. The commercial traveller also had a mixed standing in some communities, like the sailor's reputation of having a girl in every port, but not all of them were so. The work often involved travel to country regions and the smaller towns that didn't have ready access to the convenience or availability of goods or services that the city suburbs offered. Most travellers had the almost impossible task of trying to sell goods and services to people who had either little need for them or little money to spend.

In many small towns, pessimism had set in, and there was a complete lack of confidence in spending. For every township that was managing to stand on its own and with no sign of rationing, another township was despondent or, as one traveller called it, '**as dead as Julius Caesar**'. The economic depression had made conditions for the travelling salesman almost impossible to make ends meet, with his expenses sometimes greater than his income. If he was a married man, he had the added stress of being away from home and family while desperately trying to make a hard-earned sale that would sustain his family and maintain a roof over their heads.

Ambrose Leslie Thomas worked for the Atlantic Oil Company, and while seeing his clients in the southern coastal town of Nowra, he received a telegram from his company asking him to return to Sydney for a meeting on the Saturday. The uncertainty of the meeting weighed heavily on Ambrose, and his return journey to Sydney would be filled with anxiety. The belief that he had done something wrong and the possibility that his future employment was at risk was like a ticking time bomb. Before Ambrose left for the return trip to Sydney, he made one last call to one of his clients, Tom Burke, a garage proprietor, where he expressed his fear of the worse. He mentioned to Tom that he felt he was going to '**get the sack**', and that he would not make it to the offices of his employer, and instead, he intended to '**go over the first big drop**' he came to.

Ambrose said farewell and then slowly made the 100-mile journey back to Sydney. Once he arrived, he parked his car within easy walking distance of the Sydney Harbour Bridge. Then making the final leg of his journey, he walked along the pedestrian footway to the centre of the great span, climbed the trellis fence, mounted the railing and took a giant leap into the water below. The following day, Sgt Foott discovered his body floating in Little Sirius Cove. Following a thorough investigation by the police, the Coroner discovered that Ambrose's work affairs were all in order, and it was determined that the poor fellow had done nothing wrong at all.

Less than a week later, on the evening of the May 17, 20-year-old typist Alon Betty Ison met with her good friend Aubrey John Veitch, a young press artist. Aubrey had noticed that she appeared depressed and distressed over some letters she posted that day and explained that the letters contained details of her future business. She began to cry, and as the evening passed, her emotional state wavered, and she discussed fatalism and reincarnation with him. From the conversation, she made a reference to going down south, which Aubrey misinterpreted as simply going away the following day. Aubrey was completely unaware of her true intentions. Aubrey accompanied her to her flat in Potts Point and 'thought she would go to bed'.

Shortly after, in the darkness of the early hours of the following morning, Alon Ison made her way to the Sydney Harbour Bridge and, at 1.45 am, asked the toll collector on duty how to get across the bridge. A short while later, a young man discovered a woman's handbag containing a pair of gloves, a handwritten note and an item of clothing near the northern pylon of the bridge, all signs indicating that Alon Ison was another bridge suicide. The note intended for the police stated that she was '**Tired of Life**', curiously the exact words uttered by Alberta

Ellks before she died. In the note, Alon also apologized **'sorry for any inconvenience'** as well as her details such as name and address.

Police then followed up, made enquiries confirming it was her address, and discovered that Alon had not returned home overnight. The news did not look good for the Ison family. The following morning at 7.00 am, the Water Police, accompanied by Alon's father, Henry, set out in the police launch and started scanning the harbour waters, only to discover her body in Lavender Bay 220 yards from the Bridge. The distraught father told police he never had any reason to suspect his daughter would take her own life. To the surprise of the police, the body showed no signs of external injuries or any signs of violence. The post-mortem examination confirmed that drowning had been the cause of Alon's death, but there were no signs of injuries consistent with a fall from the harbour bridge.

The police raised the possibility that Alon may have intended to jump off the bridge but changed her mind, left her personal items on the bridge, and plunged into the water from the Lavender Bay foreshore. The Coroner's report was consistent with the police findings and the post-mortem, and as there was no witness to her having jumped from the bridge, the verdict of the coroner was drowning after willfully casting herself into the waters of Lavender Bay.

Even in relatively quiet times, the Bridge and the Harbour waterways still carried an unnerving certainty that illegal activities and tragedy were a possibility at any moment, and in the dark hours of the evening, while most of Sydney's residents slept, the average citizen had little knowledge of the nocturnal watch maintained by the water police over the harbour. A vital part of the port's success was the critical role played by the Sydney Water Police as it managed the vastness of the harbour and the relentless task of maintaining law and order. Interestingly the Water Police have a long history as harbour caretakers and hold the distinction of being the first civilian form of policing established in New South Wales. In 1789, one year after the colony was founded, Governor Phillip created the 'Rowboat Guard'. Its main task was to patrol Sydney Cove for smugglers and convicts attempting to stow away on departing ships. By the early 1930's with the exception of escaping convicts, little had changed, and not forgetting, the Water Police still maintained a Rowboat patrol.

At night, Sydney Harbour was a massive playground for underworld activity, a mix of opium smugglers, illegal gambling and sometimes murder. On the night watch, there was never a dull moment, with the police keeping a constant lookout for the elusive harbour pirates who plundered cargo and stole yachts moored in the harbour. They maintained a watchful eye over the dockyards and any suspicious activities on wharves, keeping watch over the vast amount of shipping anchored in the harbour.

Day or night, strange happenings on Sydney Harbour were inevitable. A few days after the death of Alon Ison, hundreds of travellers over the bridge looked skyward and noticed the lifelike effigy of a man hanging by the neck. The 6ft moustachioed dummy was swinging in the cold driving rain, suspended from the great arch at the end of a 100ft rope. Newspaper reports of the 'First Bridge Hanging' and that the identity of the practical joker was 'shrouded in mystery' only added to the reputation of the shadowy and sinister presence of the Suicide Bridge.

Occasionally a strange happening for the Water Police was a shift away from tragedy and may have been a welcome relief, as was the case when the Water Police arrived on the scene of a naked man standing proudly on a buoy in the middle of the harbour. While swinging from his perch, he started yelling at the top of his voice, boasting that he was the former secretary of Mussolini, that he was also a painter of the Vatican in Italy, the son of a millionaire, and the founder of a middle-class association asserting a White Australia policy. Continuing to swing merrily from the buoy, he yelled to the police that his newly formed association already had majority support from the civil service, and he was now on his way to enlist further support from the navy and intending to address the sailors on such matters. Greatly amused but genuinely concerned about the man's state of mind, the Water Police pulled up alongside the buoy, and without any opposition, the man was taken on board the launch, clothed, and naturally taken directly to the Reception House in Darlinghurst. Unfortunately, comical moments like the nude orator were extremely rare for the Water Police, but the comic relief hopefully made for an excellent end-of-day story.

Four days later, the murky mood of the harbour returned when 21-year-old commercial traveller Thomas Richard Sewell jumped from the bridge on the evening of June 6, 1933. Thomas had been at his place of work the entire day, and when he hadn't returned home that evening, his parents became alarmed and alerted the police that he was missing.

As it so happened, young Thomas was the son of Captain Thomas Bartlett Sewell, who escorted tourists through the harbour on the *'S.S Maunganui'* to view the bridge before its grand opening. It was on his voyage that the bold American described it as looking like a large coat-hanger. It was a memorable day for Captain Sewell, but the tragedy of his son's death would change his view of the SHB forever.

The following morning, Sgt John Slaney, a veteran of the Water Police, was on duty and conducted a search of the water near the bridge on the off chance that Thomas had possibly jumped from the bridge the night before. Sgt Slaney, better known as 'Jack,' was a certified harbour master and a formidable police officer. He was a devoted family man with three daughters and a World War 1 veteran, having served in the 3rd Battalion at Gallipoli and France. Before going to war, Jack had already served five years with the Sydney Water Police alongside his close colleagues Charles Bebb and George Day. Like his colleagues, Jack had lost count of the many rescues and the number of lifeless bodies he had recovered from the harbour, and like his colleagues, he was particularly uncomfortable with the number of young lives thrown away.

That morning Sgt Slaney's hunch was confirmed when he discovered Thomas Sewell's body washed up on the rocks at Mrs Macquarie's Point. All the evidence confirmed that young Thomas Sewell had jumped from the Sydney Bridge, and his death was later confirmed at the Coronial inquest as suicide.

A few weeks later, news of another bridge suicide was circulating, with reports that 65-year-old Peter McVerry had jumped from the bridge and drowned. This, however, was not the case, and the circumstances of Peter's death were quite different. McVerry was a native of Armagh, Ireland, a cook who lived at Kent Street in Sydney. Before Peter left his lodgings on the night of June 19, he left a note stating, '**If you are looking for me tomorrow, you will have to look about Central Wharf**. The following morning the Water Police discovered his body floating face down under the Central Wharf. McVerry's death could only be described as a 'determined suicide'; after leaving his walking stick and hat at the edge of the wharf, he took a dose of poison, manacled his wrists behind his back with a buckled strap, and then jumped into the harbour.

On the same day, Peter McVerry's body was discovered, Sgt Bebb made his way out to sea on the Police launch *'Cambria'* with a large consignment of over 1500 firearms comprising rifles, shotguns, revolvers, and automatic pistols, all of which were confiscated from acts of crime. Each year the water police disposed of vast numbers of firearms, and secretly took the consignment out through Sydney Heads into the choppy sea to the 3-mile limit, where the guns were dumped overboard to rest at the bottom of the Pacific Ocean, approximately 200 fathoms below. A history of crime now laying at the bottom of the sea.

A few days later, there was another report of a bridge victim after a wallet had been found on the footway of the Bridge. As was the practice of most bridge suicides to leave a note or possessions behind before jumping, it was a safe bet that the victim was somewhere in the harbour below. Sgt Slaney once again started the search below the bridge, when, fortunately, on this occasion, it was a false alarm as later in the day, the owner of the wallet had been found alive and well.

The following month, it was announced that the Sydney Harbour Bridge was losing money at the rate of two hundred and thirty thousand pounds a year, with the Minister for Transport, Mr Bruxner revealing that there would be a colossal loss on the bridge for many years to come if revenue did not improve. This must have put a dim light on the prospect of fencing the bridge. Without money coming in, it was highly unlikely amidst a great depression that the spending priority would be bridge related. But it was still early in the life of the Sydney Harbour Bridge, and one thing was certain, life on Sydney Harbour was unpredictable, and bridge mayhem could strike at any time.

16

BRIDGE MAYHEM

'Sensational Suicide'

On Friday, August 4th, 1933, Robert George Graham, a 16-year-old schoolboy, was reported missing from his home in Lombard Street Glebe. His concerned parents, Robert and Bertha Graham advised police that their son, affectionately known as 'Bobby', was studying accountancy, and preparing for his examinations but was deeply worried about his progress. They then provided the police with a detailed description of their son in the hope that he could be found.

Chillingly on the same day, it was reported in the evening to police that a young man had jumped from the Bridge, but much to the relief of the Graham family, it was not their young son Bobby. The young man was 20-year-old Eric Clements, who, on that afternoon, jumped from the centre of the bridge and narrowly missed striking a rowing boat below. The lucky occupant of the boat was Albert Baker, a Harbour Trust employee who composed himself and quickly recovered Eric Clements's body from the water only to find that he was dead. At the inquest that followed, Eric's tragic story was revealed by Sgt Bebb, as well as the testimony of Eric's only friend James Murphy.

It was revealed that young Eric Clements was a native of Surrey, England, and in 1930 arrived in Australia on his own when he was just seventeen years of age, being one of the last teenagers to arrive under the youth migration initiative known as the Dreadnought Scheme. The scheme involved the migration of British teenagers between the ages of 15 and 18 for training as rural workers, which were in short supply. The scheme advertised for youthful boys to go to Australia on the promise of a job on a farm after completing four months of training and then placed on a minimum wage of £1 a week. The cost of the passage to Australia was usually £87, but for a Dreadnaught boy, it was considered cheap at £22.

On arrival in Sydney, the boys were moved to an established farming school known as 'Scheyville' at Windsor, west of Sydney. Once the boys completed their apprenticeship, they were sent to work on rural properties across New South Wales. This was a difficult transition for many of the boys, who for many months, were comfortable and feeling at home with other Dreadnought boys but were now expected to make it on their own. While many Dreadnought boys relished the new beginning, some found it difficult, and there were reports of the boys being open to exploitation, experiencing poor working conditions and some never being paid.

At the inquest, Sgt Bebb explained that Eric, like most of the young Dreadnought boys on arrival, was sent to the 'Scheyville' training farm and later went to work at, Goolgowi and Tarcutta and was last heard of by the Immigration Department in 1931, when he was still owing £7, the balance of his passage money to Australia. As for Eric's character, Bebb confirmed that various reports from employers declared that Eric was sullen and often hot-tempered. Eric's friend James Murphy followed with his testimony and stated to the coroner that he had known Clements for about two years and stated that Eric had no known relatives, his father having died in the Great War, and his mother was also deceased.

James Murphy explained to the coroner.... **'When I first met him, he had no food, and his clothing was in tatters. He said I was his only friend. I came down with him from Gundagai at his request. On the way down in the train he did not speak, and I had a job to get him to eat anything.... He was always a silent sort of a chap'**

'We were nearly frozen when we arrived, so after finding a room (in Regent Street, City), we had some food and then walked to the Bridge, to warm ourselves.'

James explained that he and Eric then went to a city talkie theatre, where Eric handed £7 to James, asking him to put it in his pocket and mind it for him, but with no mention of what it was for. In the middle of the screening, Eric walked past his friend and without a word, left the theatre. James explained that he thought Eric would return, but when he didn't, he learned from a girl that Eric had gone down the street. James Murphy stated to the court... **'I wasn't alarmed, I didn't like the picture either.'**

The inquest uncovered not a single clue as to why Eric Clements jumped from the SHB, but it was a sad and lonely end for a young man who came to Australia looking for much more out of life. After hearing the evidence and testimonies, Coroner Farrington returned a verdict of suicide but also witnessed a sincere deed when Eric's only friend James Murphy revealed he had always safely held onto the £7 that Eric passed onto him. At the inquest, James presented the money to the court, which was then paid to the Australian immigration authorities and officially, Eric Clements had repaid his debt.

Just three days after Eric Clements's death, the Bridge made headlines again with one newspaper reporting **'Young Girls Sensational Suicide'**. On the morning of August 7th, Marjorie Elizabeth Cummins left for work at her usual time of 8.30 am, but something diverted her from her normal path, and within an hour, she had plummeted to her death.

Several witnesses saw Marjorie leap from the Bridge. One witness, James Smith of Glebe, was below the bridge on the foreshore at Dawes Point talking with his friend Alfred Williams when he looked upward and noticed Marjorie sitting astride the railing of the footpath. Smith watched helplessly as Marjorie poised herself for a few moments, and then with her arms outstretched, she fell forward before somersaulting and then striking the water headfirst with tremendous force, ripping the shoes from her feet.

Smith then ran immediately to the Water Police stationed nearby and informed Sgt Day who was on duty. Meanwhile, William Kemp, an employee at Mort's Dock, was passing under the bridge in a launch, and he also witnessed the fall. He reached Marjorie within minutes and quickly dragged her from the water. It wasn't long after when Sgt Day and Constable Bent of the Water Police arrived, took charge of the body, and declared that Marjorie had died instantly on impact.

Marjorie Elizabeth Cummins was only 20 years old and had a full-time position as a bookkeeper with the well-known funeral director, Wood Coffill Ltd. She also lived with her family at Bellevue Hill, a lovely home she shared with her mother, Bertha, her father, John, her brother Bill, and sisters Dorothy and Audrey.

At the inquest, her father, who was also the accountant with Wood Coffill, explained that he was never concerned about his daughter's health or state of mind as she appeared to be in excellent health and high spirits and never at any time suggested that she might take her life. The inquest into her death revealed no conclusive reasons for her suicide, except for an accident three weeks earlier when she fell while ice skating. A few days later, she complained of an injury to her neck and that she was having difficulty sleeping. There was speculation that perhaps there was an underlying problem that went undiagnosed, and the injury she sustained days earlier may have caused a brain trauma.

Another consideration was that her work environment may have created an atmosphere of anxiety and melancholy. Marjorie was probably very grateful she was employed, but perhaps the constant exposure to the grimness of death whilst in the employ of a funeral director was a mentally harmful experience and often weighed on her mind. It may have been neither of these theories, but whatever troubled Marjorie, a seemingly happy young woman with so much to live for, will remain a mystery. Even Coroner Farrington was saddened and had difficulty reconciling why young Marjorie had taken her life and openly expressed, **'there was absolutely no reason why she should have done it. She lived very happily'**. Marjorie was later buried at the Church of England Rookwood Cemetery, Wood Coffill Ltd. of course, was the funeral director.

Meanwhile, a Western Australian newspaper made a brief but unsympathetic remark... **'During last week, the Sydney suicide bridge added two more victims to its already long list. A young woman did the trick early in the week and a young man in the latter part'.**

The following morning after the so-called 'Sensational Suicide' by Marjorie Cummins, a young married woman attempted to climb the railing and jump from the same spot as Marjorie. As she started to straddle the top railing and was close to toppling over, she was fortunately grabbed by two young men who were nearby.

'Let me go', she kept repeating as the men held her and brought her safely onto the footway. Bridge patrolman McDowall was also close by and raced up and took charge of the young woman as she kept repeating, **'I want to go over and end it all.'** The woman claimed she was married and living with her husband in Newtown but didn't elaborate on why she wanted to end it all. Shortly afterwards, Constable McDowall took the woman to the Reception House.

Two days later, on August 10th, Arthur Grayson, a 31-year-old miner from Newcastle, jumped from the railing of the bridge at around 4.30 in the afternoon. The month of August was shaping up to be horrific. It must have appeared that people were lining up to jump from the bridge, with Grayson being the 3rd victim within six days and each of them in broad daylight. Arnold Pritchard, a witness to the jump, said he saw Arthur at the centre of the bridge a good distance away.

He saw him climb up to the railing, then paused and took a good look around **'as though taking a last look at the world he was leaving'**. It was at that point that Pritchard started running towards Arthur. Staring down at the water below, Arthur then leapt forward. Pritchard could not get there in time and watched as Arthur struck the water and disappeared. Soon after, Sgt Slaney, in the police launch recovered the body from the water and Arthur was later formally pronounced dead at Sydney Hospital.

Another bridge tragedy and another inquest for Coroner Farrington provided no clue as to why a healthy young man like Arthur Grayson would jump to his death.

Unfortunately, the news of bridge suicides wasn't getting any better, and it soon took a more sudden turn for the worse. Two weeks had passed since the disappearance of young Bobby Graham, and the Sydney *Sun* newspaper posted a picture and a complete description of the youth in the hope that the mysterious disappearance could be solved. Unfortunately, a few days after posting the photo, Bobby Graham's body was discovered in the harbour near some rocks at Cremorne Point, and the injuries on his body proved to be consistent with a fall from the bridge.

More than three weeks after his disappearance Coroner Farrington held the hearing for Bobby Graham as well as two deaths connected with victims being struck by electric trams, two victims hit by motor lorries, one suicide by poisoning, another suicide by hanging and another suicide at the Gap. The coroner heard evidence from Bobby's father, stating he was not a healthy child, and that Bobby was concerned about his forthcoming exams. Bobby mentioned to his father, **'I am not so keen on passing this examination as the last one'**, suggesting the young teenager was suffering from the fear of failure. There was no further evidence to alter the coroner's findings, and he gave his ruling of suicide.

After discovering Bobby Graham's body, a sense of calm fell over the bridge and the harbour. The mad rush to jump off the bridge suddenly seemed to ease, with no attempts or reports of suspicious behaviour; a few weeks of respite from bridge suicides followed. But as incredible as it must have seemed, by the end of the month, the *Sun* newspaper described the 30th of August as the blackest day in the short history of the Bridge, a day when the grim suicide toll of the Harbour bridge was increased by two when a man and woman crashed to their death.

On that day, at around 9.00 am, an older man jumped from the southern approach of the bridge, crashing onto the grass at Dawes Point Reserve below and was killed instantly. A gardener attending to the trees at the Dawes Point Reserve witnessed the man hurtle through the air falling 100 feet and striking the ground with such force that a deep impression was left on the grass. The unknown man's description was quickly circulated as being about 55 to 60 years of age, approximately 5ft. 4in. tall, of medium build, hair turning grey, bald on top, medium complexion, grey eyes and eyebrows, no teeth in his upper jaw, some back teeth on the bottom jaw were missing, and the others stained by tobacco. There was a small scar on his right knee. He was dressed in a blue serge coat and vest, bearing a tailor's tag, marked 'J. F. Hole,' patched blue serge trousers, and singlet, marked. 'A. Green.' He was also wearing a pair of old boots, size six with iron protectors. His pockets also contained a few coins and two pipes.

While the Water Police endeavoured to establish the victim's identity, they were informed that an agitated woman with a child had enquired in Argyle Street for the easiest way to the Bridge. Perhaps it was an innocent enquiry, and nothing sinister was intended, but with what seemed like the season for suicides, there was a heightened alert. The police on bridge duty were quickly informed and advised to keep a close eye out for a woman with a child. The police patrolled the bridge and all the adjacent streets, maintaining a careful lookout.

Just after midday, while Sgt Bebb and the police team were still investigating the earlier suicide at Dawes Point Reserve and the bridge patrols above were still on the lookout for a woman with child, Mrs Jessie Daly quietly made her way along the pedestrian path on the western side of the bridge. She stopped at the centre of the bridge, took off her coat and placed it onto the footpath alongside a brown bag.

A witness, Frederick Rogers of Leichhardt, although some distance away, noticed her scale the lattice-work fence, sit for a moment on the top railing and then let herself fall forward. Still a distance away, Rogers made a desperate run towards her only to witness her hit the water where he claimed '**she sank like a stone**' not far from a passing ferry below. When she resurfaced, the deckhands on board the nearby ferry *'Lady Chelmsford'* recovered her body from the water only to discover her shocking injuries had proven fatal. On further investigation of her brown bag left on the bridge, the police found a receipt from an Annandale dentist, which helped discover her identity.

50-year-old Jessie Daly was originally born in Christchurch, New Zealand, and lived alone in her home at Surry Hills. Jessie had contemplated suicide for some time and had written a letter and posted it to her friend Miss Johnson who received the letter on the day Jessie made her fatal jump. Jessie's last thoughts were of her pet canaries and in the letter, asked if her friend would take '**the greatest care of her birds**'.

Miss Johnson later had the distressing task of formally identifying Jessie's body at the city morgue and explained to the police that she knew Jessie lived alone and led a lonely life, but she never showed any sign of unhappiness or depression. It was known that she had been married, but it could not be ascertained if her husband was alive. Miss Johnson also indicated that Jessie had a son living in Leichhardt. Jessie's son, John Daly, later appeared at his mother's inquest held by Coroner Farrington. He testified that his mother had recently referred to a shortage of money. It was worry over the lack of money that preceded his mother's desperate act. While John was only working intermittently, he offered her assistance; however, his mother refused to take what little money he had. He knew his mother had previously found employment, but the work was also intermittent. He claimed that she had never suggested taking her own life. Jessie died with an estate valued at £19. The public trustee handled her probate, and she was buried at Rookwood Cemetery, where today her grave is cared for by the Cemeteries Reserve Trust.

Meanwhile, the identity of the man who jumped the same day as Jessie Daly remained a mystery, and the coronial inquiry into his death failed to positively identify him. The only witness at the enquiry was Amos Wilkins, a florist from Darlinghurst who explained at the inquest that he had talked to a man fitting the description in Cook Park in William Street. They discussed the weather while the man drank from a bottle of methylated spirits. During the brief conversation, the man told him his name was Fred Brady and how he had come to Australia from England. He told Amos that he intended to go over the bridge and asked if he wanted to join him. Amos said he made a joke about it, said no, and walked off. The evidence presented to the Coroner was thin and inconclusive. The Coroner confirmed that the man's identity was unknown, and although it was possibly a man named Fred Brady, he was later buried as 'Unknown'.

August 1933 would prove to be one of the most horrific months in the history of the Sydney Harbour Bridge, with six bridge deaths, a combination of seemingly unimaginable suicides involving young adults and a schoolboy. Interestingly, one report indicated that the Water Police believed there had been even more Bridge suicides than were reported, and the suicide roll could be more significant than was on record. They stated that in the past months, at least four men had been recovered from the harbour waters many days after their deaths, but the evidence presented to the coroner was not absolute proof that they had jumped from the bridge.

By the end of August, the Bridge 'Red Roll' had jumped to 32 suicides, and the newspapers across the country were rolling out headline after headline, 'Over the Bridge', 'Instant Death', 'Bridge of Doom', 'Headfirst into The Harbour', 'Bridge Claims Another Victim'. It could not have been a worse time in the history of the bridge, and unbelievably there was not a single mention of fencing the bridge during the entire time. Perhaps the fencing campaigners were just waiting for such a horrific month like August and then be better placed to push their case. With the approaching sitting of Parliament in September, the time to push for fencing was certainly at hand.

17

WIDOWS OVER THE BRIDGE

The curious magnetism of the Harbour bridge...A magnetism that draws not only the harassed to a dreadful death, but also grips vice-like, those whose lives are leavened with sunshine!'

'Does the Harbour Bridge cast some uncanny spell over some people; does its ponderous magnificence entice and hypnotise?'.... The popular Sydney newspaper *Truth* certainly believed it was so and expressed the following...

'The bridge! in flesh and blood, it has claimed thirty-two lives. It seems that this great parabolic arch of interlaced steel is casting a sinister, menacing spell over the city as each week, almost, its grim total of deaths, of lives blotted out with appalling swiftness, grows, and grows. Finest of its kind in the world, Sydney's great bridge is casting a lengthening shadow of destruction over the city'.

As you would expect from a newspaper named *Truth*, it took itself seriously and delivered the news differently from the mainstream newspapers. Declaring itself the people's paper, it loved a headline and often outraged the establishment with its no holds barred approach to a story. By some, it was considered scandalous, but its straight-talking and often sensational journalistic approach had a popular following, stirring up interest and public opinion. As the suicide numbers increased, it wasn't just the *Truth* that enjoyed a bold and daring headline, the more conservative papers tired of just using the usual heading, 'Another Bridge Suicide', also became more audacious.

Less than a week following the Jessie Daly tragedy, two more women would take the terrible plunge with the headline from the *Labor Daily* reading **'WIDOWS OVER THE BRIDGE'** and describing how two women **'hurled themselves'** over the harbour bridge. Millicent Dymock was 42 years old and had been a widow for nearly ten years, she had two sons and a daughter, all of whom were teenagers, and all lived comfortably in a splendid home in the suburb of Ashfield. Millicent was what they described as 'well off'; she owned her own home and had £500 in her bank account. On the morning of September 6th, without any reason or sign of distress, Millicent left her house without telling anyone and never returned.

On the morning of the 6th, Millicent made her way to the city and ultimately arrived at her final destination, the now familiar 'stepping off point' of the SHB. Walter Kinross, a decorated war veteran and bridge worker, was walking along the eastern footway towards the northern pylon and noticed Millicent ahead of him. Kinross could see she was acting strangely. Millicent must have noticed Kinross approaching and suddenly scaled the trellis fence and sat astride the top railing. Kinross ran forward and managed to grab her by the neck and arms as she started slipping off the railing.

The awkwardness of his grip against the weight of the struggling woman quickly overwhelmed him, and Kinross was gradually losing his grasp, and although he called out to other pedestrians close by, none of them responded to his desperate calls for help. Kinross thrust his arm underneath the steel railing to help grasp Millicent, 'but the leverage of her body proved too great, and gradually her weight overcame the strength of his grip'. Millicent shouted **'Goodbye'** as she fell into space.

Whilst the body of Millicent Dymock was being recovered from the water beneath the bridge, Sgt William 'Bill' Hamill of the Water Police was attending to the disturbing discovery of baby's body which had been recovered from the harbour near Darling Point wharf. Sgt Hamill was shocked to discover the infant child had been murdered; the child smothered before being thrown into the harbour. As alarming and distressing as this was, it was not uncommon for the Water Police to recover infant children, some stillborn or sadly unwanted at birth, often cocooned in a blanket or hessian sack and laid to rest in the harbour. This was the darkest side of Sydney Harbour that was rarely seen or spoken about, a painful and disturbing social dilemma.

By 2 o'clock in the afternoon, the news of Millicent Dymock jumping from the bridge had hit the telegraphic wires around the country. Around an hour later, 65-year-old widow Susan Davis was caught shoplifting, stealing a single pair of stockings and a doyly with a combined value of 7 ½ shillings from the Farmers Department store. Susan was charged by the police and ordered to appear before the Magistrate at the Sydney Central court the following day. After the sudden humiliation of being caught for shoplifting and the enormous shame of fronting up at court the next day, the 65-year-old later faced quite a predicament and one she had difficulty dealing with. Without question, Susan was in complete despair and mentally disorientated by the whole incident. Instead of making her way home to Darlinghurst, she went in the opposite direction and made her way to the Sydney Harbour Bridge and jumped.

The following day when she was due to appear at Sydney Central court, the charges were called, and Susan's name was read out by the Magistrate. The police revealed that she was the same woman reported to have jumped from the bridge the day before and was, unfortunately, now deceased. Susan Davis was not penniless, and she could have easily paid for the stolen items, but at her stage in life, having just £20 in her bank account was like having insurance. Possibly it was all that was left of her life savings, her 'rainy day' money, but that is all she had, and no doubt she felt determined to make it last for as long as she could.

What was Susan's motive for stealing? Had she done it before, and if so, was she hawking them for money to buy food? Or perhaps it was the first time she attempted anything like this, a brain snap, a total lapse in judgement, and the items took her fancy. Whatever the reason, we will never know, but Susan's readiness to commit suicide rather than face the shame of court and a shoplifting charge was telling testimony to the fragility of her mind and her quality of life during the depression. Like many people of all ages and circumstances, she was on the edge of breaking point.

About the same time Susan Davis plunged to her death, the Harbour Police were alerted to another person who was seen struggling in the water at Darling Harbour Wharf southwest of the bridge. Sgt Hamill was already having a long and challenging day and when he arrived at the scene discovered, that 42-year-old Arthur Madden had jumped from the Erskine Street Wharf and, despite efforts to rescue him by local 'wharfies', he became exhausted and drowned. Arthur Madden was a waiter but had lost his job and was sleeping in one of the charitable hostels in the city. Evidence later revealed that while a lifebuoy was thrown at Madden, he made no attempt to reach for it.

A few days later, as unbelievable as it must appear, Sgt Hamill recovered another body from the harbour. This time it was 19-year-old Allan Ashwin Scott who was found floating in the water near Kirribilli Point. He was a young poster artist reported missing for over a fortnight. Initially, Sgt Hamill thought he was another bridge victim, but a medical examination later disproved this theory on account there were no injuries to the body, but it was certain Allan had drowned. On further investigation, however, the circumstances leading up to his death were highly suspicious, and it was possible he was murdered.

The past six weeks had been plagued by a series of horrific events. A combination of seemingly unimaginable suicides involving young adults, a schoolboy, widows, the murder of an infant and the possible murder of a young artist. As the *Truth* newspaper indicated, **'Sydney's great bridge was casting a lengthening shadow of destruction over the city'**. While tragedy was continually unfolding around Sydney Harbour, there was a sitting of the State Parliament. Unsurprisingly, the horrific events of the preceding weeks raised further questions among parliamentarians.

The state member for Willoughby, Mr Edward Sanders, asked that the Government consider placing a fine mesh fabricated roof over the footwalks to deter persons who contemplated jumping over. The Premier, Mr Bertram Stevens, replied by mentioning that the idea of mesh guards had been suggested some time ago but was not considered a sufficient deterrent in the way it was suggested. Mr Steven's stated the Government was quite prepared to consider any such proposal; the difficulty was to adopt a course that would be effective. But he still brought out the old favourite that **'People who wished to take their lives would probably do so, regardless of what was done in an endeavour to prevent them'**.

The reply by Mr Stevens wasn't a complete refusal; he did at least concede that the government was willing to consider any such proposal. It was a cautious answer, the sought given when wanting to buy time. But it was clear that the pressure on the government was mounting, and before long, a groundswell of discontent from some influential public figures would emerge.

A few days before the Coronial inquiry into the deaths of Millicent Dymock and Susan Davis, the *Australian Women's Weekly* magazine ran an editorial titled 'Bridge Tragedies' Lesson'. The Women's Weekly was a new magazine launched on the 10th of June 1933 and printed in black-and-white newspaper format. Priced at two pence and claiming to be 'the biggest value in the world', the first issue was sold out by lunchtime, and it soon became the most popular magazine in Australia.

The new publication followed the story of the 'Widows over the Bridge', and the editorial published its view on the recent Bridge suicides and suggested that in the end, everyone, rich or poor, should count their blessings.

'Last week saw the Sydney Harbor Bridge's grim record of suicides swollen by two deaths in a single day...Two reflections suggest themselves.

First, it is remarkable that during the 18 months since the bridge was opened not a single person has jumped to death from the Gap, whence the tide of fashion has swung to the bridge. It is pathetic that there should be fashion even in suicide, but it is a fact.

Similarly, the intending London suicide invariably selects Blackfriars, from the several Thames bridges, to be the stage of his last act. Perhaps the unhappy soul about to launch itself into eternity has an impulse to mitigate the sordidness of self-destruction by conforming to a convention.

Then, delving deeper into the motives of those who are weary of the world and would 'shuffle off this mortal coil', it must have been observed that not every suicide from the bridge has been penniless, homeless, desperate because of economic adversity. True, economic pressure seems, sad to say, to have pushed most of them over the brink. But there have been people of means and position among the bridge's victims, people with homes and, as it has seemed to the outsider, security.

Evidently, they found that money alone was not enough to make life worth living. So those of us who haven't much money, and are uncertain of our material prospects, can count our blessings in other currency than coin of the realm, not placing too high a value on that which rust and the moth corrupt, and thieves break through and steal'.

On September 12th Coroner Farrington held the inquiry into the deaths of Millicent Dymock and Susan Davis. The investigation revealed that neither woman was penniless nor suffering from any life-threatening illness, and the Coroner returned a verdict of suicide in both cases. Since taking on his position back in July 1932, Coroner Farrington held proceedings over most of the bridge victims and was deeply troubled by the large number of suicides not only from the bridge but the relentless number of cases that occurred throughout Sydney and the country regions.

Off course, it was a challenging time for all, but Farrington was irritated by the ease by which people could jump from the bridge. He openly showed his displeasure by publicly expressing his concern stating, '**It seems to me that people can climb up the rail and go over the Bridge with ease**'. He then urged authorities to take action to prevent the '**death leaps**' and suggested they consider putting up a fine wire mesh as a protective measure which would act as a deterrent in a significant number of cases. Little did anyone realise at the time, but this was a pivotal moment in the history of the Sydney Harbour Bridge as Coroner Farrington's voice quickly became the catalyst for change.

Mr Sanders, the member for Willoughby, encouraged by the remarks from the Coroner, seized the opportunity and quizzed the Minister for Transport Mr Bruxner, on the suggestions from the Coroner for protective measures. Mr Bruxner declined to comment but confirmed that it was being discussed and the proposal was being considered.

Pressure on the government was mounting, and after reading the comments from the City Coroner, Police Commissioner Mr Walter Childs weighed in and stated he agreed with the Coroner that something should be done. He suggested a '**big canopy erected over the footways would render suicides impossible**'.

The Editor of the *Daily Telegraph* also took an ardent stand and expressed his dim view and disappointment at the authorities' lack of insight. The editorial was timely and impressive and read as follows: -

'It puzzles the man of ordinary experience that "authorities" of lethargic mind should have hesitated so long to interpose, on the Bridge, some barrier between the would-be suicide and his or her leap to death. The repeated reply that 'If people want to destroy themselves, they will do it in spite of obstacles' is surely the last word in stupidity and lack of imagination. Impulses towards suicide come to countless numbers of people; they rise and fall like a fever chart, now raised to a height at which the terrors of death are forgotten, and again weakened below the resolve upon one final desperate act. There is a level at which the slightest deterrent will make the victim of melancholia turn back from death to life. Merely to have to clamber up a difficult netting, with the fear of being seized and rescued, will stop many a man or woman from going over'.

It was hard to tell if cracks were starting to appear in the Governments position on fencing. The combined weight of the Coroner, the Police Commissioner and the rallying of the newspapers surely had to have some influence, but Mr Stevens and Mr Bruxner were holding their cards close to their chest and were still unwilling to offer up any sign of a solution. Meanwhile, the persistent presence of death on the harbour continued undiminished.

On the 3rd of October, the tally of bridge suicides reached thirty-five with the death of John Fraser Proctor Cocks. John was 23 years old, the son of his late father, the celebrated Congregational leader Reverend N. J Cocks. John was described as tall and good-looking, a happy-natured young man with ample money in his own right. He had a host of friends and was living in a fine home with his mother and sister in North Sydney. He attended University and by all reports, made excellent progress with his law studies and was almost at the point of obtaining his degree. John was also apprenticed to the well-known legal firm of Maund and Kelynack, where his work was highly regarded. John was on the threshold of a successful career.

Nobody witnessed John climb over the rails and fall to the water below, but around 11.00 am, local resident Mr George Pierce and his son were passing under the bridge on their launch when they discovered John unconscious and floating in the water. Mr Pierce then dragged John from the water, his torn clothes hanging from his body, revealing no indication of the severity of his injuries. Pierce then motored the launch as quickly as he could to the nearby Water Police boatshed, and as John was brought ashore, he suddenly regained consciousness and started raving deliriously and calling out for death, '**Give me a needle and let me die.**'

When John was admitted to the hospital, he was bleeding slightly from the mouth and nose, but it was clear to the medical team he had sustained severe internal injuries. After the first injection from doctors to stimulate his heart and soothe his nervous tension, he opened his eyes and remained conscious only for a few minutes when suddenly he moaned, '**Oh, let me die!**' John then closed his eyes and died. The inquest into John's death revealed that he suffered from depression and a year earlier had written a note to his mother and sister explaining that he was going away. He then disappeared without a trace, and his concerned family reported him missing. It wasn't long before his family held genuine fears that he had committed suicide. But after a few months had passed, John suddenly returned home.

Looking healthy and in good spirits, he explained to his family that he had been overwhelmed by awful spasms of depression and despair and was becoming a victim of melancholia. Believing he needed a complete change from his studies and his environment, he decided to 'go bush' and made his way as far as North Queensland, where he became a jackeroo on a cattle station. After a few months and feeling physically and mentally restored, John began to think fondly of his home and his postponed studies and returned to his family, studies and law work. Unfortunately, a year on and John had not wholly escaped the evils that haunted him; his sister revealed to the Coroner that just before his suicide John had taken an extended vacation which was due to health reasons after suffering a nervous breakdown.

The *Truth* newspaper followed the story of John's death intensely and declared it '**was a pathetic case: the story of a fine boy who fell prey to the curious magnetism of the Harbour bridge.**' The *Truth* was convinced that the death of John was '**entirely due to the spell which the bridge cast over his mind.**' The newspaper revealed that John had mentioned to his friends about the unnerving attraction of the bridge as he travelled over the bridge each day, his mind often feeling the intolerable desire to leap towards the blue water far below.

The feelings that John expressed were not considered unusual; psychiatrists had long theorised that great heights have a singular and unnerving attraction for most people and can exert a frightful influence on the mind. Perhaps the *Truth* was on to something, and their long-held suggestions that the bridge was a sinister entity was not so overstated.

Only a week following the death of John Cocks, on October 10th, Sgt Slaney and Sgt Foott were patrolling the foreshores of the harbour when they received reports from two girls that they saw a man jump from the bridge railing. They immediately made their way to the bridge, started circling and searching for a body, and found only a cap. It had been in the water for a brief time as it was only partially wet, a clue that the suicide attempt may have only just occurred. Shortly after, another clue, a search by a patrolman on the bridge footway, also turned up a man's coat. The clues appeared to tie in with the reports, and the search continued for days, but there was still no trace of a body. Eight days later, Sgt Hamill of the Water Police received an anonymous phone call from a woman who could see a body floating on the water's surface near Kirribilli Point.

Sgt Hamill had the ominous task of recovering the body which had been in the water for eight days and was in an advanced stage of decomposition. The man was identified as Desmond George Cleary, the owner of the cap and coat discovered days earlier. Desmond was 30 years old, a single man who lived at home with his parents and brothers Osborne and Roy. He was unemployed and had been depressed by his circumstances for many days. His father, George, who reported him missing to police, indicated that his son had never mentioned being suicidal, he appeared to be in good health and confirmed that he wasn't a drinker of alcohol. His father was completely mystified and explained that Desmond had just left one morning to get some fruit and never returned home.

With little reason to explain the death of Desmond Cleary, was it possible that he also **'fell prey to the curious magnetism of the Harbour Bridge.'** As psychiatrists warned, did the giddy height of the bridge truly have this fatal attraction to the melancholy and was the *Truth* again exposing more than just a spooky tale? If this was the case, the Bridge's fatal reach extended well beyond the city dwellers and the fringes of Sydney.

On the 24th of October, 67-year-old Lucina Lilian Moye left her home in Wagga, a country town 300 miles southwest of Sydney. After an overnight journey, she arrived in Sydney the following day and by all accounts, made her way directly to the SHB.

Having been missing from home and unsure of her whereabouts, her husband George had contacted their eight adult children, some of whom were living in Sydney, but all of them were unaware that she had arrived in Sydney. It was mid-morning on the 25th of October when several men witnessed Lucina climbing the pedestrian fence, but they were too far away to prevent her from throwing herself over the railing. Two men below at Dawes Point also witnessed Lucina crash into the water and alerted the Water Police. After they recovered her body from the water, they confirmed Lucina had perished, and she was later taken to the morgue, where her eldest son George Raymond Moye identified her body.

At the inquest, her eldest son revealed that Lucina had been in poor health and suffered from anxiety for nearly twenty years. It was thought that her condition was likely worsening, and she had no intention of burdening her family with her troubles, so Lucina Moye chose her path to eternity, and like many others before her, she made the journey to Sydney Bridge.

18

UNREQUITED LOVE

Tired of life on this old mud ball and decided to get off it'
- Charles Payne -

By November of 1933, the death toll from bridge suicides had reached the staggering tally of thirty-seven. Despite the controversy surrounding the relentless run of bridge suicides, there was still no conversation about fencing the bridge. The government once again was silent. Then on the 6th of November, war veteran Jesse Stunt became victim number thirty-eight.

Jesse 'Harry' Stunt was a war veteran, a survivor of the original 53rd Battalion Australian Imperial Forces. His battalion saw their first involvement in the Great War at the 'Battle of Fromelles'. This first stage of the allied attack on the western front was a disastrous assault, described as the soldiers' bloody initiation to warfare. A battle considered by many as the most tragic event in Australian war history, with the greatest loss of life by a single military division in twenty-four hours. Jesse was wounded at this dreadful battle, a gunshot wound leaving his left arm crippled. Jesse Stunt was never the same after that agonising day at Fromelles, the experience also shattering his nerves and leaving him mentally scarred.

Like bridge victims Lewis Dyson and William Lewis, Jesse was also an immigrant from England, born in Limehouse London in 1884. All of these men arrived in Australia hoping to start a new and exciting life in a vast country full of promise and offered plenty of opportunity. Then World War 1 interrupted their plans, and all three men didn't hesitate to enlist in defending their motherland as members of the Australian Imperial Forces. When the war ended, these men returned to Australia under vastly different circumstances from when they first arrived. The country once considered a land of opportunity was now burdened by war debt and unemployment. The skills and trades they once mastered were now being offered to younger, healthier men, and as time pushed forward into the depression years, veterans like Jesse, Lewis and William understood that time might be running out for them.

49-year-old Jesse worked as a kitchen hand for a few years and then later as a lift driver and received a war pension of £2. 2 shillings a fortnight. He was not addicted to drink and was described as having a noticeably quiet disposition. However, Jesse's nerves were shot, and even the noise of the radio worried him. On the morning of the 6th, Jesse packed all his personal belongings into a suitcase, along with his war decorations. Before he left his lodgings at Greens Road Paddington, he asked his landlady if she would mind his suitcase as he was moving on and **'going to get another place'**. About midday, Jesse made his way to the 'Suicide Bridge' and walked the same path as troubled veterans William Lewis, Augustus Gallen, and Lewis Dyson and stopped at the middle of the bridge. He placed a handwritten note on the footway, climbed the pedestrian railing, and jumped to his death.

The master of a passing ferry below saw Stunt falling into space and immediately gave four shrill blasts of the ferry whistle, now a familiar sound in Sydney Harbour, a signal that alerted the nearby Water Police that another person had jumped from the bridge. Sgt Bebb, on board the police launch *'Osiris'*, immediately made his way to the scene and removed the body from the harbour. Sgt Bebb recognised that Jesse had been killed the instant he hit the water, noting that the impact was so terrific that all the clothing had been stripped from Jesse's body. Later the note Jesse left behind on the footway was discovered. It gave details that a suitcase he owned should be passed on to a woman in Paddington. The woman was his landlady, Mary Finnigan.

Whatever tormented Jesse was well hidden beneath his peaceful disposition. Jesse, feeling tortured and suffering from a serious nervous condition, was desperately seeking peace. When he mentioned to Mary Finnigan, he was going to find another place, he meant he was looking for a place of peace and the 'Bridge of Eternity' offered him that peace.

Not surprisingly, it was only two days later when there was yet another bridge jump. 15-year-old Francis Madge Hope, known as Madge, was from Woonona on the south coast of New South Wales. The night before she jumped, she was described as the **'Belle of the Ball...a graceful figure at the Woonona Queen competition ball in the local school of Arts.'** Whilst at the local dance, everyone noticed that Madge was enjoying herself as she danced with the 'effervescent gaiety of youth'. During the evening, she openly admitted to friends that she intended to jump off the bridge. Giving no explanation as to why she intended to jump, her friends laughed, thinking she was merely joking.

No one took any notice of her threats. And then, early the following morning, she was given a lift to Sydney by her auntie who dropped her off believing she was meeting up with a friend. Madge wasted little time on her arrival in Sydney and made her way directly to the bridge. At the height of the morning traffic, Madge walked along the eastern side of the Bridge and scarcely pausing to think of the consequences, she climbed the railing and threw herself over. **'Hurtling like a great stone through the air she fell into to water'.**

Henry Ingle, the driver of a Harbour Trust launch, was below the bridge and witnessed Madge jump. He gasped in horror and yelled **'Good God'** as he watched Madge with her brightly coloured dress fluttering through the air, strike the water 'with a report like a pistol shot near his boat'. He grimaced as she hit the water, and then, snapping himself out of his stunned gaze, Ingle then rushed to her aid. Madge hit the water feet first and then quickly rose to the surface, and much to Ingle's surprise, she was treading water but was visibly struggling. Ingle pulled up close, and according to reports, incredibly Madge needed little assistance climbing aboard. Henry Ingle then made his way to the Water Police shed, and it was only then that Madge stumbled and fell unconscious.

Now more than familiar with bridge victims and life-saving techniques, Sgt Bebb lifted Madge from the launch and began resuscitation treatment until the ambulance arrived, which then transported her to Sydney Hospital. Dr Andrew Findlay, the medical superintendent at Sydney Hospital, like Sgt Bebb, was equally familiar with Bridge victims, and as the *Truth* newspaper passionately described, Dr Findlay **'commenced his fight to fan into flame again the spark of life still feebly burning in the breast of the pretty girl'**.

Naturally, the *Truth* followed the Madge Hope story closely. It was a sensational story and one that only the *Truth* could deliver in its usual unrestrained fashion...'**The huge drop, the terrific strain on the nerves, the blow to the heart and the delicate arteries had been so severe that the girl's entire system was numbed by the shock and life was only retained by a very slender thread**'.

With hot packs placed around her body and what they described as restoratives and saline fluids with a sedative influence injected into her bloodstream, Madge received excellent care. Whilst lying in bed, she opened her eyes, and her first words were, '**Oh! I feel dreadful... where am I.**' The nurses quickly assured her that she was alright and then asked, '**Who are you**'? She replied, '**Madge Hope.... Madge Hope of Woon...Woon....it's on the South Coast**'. Feeling dazed and confused, this was all that Madge could recount before the nurses encouraged her to close her eyes and told her she would be well when she woke up.

While Madge Hope was quietly recovering in Hospital, another late-night attempt to jump took place. Fortunately, two pedestrians noticed a man taking off his coat and hat and started to climb the railing. They managed to grab the man, and after a fierce struggle, they pulled him back to safety. His attempt thwarted, the police were notified, and the man declared he had been worried over business and added, 'It's all **right now. I'm glad they stopped me. I shouldn't have tried it'**.

Two weeks later, miraculously, Madge Hope made a full recovery after her jump and suffered no permanent injuries. It was suggested that like previous bridge survivors Robert Anderson and Susie Boulton, she entered the water feet first, which significantly minimised the force of impact and her injuries. It was never revealed what motivated Madge to attempt to take her life. Apart from what was considered a joke to her friends the night before, her parents were baffled, and Madge could not explain what motivated her to jump. Even the tenacious *Truth* had no answers and could only surmise, '**A young girl without a care attends a ball, enjoys herself immensely, leaves home at 5 a.m., and comes nearly 60 miles to throw herself to her doom. As 'Truth' has asked before... Does the Harbour Bridge cast some uncanny spell over some people; does its ponderous magnificence entice and hypnotise?'**

Many theories surrounding the teenagers' attempt at suicide were certainly circulating, but there was surely no doubt that Henry Ingle helped save her life, for had she lingered much longer in the water unnoticed, she would have likely fallen unconscious and drowned. Six years later, Madge Hope married and had two children. She lived a long life and carried with her the memory of a unique life-or-death experience, a shockingly grave event that she may have never had the courage to share with her husband or children.

After the sensational survival of Madge Hope, the suicides seemed to keep rolling on, and by the month's end, there would be another five suicides to add to the 'red roll' as well as several failed attempts, and still, no decision had been made by the state government to curtail the would-be suicide.

On November 12th, less than a week after Madge Hope's attempt, 24-year-old Gwendoline Cummins (Cummings) made the ultimate sacrifice to unrequited love and plummeted to her death. At 8 pm on the evening of the 12th, two youths, Joseph Wall and Bernard Phillips were walking across the bridge, and when halfway across, they noticed a woman about 20 yards ahead of them. The youths watched as she suddenly stopped and at first, they thought the woman had dropped something, but then they realised she was taking off her shoes. They watched as she flung off her jacket and then threw her handbag to the ground and started to climb over the railing. Joseph Wall had already anticipated what was happening and raced forward, jumped onto the steel latticework, and grasped her under the arms just as she let go of the top rail.

Joseph Wall described in detail exactly what happened next…. '**I was hanging half over the rail, and only the toes of my boots caught in the railing saved me from slipping over, she turned an agonized face up to me and said, 'Let me go,' but I hung on, expecting my mate to arrive any second. Then she gave a convulsive wriggle, and her dressed ripped. In a last effort I snatched at her hair, secured a hold, then felt her weight slip away. I was left with her beret in my hand, and she dropped like a stone into the water.**'

As soon as the horrified youths saw the body strike the water, they ran to inform the Water Police and Sgt Day immediately put out in the police launch in search of the body of young Gwendoline. Seven days later, her body finally resurfaced at Kirribilli Point and once again, Sgt Bebb was there to recover the body from the water.

A week later, Coroner Farrington held the inquiry into her death, revealing an unfortunate story of unrequited love. The court initially heard evidence from Gwen's employer Michael O'Regan, the licensee of the Five Dock Hotel on the Great North Rd, at Five Dock. He informed the Coroner that he had employed her as a nurse for nine months prior to her death. He also pointed out that he knew of no reason for her to 'destroy herself' and that she never drank at the Hotel, but he had since discovered that she used to take doped wine at a chemist shop. The next witness was young Joseph Wall, who told of his courageous attempt to save Gwen. Then followed the testimony of Thomas O'Regan, the brother of the Licensee. Thomas was the night-watchman and stated, '**I had seen a good deal of her at the hotel, but I had never been out in her company. However, we had a bit of a quarrel on the Sunday afternoon, but she used no threats to me. She never threatened to make any trouble for me. She was a very 'deep' kind of girl.**' Thomas O'Regan then added '**I can ascribe no motive to cause her to jump off the Bridge.**'

The final witness was none other than Sgt Bebb, who produced a letter Gwen had written to the Editor of the *Truth* newspaper which he discovered inside her handbag after her death. The letter, which was later published by the *Truth*, was censored, and any references to individual names were omitted. Gwen's letter to the Truth revealed the tragic circumstances behind her quest for love, a love that she reveals was unrequited. The letter also offers insight into her past and a clue as to the possible identity of the man she so desperately loved.

Gwen revealed that her life had been marked by unhappiness, and after being a sister at St Michael's Novitiate in Goulburn, which she described as her true vocation, she left to seek pleasure in the world, and sadly admitted, 'I found it not'. The letter told of how she had travelled to Sydney three years earlier, and among all the admirers she came across, she fell for this one man with all her heart. '**The boy I love, and still love, has turned me down completely. I have just asked him to say the last goodbye and he turns his back on me, but still, at this moment, I love him better than life itself**'. With eternal hope, Gwen wrote, '**I will pray for him in Heaven, some people meet in Heaven, perhaps our wedding-bells will sound there too**'. Gwen's final thoughts also revealed the deep love she had for her child, which she had given over to the care of others, and in her final thoughts wrote, '**keep her always and god will bless her**'.

Gwen's tragic story is not unlike the ancient mythology of the Greeks or a hangover from the Victorian era of tragic romance novels, which romanticised the notion of a broken heart and the tragedy that followed. For decades, Blackfriars and Waterloo Bridges in London had been popular destinations for broken-hearted women attempting suicide, and Ancient Greek mythology tells of similar tales of desperate love gone tragically wrong. There is the story of Queen Artemisia of Caria who fell in love with a man named Dardanus. When Dardanus ignored her, the great oracle told Artemisia to jump from the Luecadian Cliff, and she would be cured of the passion of love. Phaedra, wife of Theseus fell in love with her stepson Hippolytus, and when he rejected her, she hanged herself. Not surprisingly, both Queen Artemisia and Phaedra were cured permanently.

But whilst the romanticised Greek and Victorian tragedies had much to answer for, it has been explained by contemporaries that delusions of unworthiness, a feeling of failure or shame, a sense of hopelessness, and feeling scared of being alone were feelings shared by men and women and similarly, a broken heart or unrequited love carries a similar mental burden and are all capable of creating a state of mind bent on self-harm. Gwen's letter confirmed that she suffered from many, if not all, of these feelings, and by the end of the transcript, the *Truth* newspaper touchingly passed on its respects, '**May Gwen secure the peace she sought in such a terrible way**'.

Five days after Gwen Cummins jumped, the body of Charles Payne, a 37-year-old labourer from Marrickville, was recovered from the foreshores of Sirius Cove near the Sydney Zoo. This was the second time Charles Payne had been dragged from the waters of Sydney Harbour, but this time he was dead. Charles attempted suicide twelve years earlier and plunged into the water from the nearby Pyrmont Bridge at Darling Harbour. The Pyrmont Bridge was opened in 1902, and it also became a popular jumping-off point, but attempts were often unsuccessful as it was not a great height, and many people survived uninjured. Those who didn't survive usually drowned because they were simply unable to swim or died from exposure.

Sgt Day could easily recall the day back in 1921 when he was patrolling the waters around Darling Harbour as a young Constable. While rowing near Pyrmont Bridge in the police skiff, he could hear faint calls for help. George Day rowed closer towards the direction of a nearby wharf and found an exhausted Charles Payne desperately clinging to a wharf pile. Day dragged the helpless man aboard the skiff, who was in a poor state suffering from the effects of the cold and immersion. Payne explained to Constable Day that he had made up his mind to commit suicide and confessed that '**there was no reason for it really. But he was tired of life on this old mud ball and decided to get off it**'. Like many suicide attempts before him, the forty-foot fall to the water left Charles Payne uninjured, but had it not been for Constable Day, he may have suffered from exposure and possibly drowned like many others.

Twelve years passed, and Charles Payne, on Friday evening of the 17th of November 1933 was making his way across the Sydney Harbour Bridge. He stopped at the centre of the Bridge, the usual spot, and asked a passer-by, Clifford Toon, a theatrical actor from North Sydney, for directions to a city street. The men spoke briefly, and without any concerns, Clifford casually assisted Charles with directions. As they parted company and headed off in different directions, Clifford briefly turned around and then stood horrified as he watched Charles Payne quickly scale the lattice fencing, mount the top railing and jump.

The body of Charles Payne was not recovered until the following day, having surfaced among a flotilla of yachts that usually populated the waters on harbour race days. Like clockwork, Sgt Bebb made his way to the scene to recover the body among the yachts. When the coronial inquiry was held, Charles's brother Henry, who was living with Charles, explained that his brother had previously attempted suicide twelve years earlier and added that he had been unemployed for a long time and his efforts to secure work was fruitless. It can only be thought that twelve years after Charles's first attempt at suicide, he was still **'tired of life on this old mud ball'**, and on his second attempt, he had a much larger bridge with a greater height from which to jump.

It was proving to be a challenging month, and no one was under more pressure than the Sydney Water Police. They had little time to recover from each bridge tragedy, and the month was far from over. Early in the afternoon of November 20th, a city tram made its usual crossing of the bridge. As it made its journey, the tram driver gazing from his window, watched in horror as he passed a man jumping off the footway railing of the bridge and hurtled to the water below. With the Water Police only a short distance away, Sgt Bebb was alerted by the customary sound of four sharp blasts from the horn of a passing tugboat that witnessed the man hit the water. Sgt Bebb, accompanied by two constables, immediately boarded the police launch and pulled alongside the tugboat, which had retrieved the body from the water only a few minutes after the man had jumped.

The police then transferred the body to the launch, but all attempts to resuscitate him were unsuccessful. On close inspection Sgt. Bebb noted that the man was powerfully built and at least 6ft tall with only a penny in his trouser pocket. Bebb noticed that the man's unkempt facial appearance, along with what remained of his torn and shabby clothes, was a sign that the man had been in a state of impoverishment for some time. The *Labor Daily* newspaper while reporting on the fatal jump, made a brief but rare reference to the reaction from the usually unshakeable Sgt Bebb. The observant reporter detected that Sgt Bebb was clearly upset and remarked, **'Although he has had many years of strenuous work of this nature behind him, Sgt Bebb was visibly affected by the latest fatality. The officer has now removed the bodies of three Bridge victims from the water in as many days.'**

The body of the 41st victim was then taken to the hospital and formally pronounced deceased. Bebb quickly followed up on any leads to help identify the victim and try to determine the circumstances behind the suicide. He soon discovered that the destitute-looking man with only a penny left in his threadbare trousers was 35-year-old Branford Bryan Angell, the nephew of none other than the enormously famous Sir Arthur Conan Doyle, the creator of 'Sherlock Holmes' described as 'the super-detective who could detect a murderer by the kind of clay that stuck to his boots or the single hair that wasn't brushed from his coat'.

Sgt Bebb continued his own detective work and remarkably found an old schoolmate of Branford's, a Dr Percival C Homer, well known in medical and sporting circles who had a practice in Macquarie Street Sydney. He stated to Sgt Bebb, no doubt in a very distinguished manner, that he and Branford both attended Durham School in England and described Branford as a man of 'brilliant intellectual attainments' who 'exhibited a most studious nature and took little part in sporting activities.' He also confirmed that he had been a teacher for some time, engaged at 'various English schools of high standard'. The doctor revealed that Branford Angell was about 20 years old when he travelled to India, where he became the manager of several tea plantations in Assam, but later returned to teaching and was appointed headmaster of Poona High School. He remained in India until he contracted malaria, and it was then that he decided to migrate to Australia in 1930. For a while, he was employed on a dairy farm at Bega, on the New South Wales south coast and shortly after, he moved to Sydney seeking employment as a journalist but was unsuccessful and remained unemployed for 18 months.

Sgt Bebb had earlier visited the lodging house in Crown Street East Sydney, where Branford had spent the last few months. Mrs Norah Franey, the proprietor, was also able to formally identify the body, and her account of Branford was consistent with Dr Homers. She confirmed that Branford was a student of classical languages, Hinduism and Indian dialects and mentioned he had been unemployed for a long time and had grown despondent. Sgt Bebb then inspected his lodging and discovered among his meagre belongings were, in fact, numerous works on classical subjects and languages. Within twenty-four hours,

Sgt Bebb had completed most of his investigations and passed on the details of his enquiries to the press, as news of Branford's death, the nephew of Sir Arthur Conan Doyle, was sure to be international news.

19

BARRIER TO SUICIDE

'There will be three rows of barbed wire, and the space between the wire and the top of the present rail will be filled in with a strong wire mesh.'

On the 22nd of November 1933, two days after the death of Branford Angell, quite unexpectedly, the State Government of New South Wales announced that they would fence the Sydney Harbour Bridge. Entirely out of the blue, under the leadership of Mr Stevens, the Government Ministers all declared that they took a serious view of the increasing number of suicides and attempts from the Bridge, and they all felt that something had to be done urgently if lives were to be saved. It was decided that the Main Roads Board would erect a mesh wire along the railings and a wire frame on the top which arched back over the pedestrian footway, a structure sounding remarkably familiar to the one described by Alexander Buckham's proposal from North Sydney Council a year earlier.

North Sydney Council were quick to claim they played a hand in having the Government finally proceed with its plans to build the suicide barriers. Once a divided council dominated by those who favoured the idea that bridge suicides were just a passing phase or advocating a springboard for jumpers, the council was no longer under the influence of the naysayers. A new broom had swept through the council, and the new Mayor, Ald. Raymond Hodgson now presided. Under the guidance of Mayor Hodgson and some persistent council colleagues, the mood towards suicides was more appropriate. As the suicide numbers continued to increase, so did the councils' concerns. The council continually urged the government to act, stating that the public conscience had been shocked, and the number of suicides was having a tremendous psychological effect on the general public.

The Sydney press could also claim to have had an enormous influence in finally getting a decision on fencing across the line. Sydney's leading newspapers, the *Sun* and *Daily Telegraph*, had long been the strongest advocates for the fitting of anti-suicide fencing. They campaigned since veteran William Lewis made the first 'Historic Jump' in April 1932 and maintained a steadfast approach in reporting the bridge suicides and continually highlighting the need for safety measures.

The Commissioner for Main Roads, Mr Newell, was initially not so enthusiastic about the need for fencing or any preventive measures. He didn't believe it was a good idea to broadcast to the world that the people of Sydney had to be protected from themselves. He suggested the Government had become agitated, its hand forced by a few angry voices, but in the end, he conceded the bridge had to be fenced.

There could be little doubt that the weight of public opinion was bolstered by the influence of official heavyweights like Police Commissioner Walter Childs and City Coroner Herbert Farrington; both men had extraordinary reputations and were difficult to ignore. But why was there such a sudden turnaround? Had the persistent agitations and a few angry voices that the Commissioner for Main Roads mentioned made a difference and convinced the government to do a quick turnaround. Or had they always intended to build the anti-suicide barrier and never wanted it to appear they were surrendering to public pressure? A familiar trade tool in politics.

The harshest cynic could claim the sudden change of heart by the government was triggered by the untimely death of Branford Angell, the nephew of Sir Arthur Conan Doyle. Branford Angell was a high-profile death; he was not just one of the long-term unemployed, a lonely widow or another shattered war veteran; he was the nephew of one of the most famous authors in the world. Could a healthy dose of scepticism be excused for thinking this high-profile death nudged the government to finally act?

Whatever the reason for the extraordinary change in direction by the Government, news of fencing the bridge was widely welcomed and must have been a massive sigh of relief for all those who actively campaigned. The anti-suicide barrier was certainly good news for Sgt Charles Bebb and his dedicated team of Water Police. Following the relentless run of tragedies over the previous months and showing signs of what could only be described as suicide fatigue, Bebb and his team knew it was still too early to celebrate. Barriers still had to be erected, and until completed, there was little doubt that more suicides and attempts would continue. They didn't have to wait long. It was as if the sudden news of fencing Sydney's most fashionable suicide location created further panic among those contemplating their end. The following day after the unexpected announcement from the government, two men jumped to their death, and numerous distress calls were made notifying the police of several more people planning to jump.

A 17-year-old girl described as pretty and from a well-to-do family was found early in the morning huddled against the footway fence, weeping inconsolably. The bridge patrolman, fearing that she intended to harm herself, contacted her parents, who came immediately to take care of her. Bridge patrolmen were also on the lookout for two women. They received early reports that both women had left their homes and threatened to throw themselves over. Police and patrolmen were given descriptions of the women in the hope of spotting them. One woman was from Bondi, and the other was a South Coast woman whose husband had discovered a note telling him that she had left for Sydney to jump over the Bridge; alarmingly, she was accompanied by their 3-year-old son.

On the same morning of November 23rd, Edward Blakeney, a bridge painter, was working on girders on the western side of the bridge near the southern pylon when he witnessed a man falling into the water. Blakeney ran to the bridge office located in the pylon and communicated with the Water Police about what had taken place. The police launch, piloted by none other than Sgt Bebb, and accompanied by Constable Benson, made its way towards the spot where they believed the man had entered the water. They found a hat floating on the surface and eventually discovered his body floating about 300 yards from where he had struck the water. When his body was recovered from the water, the police found his clothes had been almost torn from his body. Sgt Bebb radioed ahead, and the ambulance wagon was already waiting at the boatshed when Bebb returned. The man was then rushed to Sydney hospital, where he was pronounced 'life extinct'.

Later, the man's coat containing a few identifying items and his umbrella was picked up on the western side of the bridge. The police confirmed that the items belonged to 42-year-old William Edward Walker, a married man from Bankstown who was employed as a tailor and working for a clothing manufacturer in Chippendale. At the inquest, five days later, William Walker's 19-year-old son Leslie gave evidence and stated that on the morning his father died, he said he was going to get an X-ray on his jaw at Sydney Hospital as he was struck by an intruder at their home. Leslie gave details that there was a quarrel with the intruder, and his father was knocked unconscious and unable to eat anything. His son also mentioned that his father had concerns that his employment as a tailor may be over by Christmas as his workplace was possibly shutting down.

The inquest revealed a strange set of circumstances leading up to William taking his life, but several issues clearly clouded his mind, and sadly like so many suicides, William's motive to end his life so abruptly remained unanswered.

The second victim that followed William Walker on that day was 26-year-old Abel seaman Richard Oliver Hickey, a native of South

Australia. Richard was a sailor on the H.M.A.S *'Penguin'* and had been married to his wife Rose for six years. Shortly after 4.30 in the afternoon, Richard, dressed in his naval uniform, made his way to the centre of the bridge. Mr Phillip Darragh, of Granville, witnessed from a distance as Richard climbed to the top handrail and began to scramble as if he had a sudden change of mind. Other onlookers also claimed they could see Richard clambering on the top rail before falling to his death. The search for his body by the Water Police continued throughout the long hours of the night, and only in the morning did his body rise to the surface, almost in the exact spot where Richard struck the water.

At the coronial inquest that followed, Richard's friend, Able seaman Walter Nolan Smith from H.M.A.S *'Australia'* had spoken with Richard only a few days before he jumped. Richard was on leave for two days and mentioned to Smith that he was suffering from pains in the head, and doctors told him if he wasn't careful, '**he was likely to go out of his mind**'. Smith's details of Richard Hickey's pain indicated that his complaint may have been severe, and it corresponded with information that Richard had received treatment at Brisbane Hospital and Randwick Military Hospital. Perhaps Richard suffered quietly and never revealed to anyone the seriousness of his condition, not even his young wife, Rose. The Coroner concluded it was suicide with no mention of his mental capacity at the time.

Within twenty-four hours after the fencing announcement from Mr Stevens, it appeared that the unexpected news may have hastened the death of both William Walker and Richard Hickey. Fortunately, there were no further reports of the two women who set out to make the same perilous bridge journey, but Mr Stevens, perhaps in a state of utter panic, thought it best to make a further announcement stating the Government was aware of the seriousness of the situation and had instructed the Department of Main Roads '**to speed up as much as possible the work of erecting the safety barrier.**' Mr Stevens also confidently pointed out that plans had been drawn up, tenders for materials were underway, and he described the exact form of the new barrier.

'It will be a barbed wire fence superimposed on the present handrail. The top of the fence will be 8 feet, 9 inches above the level of the deck and will be curved inwards for about two feet. There will be three rows of barbed wire, and the space between the wire and the top of the present rail will be filled in with a strong wire mesh. It is claimed that it will be practically impossible for anyone to climb this barrier. The new fence will extend the full length of both main and approach spans on the outer rail on each side of the Bridge.'

The proposed fencing was substantial and similar to many options that had been suggested earlier, and of course, it was considerably more sophisticated than the concept mockingly put forward by the *Perth Mirror* the previous year. It did, however, include rows of barbed wire which the *Mirror* suggested was a simple and inexpensive addition. More surprisingly, the *Perth Mirror* made no further comment or even a cynical told-you-so.

After matching the record of six bridge suicides in a single month and the long-awaited decision to make the bridge suicide-proof, November 1933 would become a defining moment for the SHB, one that would change its path forever. However, the year wasn't quite finished for the SHB, when on a Saturday morning, December 17th, a North Sydney woman looked out of her bedroom window and was shocked to see a body hurtling from the bridge towards the water. She was not the only witness who watched in horror as 23-year-old Sarah Evelyn Semlitzky climbed the railing, then resting her knee on top, pulled herself over and went hurtling to the water. Pedestrians on the bridge panicked, rushed to the fence and watched as Sarah hit the water feet first. As she rose to the surface, to everyone's disbelief, she was still alive and started to make a feeble attempt to swim. A passing motor launch had also seen the fall and raced to rescue her from the water. She was immediately taken to the water police sheds, and without delay, Sgt Bebb treated her for shock and applied hot blankets. **'Let me go! Let me go!'** she moaned. Bebb continued to comfort Sarah while waiting for the arrival of the Central Ambulance, which then rushed her to Sydney Hospital. Sarah remained conscious most of the time but did not reveal to anyone why she made the leap. Unfortunately, Sarah died within half an hour of being admitted to the hospital.

Sarah Semlitzky was 16 years old when she married her husband, 24-year-old Harold Semlitzky. Together they had a daughter Rita, but it wasn't long after the marriage proved unsuccessful, and they were soon living apart. Some years later, in July 1931, Harold's body was discovered upriver from the harbour near Abbotsford wharf. He had drowned, and coincidentally, Sgt Bebb recovered his body from the water, but how Harold drowned was never determined. A good two and half years after her husband's death, Sarah had moved on and was looking forward to getting on with her life. In fact, Sarah had made plans to be married again and had every reason to be happy, with family and close friends describing her life as 'on the up'

Everyone remained confused as to why Sarah had taken her life when things seemed to be going so well. There was no evidence to suggest a motive for her suicide at the coronial inquiry, and the police presented one possibility. They were inclined to believe that Sarah may have received a knock to the head when she fell from a tram the night before when she went out with her fiancé. Even after she was treated at Sydney Hospital for slight injuries, the police thought she may have had an undetected brain injury that caused her to leave home the following morning, make her way to the bridge, and jump. It was all they had in the form of a possible explanation.

Coroner Farrington held his last bridge inquest for the year and determined that Sarah died from 'Shock and injuries after wilfully casting herself from the Sydney Harbour Bridge'. The final week of inquests that followed was another graphic summary of suicide and tragedy, with the court sessions recording one throat cutting, three poisonings, two hangings and one gunshot, all of which were self-inflicted, as well as a woman struck by a train and three drownings.

As 1933 came to a close, it was also time for the remarkable Sgt Charles Percy Bebb to move on. His distinguished and outstanding service in the Water Police had come to an end. He had seen enough tragedy on the harbour, and the last few months had undoubtedly been some of his long career's most disturbing and taxing times. He had witnessed many tragic and pointless deaths, and perhaps the deaths of the brilliant Branford Angell and the young single mother Sarah Semlitzky were the final emotional stumble. As reported earlier by the *Labor Daily* newspaper, this was perhaps a sign for Charles that he had seen enough. It is uncertain if he requested a transfer, but in the new year, he started a new position at Redfern Police station with an impending appointment as Inspector of Police.

There was at least some good news in the final weeks, when work on the anti-suicide fencing commenced on the 20th of December and with an estimated completion date of February 1934, it was now a race against time.

Fig 8. Proposed Bridge fencing with three strands of barbed wire

Fig 9. 'Colonel' Michael F Bruxner - Courtesy Aust. War Memorial H19224

Fig 10. Headstone of William James Lewis - Rookwood Cemetery NSW

20

THE WILD RUSH

'Suicide season was once more in full swing in Sydney'.

During the depression in Paris, a 75-year-old woman read in the *Le Petit Journal,* a popular daily newspaper, that the French authorities were contemplating closing the local cemeteries for good, and thereafter the dead would be interred 20 miles north of Paris in the tiny township of Merv-Sur-Oise. In complete panic and despair, fearing she may not be buried in her beloved Paris, the woman took her own life that same day. The unfortunate woman left a note saying she had made up her mind to be buried in Paris and hoped she would not be too late. The fear of missing out by the elderly woman led to an extreme act; however, the unfortunate event in Paris bares a similarity to events that were to follow in Sydney when the fencing of the Sydney Bridge was finally announced.

For anyone contemplating jumping from the bridge, the news of suicide-proofing raised the possibility that they may miss their opportunity. Just like the poor old lady in Paris, the fear of missing out was a trigger that could prompt a suicide attempt sooner rather than later. The police and the bridge authorities prepared themselves for the possibility of a 'wild rush' to suicide. Sgt Bill Hamill, now Senior

Sergeant in charge of the Water Police, prepared himself and his team for a more than ordinary month ahead. As always, they were on the alert, and the special police patrol on the bridge increased its numbers in anticipation of more suicide attempts.

With such a high suicide count in November, a gambling man would have felt confident that December would be a record month of suicides. But to the authorities' surprise, it appeared the sudden presence of fencing workers spread across the bridge and the extra bridge patrols had been a deterrent, making any attempt to jump a lot more complicated. Unfortunately, it was just the calm before the storm, a short-lived pause before it all changed on the last day of December, when around sunrise, two local fishermen, Thomas Mallon and Cecil Little, witnessed a naked man fall from the bridge and plunge feet first into the water.

The naked man was 43-year-old unemployed labourer and war veteran Charles Gallagher. Charles made his way to the centre of the bridge early that morning, stripped off all his clothing, placed it neatly on the footpath, climbed to the top railing, paused for a second and then flung himself into the water below. Charles Gallagher was described as 'a tough nut to crack'. Not only did he survive his fall from the bridge, but he also managed to swim around in the harbour for up to twenty minutes before being picked up by the water police; only then did he suddenly lose consciousness. He was hauled on board the police launch and then rushed by ambulance to Sydney Hospital. Still unconscious on arrival, he later awakened and started singing, then asked if it was true, did he jumped off the Bridge and if he could have something to eat.

News that a war veteran had survived the great fall from the bridge travelled fast. The following day, a welfare officer from the RSL (Returned Soldiers League) and the AIF Pioneer Battalion Association secretary visited Charles. Both representatives offered him support and a few little luxuries, such as tobacco and offered help to find Charles work when he left the hospital. On the same day, Charles was interviewed by Sgt Slaney and the newspapers, and it was clear that Charles had quite a personality and a fascinating story to tell.

Charles explained he travelled to Sydney from the bush only about six weeks ago and was penniless the day he arrived. He made an application for the dole but was told he needed to prove his identity and be established in a permanent address for at least three months. Undaunted by the rules of the dole, Charles fell back on the one talent he possessed. According to Charles, he was considered a good singer, so he reinvented himself as the 'singing soldier' and toured the streets of Sydney's suburbs in the hope of an appreciative audience who would pass on a few pence for his effort. Charles explained to the newspapers, **'I took this on because I have always been fond of music, had a good voice and have been praised by a good many music teachers. But things weren't going too good, and when my 'nobber' the chap that takes round the box left me suddenly, I began to worry about making ends meet. I had to sing forty to fifty songs a day, which is a big strain, but when I had to do my own house-to-house collecting as well, I could hardly manage to make enough coppers for a pie. On good days the 'nobber' and me have been known to make five bob, but it was hard work.'**

Charles attributed his survival to his experience with high diving; whether we believe him or not, it is still an astonishing story that defies the odds. Four days after his astonishing tale of survival, except for a ruptured ear drum and suffering some bruising, Charles Gallagher was released from the hospital. Three weeks later, he had to appear in court charged with attempted suicide. At his court hearing, Charles was defended by a representative of the RSL, and he pleaded guilty. Charles explained to the magistrate that on the night before he jumped, he had no money and had been sleeping in Sydney's Domain Park **'when something told him to go to the Bridge and jump over'**, and he could not recall anything after that. Charles was bound over for 12 months 'to be of good behaviour'.

Fig 11. Bridge Survivor Charles Gallagher the 'singing soldier'

While Charles Gallagher lived to tell the story of what he called '**the horrors of the Harbour Bridge rail.**' a very different story awaited a determined 33-year-old unemployed labourer who decided his fate with the simple flip of a coin. Frederick Charles Bootman was 23 years old when he migrated to Australia from England in 1923. Looking for a new start in life, he was attracted to the old goldfields, where he spent his early years working as a labourer in Bendigo, Victoria. As the depression took hold, he travelled more extensively seeking work and settling in another mining town in Broken Hill, New South Wales and eventually worked at Major's Creek, another well-known but expired gold town.

Frederick remained a loner; he never married and had few acquaintances, and by late 1933, unemployed and his money running out, he was desperate for work and moved to Sydney. Still out of work and with no friends or family to call on, Frederick soon found himself homeless and became a resident at a hostel in Pitt Street Sydney run by the Salvation Army known as the 'People's Palace'.

The People's Palace was opened in 1899 and was sometimes home to as many as five hundred people at a time. The Palace offered affordable shelter for the 'poorest of the fallen'. The accommodation was available for men, women, and homeless boys, a swag room was provided for weary travellers and a 'drunk ward' was made available where instead of being taken to a police cell, unfortunate men and women were given a decent bed for the night. For three months, Frederick continued living at the People's Palace and maintained his desperate search for work, but with his money about to run out, he spent what little he had left on lottery tickets in nail-biting hope that his luck may change.

On New Year's night, 1934, North Sydney residents Miss Amy Watson and Miss Josie Leonarder were taking their regular evening stroll along the eastern footway of the bridge towards the city and taking in the glorious night views that many locals enjoyed. They were making light conversation when Josie remarked, **'I have been across so often, but I have never seen anyone jump over.'** Amy replied jokingly, **'Just wait till we get to the middle, and I'll oblige'**... **'Perhaps this man will do so instead'**, Amy added, indicating a man standing with one foot on the latticework, and as Amy spoke, Frederick Bootman pulled himself to the top rail and leapt over.

Both ladies were stunned and stood silent as if frozen to the spot, unable to move or call out. Soon they heard a splash in the water below, and the ladies managed to move towards the fence. They slowly gazed over the railing and noticed the ripples and the widening of circles in the water where Frederick Bootman landed. The ladies then ran to the toll station and informed the duty constable of the extraordinary event that had just taken place. The water police were immediately informed, and the night search for Frederick's body proved unsuccessful.

Early the following morning, Sgt Foott searched the waters beneath the bridge, but his effort to find the body of Frederick Bootman proved unsuccessful. Foott then made his way up the harbour to Blackwattle

Bay at Rozelle, where the body of a stillborn baby floating in the water had been discovered. After a lengthy day of investigations and the distressing recovery of the stillborn baby from the water, Sgt Foott proceeded to make his way back to the police sheds at Dawes Point. As he made his approach under the bridge in the police launch, Foott continually scanned the waters looking for any sign of the body of Frederick Bootman.

Suddenly a body plummeted from above and landed in the water only a few feet from his launch. The force of the body hitting the water was explosive, and the wake created by the force unsettled the launch. Sgt Foott, already shaken from the morning's events, was now desperately circling back, looking for the victim who nearly landed on his launch.

The victim was Donald Stewart Sullivan, a 46-year-old accountant who had hurled himself from the western footway above. Within minutes Foott hauled Donald Sullivan's battered body from the water. Donald's face was badly smashed, but he was still breathing. Sgt Foott then rushed to the police boatshed, where Sullivan was transferred by ambulance to Sydney Hospital. Donald died three hours later from his injuries. The reason for Donald taking his life was a complete mystery to his family and the authorities. By all accounts, he was faring well and seemingly settled after finding gainful employment with motor car dealer Boyd Edkins Ltd for over a year. He had even earnt a rare pay increase of 1 pound per week just three weeks before his death. It was said Donald was quietly enjoying domestic life with his wife Elsie and their five sons, one of which was just one month old.

At the Coroner's inquiry, his younger brother Cyril suggested it could have been a 'brain snap'. Cyril mentioned to the Coroner that Donald had previously been unemployed for three years, and perhaps he was greatly concerned by the pressure of having to earn his increase and maintain his job. Was it as simple as Cyril suggested, was Donald overwhelmed by the anxiety of the past and the uncertainty of the future? With little else to go on, the Coroner recorded a verdict of suicide, stating that Donald died in Sydney Hospital from shock and concussion willfully caused by casting himself from the Sydney Harbour Bridge.

It had been just two days into the new year, and the signs of what had earlier been described as the wild rush to beat the 'foolproof' fencing quickly became all too true. A nervousness surrounding the sudden frequency of suicides placed pressure on the authorities to keep the public informed on the progress of the fencing. The transport minister Mr Bruxner assured the public that work on the fencing preparations had been accelerated. He explained that work had continued through the holidays and given the recent suicides' workmen were working as quickly as possible to complete the rigging so that the fencing panels could be installed. He also announced that the first sections on the eastern side of the bridge between the arches would be completed within two to three weeks, and there were no delays with materials.

Bridge chaos ensued, and the following day after the fencing update from Mr Bruxner, retired mariner Captain T. Jones was standing on the verandah of the Imperial Hotel at Milson's Point, which stood close to the water's edge in clear view of the Bridge. By chance, he was looking at the bridge through a pair of binoculars when suddenly he saw a man somersaulting through the air and plummet headlong into the water. Mariner Jones then alerted his friend Frank Graham a well-known amateur wrestler who was also at the Hotel. Together they could see the man's body floating under the middle of the bridge. Frank Graham noticed that nearby boats were utterly oblivious to the man in the water, and they simply passed him by.

Thinking that the man may have survived the terrible plunge, Frank Graham took off his coat and boots, launched himself into the water, and started swimming towards the victim. In the back of his mind, he knew **'that several of those that had gone over had been rescued alive'**. Soon a crowd gathered on the shore and watched the heroic attempt by Graham. He wasn't far from the victim when suddenly suffering from cramps and gripped with pain, he started signalling for help. A boy in a tin canoe was nearby and immediately paddled out to Graham, who was able to clutch onto the stern of the canoe while the boy paddled him safely back to shore. Frank Graham's attempt failed, but he thought it was his duty to help and said he **'had to give it a go'**.

As the dramatic rescue attempt by Graham unfolded, the Water Police had been alerted and made their way to where the body of Sidney Cecil Stephenson was floating. His head and body had sustained terrible injuries, and it appeared he was killed instantly. Sidney Stephenson was the 47th suicide victim, a 43-year-old bootmaker from Artarmon. Little was known as to why Sidney committed suicide, but the brief details at his inquest explained that his circumstances were like so many other suicide victims; he lived a lonely life and suffered from depression. At the inquest, his brother Charles testified that Sidney had been separated from his wife for thirteen years, and he lived a solitary life but was 'addicted to liquor'. Charles said that he had only seen his brother on a few occasions in fourteen years.

The day after Sidney Stephenson's body was recovered from the water, the new rigging for the fencing of the bridge was completed, and the workmen started erecting the protective fencing panels. That same day the *Newcastle Sun* newspaper reported that there had now been eight suicides in six weeks since the Government had announced the construction of the protective fencing. Since the fencing would take another eight weeks to complete, the newspaper predicted that at the current rate, Sydney could expect another ten or eleven victims before the fence was completed.

On the 7th of January, Robert Perry, a resident at McMahons Point, spotted Frederick Bootman's body floating in Berrys Bay. He telephoned the Water Police, and Sgt Hamill and Constable Richardson retrieved the body and took it to the city morgue. After a formal identification, the police later searched Frederick's room at the 'Peoples Palace' and discovered a loaded rifle lying on his bed. Among his belongings, they also found a bundle of lottery tickets drawn only a few days before his death.

On further investigations, it was revealed that Frederick had mentioned to an acquaintance at the Palace that if his luck didn't change soon, then the **'spin of a coin'** would determine his fate. Frederick mentioned he would carry out **'something desperate'**. He said, ' **If it comes down heads, I'll do what I have made up my mind to do one way.... if it comes down tails .... I'll do it the other way.'** The investigation was complete. Frederick had decided his fate when the final few shillings he spent on lottery tickets failed to draw a prize, a simple 'spin of a coin', heads or tails, determined either shooting himself or jumping from the bridge.

In the coming days, the number of suicide attempts ramped up, and the *South Coast Times* summed it up, claiming that the **'suicide season was once more in full swing in Sydney'**.

21

A LIFE WELL LIVED

'Am going to do the high dive tonight' – Jeremiah Sullivan

There have always been mixed views on suicide; the most discernible being is the act of suicide, one of courage or the act of a coward. Many people also express the idea that suicide is unjustified because it leaves a stigma of insanity, which the relatives must bear, and Doctors are justified in giving incurable sufferers unlimited medication to ease their pains and help them avoid the idea of suicide.

Mr A B Kempster of Sydney, who, for reasons unknown, gave himself the title of **'Australia's Outcast Poet-Orator'**. He believed that only a coward would commit suicide and his poem titled 'The Sydney Harbour Bridge - The Bridge of Sighs' was curiously published in the *Tasmanian Voice*. His poem read…

A speedy exit to the gates of paradise.
But why not stay,
And fight for justice here?
Instead of leaving it to those who do not fear.
Cowards are not wanted in after life,
If they have quitted

When the world is full of strife.
The Bridge denotes man's skill to arch a gap,
So why should any, amidst plenty, suffer lack?

An alternative view of the 'Outcast Poet' was expressed by a British Coroner at the inquest into the suicide of a man with cancer. The Coroner was outspoken and he made the assertion that.....'**This poor man suffered the tortures of hell. He knew he was under sentence of death. Why should he not have the right to say he would suffer no more? I think he did perfectly right**'.

Sir John Bland-Sutton, an eminent London surgeon, agreed with the Coroner's comments, stating..... '**He respects a man who, doomed to a painful, lingering death, has the courage to end his life. Why should he be expected to continue living in agony? Juries and coroners try to spare families, cloaking that brave act in the guise of Insanity. Surely it would be better to honour the man's courage. The danger is that many who think they have cancer will commit suicide through sheer fright.**'

The Dean of Canterbury countered the view of both the Coroner and the surgeon and said....'**he would hesitate harshly to judge a suicide who knew that his continued existence would cause untold agony to his friends as well as to himself. Yet, if it needs courage to take one's life, even greater courage is required to bear pain until the end, as many splendid men and women racked with agony do. So, I should be loath to see an increased acceptance of the easy way out. Our character would suffer.**'

69-year-old Jeremiah Michael Sullivan was a native of North Ireland and an Imperial war veteran who spent many years travelling the world but finally settled in Australia, where he felt most at home. Far from insane or suffering any mental distress, he was suddenly diagnosed with tuberculosis. Under the sentence of a 'lingering death', he favoured the view of not waiting around for death to creep up on him. Having lived a full and adventurous life on his terms, Jeremiah decided to end his life on his terms.

Confident in his decision, he made no attempt to hide the fact that he was not a well man or that some may consider him a coward; he sampled everything life had to offer and thought it a life well lived.

Jeremiah made the decision to go out in style, and the Sydney Harbour Bridge was the best place to do so.

On January 11, around 5 pm, Jeremiah crossed paths with Miss Mary Coasby, a local resident of Leichhardt, with whom he had boarded for several months. They struck up a conversation, and she noticed that he was unusually well-dressed and asked him where he was going. Jeremiah said.... '**I am going on a long expedition. You will read all about it in tomorrow evening's paper. A man might just as well go and meet his maker six months before or wait six months for him to take him.**'

'**Keep this for a souvenir to remember me by**, Jeremiah added and handed her a threepence coin. Mary recalled how they 'had a little conversation about the ordinary things for a while', and then a tram came along. Jeremiah patted her on the shoulder, shook her by the hands, raised his hat and said 'Goodbye', and got on the tram. Mary, greatly concerned, then rang the local police and told them of her peculiar encounter with Jeremiah.

It wasn't long after his chance meeting with his old landlady Mary Coasby when Jeremiah arrived at his final destination. Making his way along the bridge footway from the city end, he was well aware of the extra patrolmen on duty, and as he approached the centre of the bridge, he encountered Constable Arthur Costello. They spoke briefly, and Jeremiah gave the patrolmen his name as O'Sullivan of Five Dock. As the police had been notified of a gentleman contemplating suicide, they were on the lookout for a man going by the name of Sullivan, not O'Sullivan and Constable Costello allowed Jeremiah to pass.

The following morning George Ford, a launch driver, discovered Jeremiah's body floating just 200 yards off Dawes Point. Sgt Hamill was soon advised and recovered the body from the water. The police then retraced the initial lead from the day before and contacted Mary Coasby who visited the City Morgue, and sadly she identified the body of the man she knew as Jerry.

The same morning the Editor of the *Sun* newspaper Mr Delamore McCay received some astonishing letters, and written on a telegram form accompanying them was the following,

'4.30 p.m - Am going to do the high dive tonight. Be faithful to my requests' signed - J. M Sullivan.

Jeremiah Sullivan wasn't the kind of man to let someone else tell his story, so he wrote his own and posted it to the Editor of the *Sun* newspaper only hours before he jumped from the Sydney Harbour Bridge, hopeful the newspaper would be faithful to his request and publish his short autobiography. Described by the *Sun* as 'Sensational letters', the newspaper's Editor was faithful to Jeremiah's request and printed his story the same day it was received. It was published as it was written, including any errors, despite Jeremiah mentioning that a proofreader would swear over his spelling.

Jeremiah Sullivan was a no-nonsense man, a raconteur who delivered a fascinating and insightful story with frankness and wit. He travelled the world and had an adventurous life, rich in experiences, where he made and lost small fortunes; he was tempted by the gold rush in Coolgardie, Western Australia, and then set off to the U.S.A. He was in the Spanish civil war, a vegetable grower, and helped construct the Yuma Dam and then later joined the British navy.

Jeremiah had a pioneering spirit, a man who was willing to try anything, anywhere and at any time. He declared a bachelor's taste for freedom but missed the **'magic touch of the baby's fingers'**, and as his grey hair started to show his years, it never slowed his lust for life or his ambitions. He was a philosophical man, influenced by the great philosophers and understood that suicide might seem by those under the influence of the church a cowardly act, but he remained true to his own beliefs.

When he thought his story seemed tedious or perhaps fanciful, Jeremiah took a moment in his letter to assure the reader, '**perhaps it is getting wearisome to the readers, but it is true, as I do not wish to go to the other shore with a lie as the last act performed.**'

The following are Jeremiah's letters, republished again for a contemporary audience to appreciate….

'**It is not my desire to start a controversy, after my departure; as I will be unable to participate in it or refute any accusations of cowardice, on my part for the course I have pursued.**'

'**I maintain that an old person suffering from an incurable complaint (advanced T.B. of the throat) that has no dependents, and has not sufficient means to ensure proper comforts, is a coward, if he becomes a public charge; or a parasite on his well-meaning friends, admitting that it is contrary to the laws of nearly all civilised countries, and all Christian creeds.**'

'**I contend that there are cases where (though not according to Christian dogma) an individual with the health, and welfare of his fellow beings considered, shows a proper spirit, by removing any possibility of contamination from him. Not alone has this cathosprey come on me, but also my lack of memory of present or recent events, I am recently unable to remember almost any future engagements, new names, or places, unless noted down.**'

'**This is what has been in vogue for the past six weeks or so. I have to pause, as I write this, to think how to spell the simplest of words, and I am sure the proofreader will swear at the many overlooked. Well, that is another reason I have for retiring so unceremoniously, as I have no desire to greet my friends, through a barred enclosure, at the Park.**'

"I can still smile, however, and am not afraid to tell a joke on myself. Now, then, what good is this old hulk of mine? Would be 70, if I lived until September 29 next, the kindly doctors give me a few months more with proper care. Perhaps I am 100 years ahead of times, as probably then I could have a couple or more glands tied in place, and my lost voice restored; two full sets of molars installed; throat swabbed out and left in O.K. order; a natural ear drum to replace the unresponsive one; a few patches on bellows; and the calendar pushed back 45 years— and all before dinner.'

'For over a month I have not had five hours of natural slumber, the rest all artificial. It is not my desire to discredit any concern at this stage of the game; but certain powders were in my case non-effective; but the empties gave a good kick off to the copper. Some of the sleep producing mixtures I had prescribed for me costing from 3s 6d to 7s 6d would give a semblance of one, but the after effects were a craving for more. Then I tried another, more pleasant, but a trifle more expensive, a visit to the pub. There I met jovial friends (with whom I am now loath to part) who were drinking the same medicine, but not for the same reason. However, like the other hop, — it called for a comeback. Yes, want of restful sleep will affect the brain and lower mentally when prolonged.'

'Fate has been both kind and unkind to me. Almost on my fourth birthday, my mother died. It Is the first event I can remember in life. A sad one, I could paint an exact picture of the scene now. As a cousin brought me to the death chamber, I ran and kissed her and said, mamma was cold and asked to have her covered. Right here is where I fall out with many, perhaps, when I say I had the best mother the world ever produced. True sons and daughters will claim that theirs was, so we will call it a dead heat.

'Next, my loved father died, when I was 18, I left the engineering college and took his place in a large distiller's distribution department, maintaining house for my only sister. At 20 I was engaged to my schooldays' sweetheart; and had furnished the neatest little dovecote imaginable, when she became ill with diphtheria, and she also died! She had all my love, and it was buried in her grave, none left to share with another.'

'I became a wanderer, seeking forgetfulness, roamed the world, made the first trip to Australia, back to America, finally settled awhile in Arizona, rode the range with the roughest, and most kindly of bronco busters. Old Mexico next, tried railroading, my unfinished engineering knowledge came in handy, worked up, had charge of arch construction work on three different lines.'

'Still the reckless devil-may-care bachelor —no tomorrow. The happy bachelor may be all right, but when you get old you are lonely; you have missed a lot, the magic touch of the baby's fingers, the warm kiss from the velvety lips, and the proud thrill of the cooing voice of the first 'papa' — oh well! I was going to substitute another letter for that 'w' and make it more forcible.'

'Well, about that time Coolgardie got on the map. Wanderlust again. Knocked around over two years, finally disposed of a quarter interest in a claim near Kanona. Off again. Spanish-American war broke out. Have a go with Colonel Roosevelt's Rough Riders.' By the way, the Colonel (Teddy) was the uncle, not the father of the ruling President there, and I wish to remark that though he is crippled in the feet, the head certainly escaped —would like to be round to find out how his desperate experiments end.'

'Well, the short war over, had a go at N.W. Mounted, a noble band of cobbers, yet with all that varied career, in lone moments the beautiful face of my schooldays' sweetheart recurred to me. Tried celery and lettuce growing in New York State, worked 16 hours daily, then a trip to Florida every winter, buying for two large commission houses. Got tired, back to Arizona, became State cement inspector, in conjunction with a cement business of my own.'

'Would rather not tell what I did in a few Mexican revolutions, it is not over-credible; It Is all right for the rough element. Saw the site of Hollywood when there was not any— helped construct the Yuma Dam that made the Imperial Valley richer than that of the Nile, but not so extensive. Buy a half interest in a big cattle outfit on Gila River, Arizona, and built up a great herd, my partner was over-handy with branding irons, yet always got by. Sold out for 80,000 dollars, big fiesta at Phoenix. Went back to cement business again.'

'Am almost exactly 50 (born September 29, 64). I was then 40 per cent, as grey as I am now. I visited the U.S.A. recruiting station at Phoenix and saw an old chum from Rough Riders who had charge, Captain W. A. Jones. Told him I wanted the once over, a thorough one, as though I was a youngster applying for enlistment. Well, I got it, and it was a hot one. Did everything but stand on my head, found a small puncture in the drum of my left ear, and tested it with a stopwatch; verdict A1— wanted me to dye locks and hop into his mob. 'No, Cap, too tame,' I said. 'The Greasers won't fight. Captain, I can take 50 of my cowboy pals and capture their biggest border town, no-gales, sever their railway from the south, and hold it also.'

Perhaps this is getting wearisome to the readers, but it is true, as I do not wish to go to the other Shore with a lie as the last act performed. However, at the hotel where I lived I did some wonderful propaganda work, telling the young doctors (and there were many of them) how wonderful it would be for them to go over and come back in a few years, and hang out a sign with a Lion and Unicorn, and beneath an emblazoned sign 'Doctor to the King'. Well, I was challenged by a French-Canadian named Greer and he asked why I didn't go, I thought a moment and said, 'I will start tomorrow at 6 a.m. Take the train for Washington, D.C, remain there for a ten days' rest, then sally forth and join the Canadian Army, or the British Army, and by God, if they won't take me, the French Foreign Legion will. I must get a few hours' rest. It is now 12.30 a.m., my last day on terra firma.'

4.30 a.m. — Well, I had a rest. I thought of all the great bridges I had ever seen. I must insert something that is a matter I have never seen published here. I predicted when they were building 'Our Harbour Bridge' that the Gap would go out of fashion, and I told some true stories about the Brooklyn Bridge, a cable suspension one, not a great deal shorter or lower than ours. If I am not mistaken, I am almost certain the first man to drop over was Robert Emmet Odlum, for scientific purposes, inventing a net for rescuing people from high buildings. He claimed that by dropping down feet first the distance made little difference, provided the net could stand the strain. However, he toppled over when near the river, and struck sideways on the non-compressible water and died.'

'There was at that time a newsboy named Steve Brody, who conceived a great idea. He advertised the fact that he could do the trick — the police guards were doubled, but on schedule, a figure dropped downward. A boat that was waiting below reached over and hauled in Steve. The joke was not made public for years. Well, Steve received 5000 dollars for his first week's presence in a dime museum, and how the people flocked to see the hero! This salary came gradually down. However, at the end of six months, he had sufficient money to start the flashest drinking saloon on the old New York celebrated Bowery, and the people rushed to see him and shake his hands, hero-worshippers.

'When his oarsmen that were in the boat with him and he fell out, about a division of the loot, some years later. It was shown that Steve was hanging to the boat before the weighted dummy was hurled over by a confederate from above, but at all events, they had made their pile! The saddest case of all, a drunken longshoreman going home one night, named Paddy Dougherty, said 'That jump is nothing', made it and after a while swam to the Brooklyn side of the shore, and next morning got six months. The laws had tightened up.'

'Now, before I finish up where I left off at 12.30 a.m, I wish to state this anti-suicide fence you folks are putting up around the bridge is a great mistake. You advertise to the world that you are so weak-minded that means must be taken to prevent you from self-destruction. Tear it down, or at least leave a few unguarded openings in it, anyway. I followed out my program, sailed from Guy Street Barracks, Montreal, in the British Royal Engineers of Aldershot and was invalided back in September

1918, on Casmanla, and by special favour given first-class passage to Arizona. Came out here at end of 1918.'

'I loved Australia and have made thousands of good friends here, and no doubt a few enemies. When the man that has not found someone to dislike him is a regular mollycoddle. I hope my friends will all forgive me, and not bother about a funeral. Any Institute may have my body, or any student that wants a skeleton to study anatomy, may have this 5ft. 10 inches one by just skinning it, that is about all that is on it now.'

'I die with one consolation, that at least 50 per cent, of all the money I have ever made I have given away, and I freely forgive those who have defrauded me of many hundreds. I can fearlessly meet the Supreme being, place my cards on the table face up, and the worst I can get is a draw.'

With his health failing him and diagnosed with only several months left to live, Jeremiah was satisfied with his journey through life. He tells a story of a rich and adventurous life many would consider fortunate, colourful and inspiring. He had no regrets and maintained a sense of humour even in the face of death.

Jeremiah also wrote letters to several friends, and although he asked that his body be given to the University, the Returned Soldiers League secured an order for burial from Coroner Farrington, the cost of which was borne by the Returned Soldiers League. It was true that Jeremiah had made many friends and acquaintances, the large attendance at his funeral at Rookwood Cemetery was testimony to his popularity. His coffin was draped with the Union Jack and a fund had been opened with the aim of erecting a headstone over his grave.

When Jeremiah declared in his letters to the *Sun* that '**I hope my friends will all forgive me, and not bother about a funeral**', he was hoping that his close friends would understand and quickly move forward and there should be no suffering from his passing. Tragically however this was not the case. 53-year-old war veteran John McGrath was part of the large crowd that attended the funeral, and the loss of his best mate affected him greatly. Jeremiah and John had been bosom buddies for many years and when John learned of his best friend's fate, he became a wrecked man. John was one among the long-term unemployed and had been feeling despondent for some time and with the added loss of his best friend, he was unable to manage his grief.

A week after Jeremiah jumped from the bridge, John McGrath's body was discovered floating in Hen and Chicken Bay, west of the harbour. Following the police investigations, the Coroner confirmed John had committed suicide.

A few months after the Jeremiah Sullivan case, his story became the focus of a Coronial inquest in London where the chief medical witness disputed the verdict of **'suicide while temporarily insane'** claiming the verdict was meaningless and referenced the case of Jeremiah's suicide from the Sydney Harbour Bridge.

The medical witness, Dr Scott Reid made the claim that **'Only sane people commit suicide. Other psychologists may have a different say-so in the discussion. Suicide is an act of flight; but whether it is an irresponsible flight from reality, which is mentally unsound, or whether a deliberate flight from hostile forces too heavy to be combated - that is another question'.**

'What are you to say of that old soldier of fortune, who wrote his long autobiography to the 'Sun' before he went over the Bridge a few weeks ago? He was dying by inches and lacked money to alleviate or to cure his trouble. He found a posthumous cure. Consciously or sub-consciously he knew that newspaper readers would say to themselves, 'That old fellow could have been helped and saved. As things were, he gave up the fight. He illustrated the conclusion reached by Schopenhauer, as an observer rather than a psychologist, that the hour of suicide comes......'When the terrors of life outweigh the terrors of death.'

Fig 12. Workmen constructing the anti-suicide fencing

22

BEATING THE NET

'Oh, I am not going over, it is rather too cold for that tonight'.

As was demonstrated by the seemingly unflustered Jeremiah Sullivan, it was proving difficult for the bridge patrolman to stop a carefully planned or determined suicide. Whilst the bridge patrolmen were constantly on the lookout for suspicious behaviour, there was still no such thing as the so-called 'suicide look'. Even the most vigilant patrol officer could be fooled by someone determined to jump. Daring and fearlessness were unforeseen traits for anyone trying to identify a stranger bent on suicide. One patrolman commented that couples and girls who walked arm in arm by twos or threes and family parties were beyond suspicion, but the solitary dawdler or even the man that walks with purpose as if late for an appointment **'may only have an appointment with death'**.

Around 8 am on the morning of January 15th, 1934, 60-year-old commercial traveller John Thomas Caves, carrying his coat and a suitcase, made his way along the eastern footway. It was pedestrian peak hour, and like everyone else, he was walking with purpose and appeared to be making his way to work. John's appearance and demeanour disguised his real purpose, a deadly undertaking from which he could not be distracted. Completely void of emotion, John suddenly stopped, placed his suitcase and oil skin coat on the footpath and, without looking over his shoulder, turned and started climbing the trellis fence. Several pedestrians were close by and were astonished at how calmly John went about his preparation to jump.

Bridge patrolman Arthur Costello who was at the scene of Jeremiah Sullivan's fatal jump three days earlier, was close at hand when he heard a voice yell, '**Look Out**'. As John Caves gazed across the harbour and prepared himself to jump, patrolman Costello and a passer-by managed to seize Caves by the wrist. Both men struggled as they tried desperately to lift Caves back over the railing. Caves described as a heavily built man, then desperately wrenched himself free from the grip of patrolman Costello and launched himself towards the water below.

Two brothers, Cedric and Lewis Thus, were cruising in their launch just beneath the bridge when they saw Caves strike the water only a short distance from their launch. As the body of John Caves rose to the surface, the Thus brothers desperately recovered Cave's broken body from the water. They then made their way to the Water Police boatsheds just a short distance away, only to have confirmed that John Caves was killed instantly when he struck the water. The Police later recovered the coat and suitcase left behind by John on the footway, and inside the suitcase, they found a note which provided Police with his identity.

John Caves was married but separated from his wife Nora, who was living at Mosman. Together they had eight children, all of whom had reached adulthood. In his younger years, John was a painter by trade and a skilled musician. He joined the AIF when he was forty-two years old and was discharged at his request before embarking overseas when his wife fell ill and could not look after their large family on her own.

As the years passed, John worked as a commercial traveller, but before jumping off the bridge, John had joined the long-term unemployed. His son Eric was present at the Coroner's enquiry and confirmed that his father had lived away from the family for over two years. There was evidence of ill health and that John had no fixed address and overindulged in alcohol, a condition the Coroner felt had aggravated Cave's state of mind.

Within days after the death of John Caves, another attempt to jump was made by a young man desperate to beat the net, only this time, he was dragged back as he was preparing his climb. Restrained by the patrolmen, they were shocked to discover he was also carrying a loaded gun. Preventing bridge suicides was undoubtedly more difficult than anyone could have appreciated. The work of the bridge patrolman was dangerous, unpredictable, and disturbing, all experiences that patrolman Arthur Costello had encountered within days of having faced two suicide victims. The deception employed by the would-be suicide was superficial and crafty, a deadly game played by men and women alike.

Special Constable John Mulville was patrolling near the middle of the Bridge at about 8.30 pm on the 21st of January when he noticed a young woman standing by the fence. John Mulville was on alert and carefully watched her movements. She had a striking appearance and was extremely well dressed in a delicate green dress, a handbag and carrying a bunch of red zinnias and white daisies.

Mulville watched as she placed one foot on the steel lattice and leaned over the rail. Mulville slowly approached the young woman and caught her eye; the woman then stepped back and smiled at Mulville. She laughed and assured Mulville, **'Oh, I am not going over, it is rather too cold for that tonight.'** Mulville replied with a smile, **'No, it's too cold.'** The young women then casually walked away towards North Sydney.

John Mulville feeling comfortable that the pretty woman was genuine and just making her way home, continued his patrol in the opposite direction. A minute later, Mulville heard screams and yelling about ninety metres from the northern pylon. The commotion caused Mulville to quickly turn back to where he had met the smiling young lady. As he ran towards the panicked crowd, he saw a girl crying and people leaning over the railing, scanning the dark harbour waters for a glimpse of the young lady who had just thrown herself over the railing.

Mulville quickly noticed a handbag and a small bunch of flowers placed neatly at the foot of the fence.

Ethel Beatrice Francis, affectionately known as 'Boffles', was 25 years old, a young saleswoman who lived in Rose Bay. She had been at home all day when in the evening, she made her way to the Bridge. When Ethel encountered Constable Mulville, she was calm and composed and displayed no outward signs of emotional distress, completely disguising the fact that she had been contemplating suicide for some days. The Police quickly established her identity from the contents of her handbag and discovered a handwritten note she had prepared and dated three days earlier, which read, '**Dear Mother, please forgive me**'.

When the Police advised her mother, Emily, of the tragedy, she mentioned that Ethel had planned to marry last year, at which time she gifted her a house. Described as a young 'woman of property' and always cheerful, it was later revealed at the inquest that Ethel had never mentioned taking her life and had not shown any signs of despondence. Her father, however, suggested that she was concerned about maintaining her job. This was the only thin piece of evidence put forward to the Coroner, and no further evidence helped solve the mystery of why Ethel jumped to her death.

The following morning Patrolman Mulville had to suffer the anguish of reading the front page of the *Daily Telegraph* as it reported on the suicide of Ethel Francis with the unfortunate headline 'PATROLMAN WAS EVADED' – 'SMILE LURED WATCHER FROM SCENE'. The same morning Sgt Hamill had the unpleasant task of recovering Ethel's body from the harbour, discovered floating face down under the old Milsons Point wharf. The same wharf that James Soden had dropped himself over with a large stone tied around his neck nearly twenty years previous.

The following day another body was found floating underneath the wharf at Dawes Point, a short distance from the Water Police shed. Oscar Descamps, a 73-year-old French cook, had been reported missing from his home for three days. At first, Sgt Hamill thought it was another bridge victim, but despite finding his body near the Bridge and the heightened alert surrounding potential suicides, there were no telltale injuries or evidence that Oscar had fallen from the bridge. After further investigations, there proved to be some mystery as to the events that led to Oscar's death, and without sufficient evidence, the Coroner could not determine how he came to drown.

A few days later, the fencing on the eastern and western pedestrian harbour spans was completed, and only the fencing on the bridge approaches needed to be erected. With the bridge approaches being guarded by patrolmen and only hard asphalt below, it was considered highly unlikely that anyone would make any attempt to jump.

Dr A H Martin, a well-known Sydney psychologist and lecturer at Sydney University, claimed '**that the man who will leap to a clean death in the Harbour will hesitate long before jumping onto asphalt, such a death would be 'messy' and even the man who has decided upon his own destruction shrinks.**'

Unfortunately, Dr Martin's assessment would be quickly put to the test when a few days later, on the 25th of January, Joseph Baxter Bryson managed to slip past the patrolman on the bridge approach and become the fifty-first suicide. 16-year-old William Sibbons from North Sydney watched as Bryson tossed a coin in the air and then jumped from the northeastern pylon. The pylon alcove parapets were level with the footway approach and remained unfenced and, at the time unguarded. It was here where Joseph Bryson climbed onto the parapet and jumped. Possibly believing he may hit the water, instead, he fell with terrific force to the unforgiving ground below, landing on the balcony garden plot that surrounded the base of each pylon. One newspaper reported that when the ambulance men arrived at the scene, they discovered a broken body, but miraculously his pipe was still clenched in his left hand.

Joseph was born in Scotland and, with his family, immigrated to Australia in 1913. In July of 1915, he joined the Australian Imperial Forces, was a gunner attached to the 6th Field Artillery, and served in

France, where he was wounded. His service continued with the 5th Light Horse Brigade until he was medically discharged, and he returned to Australia in February 1919. Twenty-five years later, Joseph 'John' Bryson was 41 years old, a Kings Cross Estate agent, and a partner with Thomas and Bryson Estate Agents. After his death, the Police reported that John, as he preferred to be known, was well-known in the area, and it was mentioned that he had many female acquaintances. It was also discovered that Joseph had been feeling despondent for quite some time and was last seen purchasing a lottery ticket. At the spot from where Bryson jumped, instead of leaving a note or pieces of clothing, he left behind a single lottery ticket. Local schoolboy Jack Holland found the ticket issued under the name of **'Over the Bridge'**, an unexpected piece of evidence but also a clear sign that Joseph Bryson intended to jump.

Joseph Bryson spent his last shillings on a lottery ticket in a final attempt to free himself of his troubles. Like Frederick Bootman, who jumped earlier in the month, both men's fate was determined by chance. If they didn't win a prize, Bootman gave himself two deadly options and decided with the toss of a coin, while Bryson already envisaged how he would meet his end and made it known by writing on his lottery ticket.

The day after the Joseph Bryson tragedy, Sgt Bill Hamill recovered yet another body from the harbour. The badly decomposed body of 27-year-old William Laidlaw, an out-of-work salesman from Edgecliff, was recovered near the Cremorne Ferry wharf.

It was taken to the City Morgue to establish his identity and cause of death. Like the elderly Frenchman, Oscar Descamps, the Water Police suspected that William Laidlaw had jumped from the Bridge, but once again, the Coroner concluded an accidental drowning, stating it was **'Asphyxia from drowning, but how, where, or by what means he came to be drowned, evidence does not show'**.

With two harbour drownings within days of each other, it was a curious possibility that Laidlaw and Descamps had planned to jump from the bridge, but the installation of the fencing and the presence of extra police patrols had prevented both men from jumping from the great height. Perhaps each of them, unable to swim and feeling completely downcast, plunged off the nearest wharf into the water and perished. We can only speculate on such a possibility.

Meanwhile, having somehow recovered from the Ethel Francis tragedy, John Mulville had not given up on his duty as a bridge Patrolman. He may have been deceived once, but he was not defeated by the tragic circumstances of having Ethel Francis slip by while on his watch and before the sad month of January 1934 had come to an end, there was yet another attempt to beat the net.

Early in the morning of the 31st of January, a sixteen-year-old girl was found clinging to a granite ledge on the Northern bridge pylon 150 feet above the hard ground below. The young girl had climbed over where the footway met the pylon which was still unfenced. She then climbed down the pylon to the granite ledge which overlooked the ornamental garden plot. She balanced herself on the ledge and appeared ready to jump when the workmen below spotted her and shouted to her, warning her not to jump. She then hesitated and looking disorientated, she appeared to change her mind.

Hearing the shouting from the workmen below, John Mulville was the first patrolman on the scene and immediately climbed down to the pylon ledge. Mulville found the girl confused and exhausted and close to falling off the ledge. He quickly grabbed her and calmed her before they both made a safe return to the footway above. The young girl revealed she had left home after a family 'squabble', a trifling dispute which she later regretted when she was reunited with her mother.

The theory of a hastening of suicides before the completion of the safety barriers was true. By the month's end, there had been a record number of seven suicides, several harbour drownings, and countless attempts at suicide from the bridge. It was still a nervous time, and the job of erecting the fencing was still unfinished.

A week later, the wild rush to beat the net still had a bit of wind left in the sails, with a final desperate attempt by a woman who tried everything to end her life. Firstly, she tried to squeeze between some fencing and rigging in an effort to jump, and when restrained by patrolmen, she then attempted to throw herself into the path of an oncoming train. Once again, she was restrained. The Police then proceeded to take her to the Reception House, when the woman again managed to break free and made one final attempt and tried to throw herself over the wall of the southern approach to the bridge, but her last attempt was again foiled by Police.

With a record number of seven suicides during January, the Sydney Harbour Bridge 'Red Roll' stood at fifty-one, and as the rush to beat the net appeared to be finally over, the Melbourne *Herald* reported that the **'Sinister Arch was nearly safe'**.

Fig 13. Pictured foreground - a bridge patrolman stands on duty

23

CLOSED FOR BUSINESS

'It will become as world famous as the Eiffel Tower of Paris and the Empire building in New York'

On February 20th, 1934, nearly two years after the official opening, the new safety fencing on the bridge footways was completed, and both sides of the Sydney Harbour Bridge were now considered safe from suicide attempts. As promised by Minister Bruxner, the project was completed in quick time and without delay. Although it could be argued that it was fifty-one lives too late, the bridge was now adequately fenced, and the extra police patrols introduced to keep the footways under surveillance were withdrawn.

The Bridge was forthwith judged as 'suicide proof', and everyone firmly believed that anyone who attempted to climb the fencing would require the skills of a world-class gymnast, by which time the police or a passerby would have prevented them from achieving their end. It was also pointed out that the aesthetics of the bridge was not compromised by the new addition, with the barrier in **'no way detracting from the symmetrical lines of the bridge.'** An outcome that would have pleased many fencing detractors but perhaps not the devoted and often uncompromising chief bridge engineer Mr John Bradfield.

Free from controversy and no longer a sinister lure for the melancholy or burdened by the title of 'Suicide Bridge', the fictional character Mr Melancholy of the satirical 'Suicide Club' that once found humour in the tragedy of others, would have proclaimed the suicide bridge, closed for business. But news of the bridge being closed for business meant some people who were considering the bridge as the final terminus in life resorted to the old ways, as was the case for 29-year-old schoolteacher Lina Craig. Before Lina died in the hospital from self-administered poisoning, she managed to explain to the doctor that she had no money and was in trouble over a man. Lina said, **'I intended to throw myself over the Harbour Bridge, but it was closed in, so the next best thing was poison.'** The night before she died, Lina confessed that she made a batch of scones laced with an entire bottle of phosphorus and later consumed them all.

Whilst there was no statistical evidence to support the fact that protecting the bridge with fencing would reduce the overall suicide rate, it certainly removed the bridge from being the most desirable stepping-off point, as well as freeing it from the frequent miserable headline of 'Another Bridge Victim'.

Within weeks the new fence was put to the test, and as predicted, none of the desperate souls were world-class gymnasts, and they struggled in their frantic like attempts, often getting entangled in the wire and giving enough time for the passerby to help restrain them and bring them back from the brink.

It was still going to take some time for the Harbour Bridge to establish its rightful place as the most loved and greatest man-made structure in the country. However, there were a few early signs that the bridge had a bigger and brighter future beyond being the popular whipping post for interstate newspapers or just a useful transport link between two shores.

One enterprising man who had a unique vision for the Sydney Harbour Bridge was Archer Whitford. Archer was 48 years old, the son of a sheep farmer, who started work as a chemist's assistant and later was a carnival spruiker at the fairgrounds before starting his various enterprises, which included a banana plantation, a newspaper, an advertising business, floodlit tennis courts, a dairy farm, a broadcasting station, a real estate business and an all-important lease on the southeast pylon of the Sydney Harbour Bridge. Whitford successfully negotiated a ten-year lease over the Bridge pylon and, in doing so, spent a further £17000 installing a lift to service the six floors of space he renovated.

He was truly imaginative and fitted an aboriginal museum, a photographic gallery, a camera obscura (photo projector), a café, and covered one of the bare stone walls with a map of the world and clocks showing the time in capital cities around the world. One of the rooms was converted into a Buddhist temple, another was used to produce a daily newspaper, and on the rooftop, he installed a battery of telescopes for the visitors viewing pleasure. Whitford also managed to have the authorities appoint him as postmaster so he could operate the smallest and only bridge post office in the world.

Known as a 'Live Wire', Whitford had an enormous imagination for attracting tourists, and after opening day on February 16th, it wasn't long before he was employing fifty people, and his vision was paying off, with takings of £70 a day. With such a success on his hands, Whitford confidently declared **'that undoubtedly in time it will become as world-famous as the Eiffel Tower of Paris and the Empire building in New York.....It is my ambition to make the Sydney Harbour Bridge Pylon exhibition a national institution and I look forward to the time when no visitor will think of leaving Sydney without paying it, and the wonderful bridge a visit.'**

Archer Whitford had undertaken a substantial financial risk, but his grand vision for the Sydney Harbour Bridge proved to be a breath of fresh air for a city that for many years had seen so much doom and gloom. It was also a small but significant step for the rebranding of the Bridge as a popular tourist destination.

The legacy of Archer Whitford's vision is maintained to this day, only in a more contemporary form, and still known today as the 'The Bridge Pylon Lookout and Museum'. It remains a popular stand-alone tourist attraction as well as the perfect partner to the now famous Sydney Harbour Bridge climb.

On the 19th March 1934, the 2nd anniversary of the opening of the SHB passed with the blink of an eye, with no fanfare, no glorious tributes, and it hardly rated a mention in the newspapers. Even the *Daily Telegraph* was solely objective and unable to report anything exciting about the bridge, marking the occasion by simply saying, '**Today is the second Anniversary of the opening of the bridge which Sydney dreamed of for generations, and will continue to pay for, for more generations. The Bridge has behaved exactly as anticipated by its designers and will apparently continue to do so indefinitely.**'

Archer Whitford, on the other hand, was proudly proclaiming that he was now operating the world's smallest post office from the grandest bridge in the world. Attempting to rouse more publicity for his expensive venture, Whitford sent telegrams to all the newspapers hoping they would share the news of his latest enterprise. The telegram read, '**This is one of the first telegrams sent from the smallest, but not the least important post office in the world, situated in the Sydney Harbour Bridge pylon. It is the only post office on any bridge in the world.**'

Precisely four months had passed since John Baxter Bryant jumped from the bridge, and unfortunately, on May 25th, the tragic death of 23-year-old Clifford John Hayden brought back memories of those dark days. Fencing the pedestrian path on the bridge had made it difficult enough for even the most determined suicide to jump from the bridge; however, the approaches to the bridge were not fenced, and the temptation, impulse, or sheer determination to use the bridge approaches as a jumping off point was still possible.

It was revealed that Clifford Hayden was receiving treatment for serious nerve trouble, and he was deeply concerned about his sick father. His worrying circumstances led him to the unfenced approaches of the bridge, where he plummeted headfirst to the solid asphalt below and was killed instantly.

The following week 48-year-old Thomas Peers, a fireman from the steamship *Ascanius*, followed a similar path as Clifford Hayden, but the police quickly ruled out suicide or foul play. The police presented their case at the Coronial inquiry claiming that Thomas **'had drunk more than he was capable of holding'** and, under the influence of alcohol, attempted to cross from the eastern side to the western side of the approaches by climbing over the lattice fencing, onto the tramlines and then slipped and fell through the maze of steelwork to the ground below. The Coroner was unable to determine if Thomas met his death accidentally or otherwise and declared an open verdict.

News of Thomas Peers's death hardly rated a mention in the Sydney newspapers, and although it was unwelcome news, it was not well publicised and not nearly as sensational as the wild rush of suicides that had not long passed. It looked certain that the fashion of Harbour Bridge suicides had run its course. However, news of the deaths of Hayden and Peers did reach as far as Western Australia and created a small window of opportunity for the critic known as 'The Tramp' from the *Albany Advertiser* to have a final taunt at the Bridge and the people of Sydney, and this is what he had to say…

Talking about suicides, as most people are aware, the Harbour Bridge for a time completely ousted the Gap from favour among Sydney's suicides. After about 50 people had hurled themselves over from the footways on the Bridge, the authorities erected a fence of wire netting and barbed wire along both sides of the bridge. 'That'll stop it' they remarked and settled down with complacency to collect tolls.

It needs to be realised that suicide is regarded seriously by Sydney people. The Bridge is costing them £10,000,000 apart from interest, and they cannot afford to have people who might pay tolls killing themselves at the wholesale rate that was prevalent.

When four months passed without a single suicide from the Bridge, it really looked as though the jumpers were foiled. Then a more determined man than usual discovered that the fence only extended along that portion of the Bridge over the water.

The approaches at either end offered excellent facilities, with the added advantage that, the fall terminating on a concrete roadway, there was less chance of an unsuccessful leap. To think was to act, and in one week, two men jumped over, landing, as one Sydney paper put it, 'with sickening thuds.'

The authorities were nonplussed, but only for a while. 'Two more toll payers gone! It cannot continue.' So now the whole Bridge is going to be netted from end to end, even the gap in the decking, between road and rail, being covered over.

'THE BRIDGE.' The pride of Sydney, the Harbour, has now become of secondary importance. It is merely fortuitous of nature which by dividing Sydney from North Sydney, made the bridge possible, even if not strictly necessary.'

The article by *The Tramp* was a simple reminder of the view expressed by John Fraser Foster, who said that it didn't take much for one state to make '**disparaging comments upon the other States**'.

With the final word from '*The Tramp*,' it appeared that the last chapter in the life of the 'Suicide Bridge' was finally written. There was now hope for a new life for the Bridge, a life that it was originally intended for, the bridge that convict, forger, government architect and once the face on the ten dollar note, Francis Greenway, had envisioned more than two hundred years earlier when he proclaimed a bridge that would...'have given an idea of strength and magnificence that would have reflected credit and glory on the Colony and the Mother Country.'

24

A NEW LIFE

The Sydney Harbour Bridge is the bargain of the century.'
- Jack Lang-

The Great Depression had undoubtedly taken a lot of good out of living, and it could be said if there had been no Great Depression, the suicides on Sydney Harbour and elsewhere around the world would have been significantly less.

For the troubled suicide victims, many were simply tired of life, their life force drained from their weary bodies, the war veteran who once had plenty of fight in him was no longer able to battle against an enemy he could not see, the widows who lived and loved, later felt nothing but despair and loneliness, and the long term unemployed were stripped of their self-worth and dignity. There were the young who had so much to live for but emotionally yielding, the vulnerability of youthfulness sometimes defeating them. Some were ill and knew that their life would soon be cut short, they found a different courage and were determined to end life on their terms, and there were those who suffered from the evils of depression and the torment of their worst fears which eventually overpowered them.

Fortunately, the Great Depression didn't last, and eventually, it appeared the good times would return, and by the end of 1934, it was considered that Australia had turned an economic corner. With the restoration of the basic wage this alone was a positive sign of change, and Australia was slowly making its way back to prosperity.

The *Labor Daily*, the working man's paper, routinely reporting on the daily struggles, also felt the tide of change and sent out a message of hope, encouraging people not to give up on life, affirming to its readers that change is just around the corner and quoting from renaissance philosopher Michel de Montaigne.

'All the inconveniences of the world are not considerable enough that a man should die to evade them, and besides, there being so many changes in human things, how can we judge when we are at the end of our hopes?' - Montaigne

Had the bridge remained suicide-friendly, bridge deaths would have surely continued unabated, and along with its sinister image, had to endure a barrage of criticism, unwarranted slurs, and the possibility of being a shadowy monolithic curiosity. But for the remarkable work of many people during the bridge's difficult beginnings, that all changed, and despite the toughest of times and the financial stranglehold of the depression, persistence from the campaigners altered the history of the bridge.

It is also important to remember the remarkable work of the Sydney Water Police. Led by the formidable Sgt Charles Bebb, the men of the Sydney Water Police had sustained much of the heavy lifting while managing the harbour during its many transformations. They could have written volumes on the life of Sydney Harbour and the SHB, but unfortunately, none of these great men put pen to paper.

Only a few months after the bridge fencing was completed, Sgt Bebb obtained a well-earned transfer of duty and looked forward to spending more time with his wife and family. Sadly, his chance to enjoy a well-deserved change was unjustly taken away. After only a few weeks in his new role as Inspector of licensing at the Kogarah Division, he passed away on October 21st, 1934, from complications related to appendicitis surgery; he was 48 years old. A year later, the Anglican Archbishop of Sydney, Dr Howard Mowll dedicated a memorial chapel to Charles at Saint David's Church of England in Arncliffe, where Sgt Bebb had been a devoted parishioner.

After the death of Sgt Bebb, life for the other main protagonists during the tragic bridge years continued, and their ambitious paths were not diverted. During the 'fenceless' years of the bridge, few politicians could have survived the troubling unfamiliarity of bridge jumpers or the scrutiny of the press. However, the determined 'Colonel' Michael Bruxner was like Charles Bebb, a fearless man with immense strength of character and devotion to duty. Mr Bruxner continued as Deputy Premier and Minister for Transport for almost ten years. Although an early opponent of the construction of the Harbour Bridge, Bruxner remained a dedicated public servant. As a Minister, his responsibilities were considerable and challenging, given the deplorable financial conditions the State Government had inherited in its time.

Despite his early reluctance to fence the Bridge footway, perhaps the only hiccup during his tenure, his achievements as Minister for Transport were outstanding. He went on to oversee the construction of over 1000 bridges throughout New South Wales and carried out the most significant program of road improvements in the history of New South Wales. He initiated the dustless road program throughout every town and village, introduced the painted centerline on main roads and highways, established motor ramps and the 30-mile speed limit in built-up areas and was the founder of the Roads Safety Council of New South Wales. All initiatives that have been carried forward similarly to this day.

In 1958 he retired from politics after serving in Parliament continuously for 32 years and as a member of the NSW Legislative Assembly for nearly 42 years. In 1959 a 260-mile stretch of Highway was built in Northern New South Wales and named the Bruxner Highway in his honour, and in 1962 he received a knighthood KBE for political and public services.

Not all public officials of the time had equally distinguished careers like Bebb or Bruxner, but even the most adverse bridge detractors, such as Alderman David 'Springboard' Hunter, managed to continue an ambitious path. Alderman David Blair Grant Hunter remained undaunted in his stance on bridge suicides. The man who unashamedly made the astonishing suggestion that a springboard be placed at a convenient spot on the bridge from which the suicide jumper could pay a shilling for the privilege surprisingly became the elected Mayor of North Sydney Council in December 1935. Later in 1954, he was appointed Chief Justice of Tonga, a position he retained until his death in 1964. His obituary included mention of his lively wit.

The four bridge jumpers who survived their unique experience lived on, and their remarkable stories of survival quickly faded, all four living the remainder of their lives in relative obscurity. War veteran Robert Anderson separated from his wife Daisy and lived a solitary life until his death in 1960. Young Jean 'Susie' Boulton, known as the 'decidedly pretty girl', never married and lived a quiet life with her mother Laura in the Riverina township of Tumut at the foothills of the Snowy Mountains. Charles Gallagher 'the naked singer' later found permanent work and lived in Wollongong until his death in 1958, and 'belle of the ball' Madge Hope died in 2007, reaching the grand old age of 88.

While the threat of suicide attempts is now a distant memory, once again, times have changed, and the foot patrolling policeman of yesteryear have been replaced with around-the-clock video surveillance and private security firms patrolling the bridge, the threat of terrorism bringing a more fearful danger. On the majestic steel arches above the carriageway, small processions of tourists can be seen tethered by safety lines to railings enjoying the now famous 'Bridge Climb'. They slowly make their way to the bridge summit for a view that is worth the price tag for the rare privilege. The awestruck tourists remain entirely unaware of the many tragedies that once took place from the deck beneath them.

The early bridge birthday celebrations that were once easily overlooked have since been replaced by the extraordinary New Year's fireworks celebrations. With the bridge as the centrepiece of this annual event, it attracts thousands of tourists and spectators from around the world to watch the spectacle, a grandness in scale not seen anywhere else in the world. The Venetian carnivals and the Sydney Festival that once attracted large crowds have been replaced with the entire city of Sydney, now a canvas for the 'Vivid' light festival, a creative masterpiece that covers the great landmarks of Sydney in a dazzling night time display of colour and themes, continuing to draw vast crowds, and each year outdoing the year before.

The 'Big Fella' Jack Lang, the embattled State leader dethroned shortly after he officially opened the bridge, against all public opinion, made the following statement... **'The Sydney Harbour Bridge is the bargain of the century'**, a bold claim in 1932, but today, most Australians would agree with him in a heartbeat.

In 2032 the Sydney Harbour Bridge will celebrate its 100th Birthday, a celebration that will be the grandest possibly ever seen in Australia and not unlike the opening celebrations in its significance and importance. A vast and exciting spectacle awaits all Australians and is worthy of the flamboyant poetic praise that once bellowed from proud Australians a hundred years earlier.

Thanks to an anonymous American tourist, the 'Coathanger' as the bridge has become affectionately known, is the jewel of Sydney Harbour, standing guard over its magnificent waterways and equally stunning harbourside companion, the Sydney Opera House. It is precisely what it was once predicted it would be, **'a mecca for tourists'** that would **'reflect infinite credit upon the engineering skill, the imaginative audacity, and the foresight and enterprise of man'**.

For close to a hundred years, the Sydney Harbour Bridge has nurtured the energetic and now glittering city it embraces; the 'Coathanger', the colossus of the southern hemisphere, has seen it all and endured. The Bridge is one of the most recognized man-made structures in the world, a superstructure that stands up equally against ancient peers like the great pyramids of Egypt or architectural greats like the Eiffel tower in Paris. And like its giant counterparts, it also has a great story, one celebrated by all Australians. As its enormous span majestically stretches across the city, it also shelters the memory of the many lives lost in the water below.

    It is a great bridge, the keeper of secrets, and the GUARDIAN OF SOULS.

CHAPTER NOTES

CHAPTER ONE – BACKGROUND

Source: Sydney Morning Herald (NSW : 1842 - 1954), Saturday 16 November 1929, page 21 – James Hunter, snared seagulls.

Source: Argus (Melbourne, Vic. : 1848 - 1957), Thursday 2 February 1911, page 7 - Sydney's Dirty Doorstep

Source: - State Archives NSW. – The Sydney Plague 1900

Source: Evening News (Sydney, NSW : 1869 - 1931), Wednesday 29 March 1899, page 3 – James Ryan ferry Suicide

Source: Singleton Argus (NSW : 1880 - 1954), Saturday 1 October 1910, page 1 – Arthur Newland ferry suicide

Source: Darling Downs Gazette (Qld. : 1881 - 1922), Friday 7 April 1916, page 6 – Edward Soden

CHAPTER TWO - THE FIRST TO JUMP

Source: Braidwood Review and District Advocate (NSW : 1915 - 1954), Tuesday 26 April 1932, page 7 - Opening quote

Source: Singleton Argus (NSW : 1880 - 1954), Monday 9 May 1932, page 1 – 750,000 people

Source: Sun (Sydney, NSW : 1910 - 1954), Sunday 20 March 1932, page 44 - Coathanger

Source: South Coast Bulletin (Southport, Qld. : 1929 - 1954), Friday 11 March 1932, page 8 – Horse drawn floats

Sources: Catholic Press (Sydney, NSW : 1895 - 1942), Thursday 31 March 1932, page 13. Townsville Daily Bulletin (Qld. : 1907 - 1954), Monday 21 March 1932, page 4 – Bridge opening

Source: Sydney Morning Herald (NSW : 1842 – 1954), Monday 21 March 1932, page 12 – Fireworks - forge of Vulcan

Source: Argus (Melbourne, Vic. : 1848 - 1957), Saturday 27 February 1932, Professor Ernest Scott

Source: The Daily Telegraph (Sydney, NSW : 1931-1954) Mon 25 April 1932, front page – Joseph Molineaux

Source: Sydney Morning Herald (NSW : 1842 - 1954), Monday 25 April 1932, page 5 – Bebb and constables

Source: Braidwood Review and District Advocate (NSW 1915 - 1954), Tuesday 26 April 1932, page 7 – Historic Suicide

Source: The Daily Telegraph Monday 25 April 1932 Page 1 – First Bridge Suicide

Source: Labor Daily (Sydney, NSW : 1924 - 1938), Tuesday 3 May 1932, page 1 - Just Another War Victim

Source: Daily Examiner (Grafton, NSW : 1915 - 1954), Thursday 28 April 1932, page 4 - new highway of life had been converted to one of death

Source: Newcastle Morning Herald and Miners' Advocate (NSW : 1876 - 1954), Tuesday 26 April 1932, page 5 - Here take this; I won't have any use for it now.

Source: Sun (Sydney, NSW : 1910 - 1954), Tuesday 26 April 1932, page 9 – No Trace

Sources: Daily Telegraph (Sydney, NSW : 1931 - 1954), Saturday 11 June 1932, page 6, Beaudesert Times (Qld. : 1908 - 1954), Friday 3 June 1932, page 3 – Robert Anderson

CHAPTER 3 - NO BARRIER TO SUICIDE

Source: Age (Melbourne, Vic. : 1854 - 1954), Friday 7 November 1856, page 7 - Opening quote

Source: The Sydney Morning Herald (NSW : 1842 - 1954) 18 April 1931, page 11 (Centenary Supplement) - Engineering triumph

Source: South Australian Weekly Chronicle (Adelaide, SA : 1881 - 1889), Saturday 11 July 1885, page 19 – Clifton Bridge, dashed to pieces.

Source: Evening News (Rockhampton, Qld. : 1924 - 1941), Tuesday 22 November 1932, page 8 – Clifton Bridge, covered fence

Source: Evening News (Rockhampton, Qld. : 1924 - 1941), Tuesday 22 November 1932, page 8 – cliffs v bridges.

Source: (1926, May 8). Observer (Adelaide, SA : 1905 - 1931), page 11 – Beauty of design

Sources: Dorrigo Gazette and Guy Fawkes Advocate (NSW : 1910 - 1954), Saturday 25 November 1922, page 4, Advertiser (Adelaide, SA : 1889 - 1931), Tuesday 11 July 1922, page 6, https://adb.anu.edu.au/ Bruxner, Sir Michael Frederick (1882–1970) by Don Aitkin, Armidale Express and New England General Advertiser (NSW : 1856 - 1861; 1863 - 1889; 1891 - 1954), Tuesday 18 July 1922, page 3 – Michael Bruxner

Source: Central Queensland Herald (Rockhampton, Qld. : 1930 - 1956), Thursday 24 March 1932, page 32 – Jack Lang Speech opening ceremony

CHAPTER 4 - SUICIDE, A SIGN OF THE TIMES

Source: Lithgow Mercury – Hospital Briefs And Some Personals, Friday 31 March 1933, page 4 - Opening quote

Source: Uralla Times (NSW : 1923 - 1954), Thursday 18 May 1933, page 9 – Mount Mihara

Source: Recorder (Port Pirie, SA : 1919 - 1954), Tuesday 12 April – Dr Frederick Hoffman

Source: South Australian Register (Adelaide, SA : 1839 - 1900), Monday 9 September 1850, page 4 – Arroyo Seco Bridge – Pasadena.

Source: Mirror (Perth, WA : 1921 - 1956), Saturday 9 July 1932, page 16 – Stepping-off point

Source: Daily Telegraph (Sydney, NSW : 1931 - 1954), Friday 16 December 1932, page 10 - Salvation Army - Are you In trouble

Source: Cessnock Eagle and South Maitland Recorder (NSW : 1913 - 1954), Friday 12 February 1932, page 8 - 'The Suicide Club'

Source: Truth (Sydney, NSW : 1894 - 1954), Sunday 1 May 1932, page 8 – Doctor Psychology of suicide theory

Source: Northern Star (Lismore, NSW : 1876 - 1954), Thursday 4 August 1932, page 7 - William Bray, Joseph 'John' Bryson

Source: Lithgow Mercury – Hospital Briefs And Some Personals, Friday 31 March 1933, page 4, Wellington Times (NSW : 1899 - 1954), Monday 29 September 1930, page 5 – Poisons and the gas bill

Source: The Week (Brisbane, Qld. : 1876 - 1934), Friday 26 September 1930, page 21 – James Brown Taxi Driver

CHAPTER 5 -TIRED OF LIFE, THE FIRST WOMAN

Source: - Labor Daily (Sydney, NSW : 1924 - 1938), Thursday 7 September 1933, page 4 – Opening quote

Source: Singleton Argus (NSW : 1880 - 1954), Monday 14 March 1932, page 2 – William Power

Source: '1932 - A Hell of a Year' – Gerald Stone - Unemployment Statistics

Source: 'Australia's Yesterdays' – published by Readers Digest text by Cyril Pearl. – 500 applicants

Source: Sydney Morning Herald (NSW : 1842 - 1954), Monday 27 June 1932, page 10 – Evicted Families

Source: Daily Advertiser (Wagga Wagga, NSW : 1911 - 1954), Saturday 20 February 1932, page 1 – Mr Jones

Source: 'Australian Battlers Remember' – Keith Smith 2003.

Source: Mudgee Guardian and North-Western Representative (NSW : 1890 - 1954), Monday June 27th 1932, page 2 – Alberta Ellks - sank like a stone.

Source: Sun (Sydney, NSW : 1910 - 1954), Wednesday November 9th 1927, page 14 – Sgt George Day

Source: Daily Examiner (Grafton, NSW : 1915 - 1954), Thursday June 8th 1933, page 4 – Const. Walter Edward Jordan

Source: Mudgee Guardian and North-Western Representative (NSW : 1890 - 1954), Monday June 27th 1932, page – Tired Of Life

Source: Labor Daily (Sydney, NSW : 1924 - 1938), Saturday July 2nd 1932, page 9 – She wanted to die

Sources: National Advocate (Bathurst, NSW : 1889 - 1954), Saturday July 2nd 1932, page 2. Newcastle Morning Herald and Miners' Advocate (NSW : 1876 - 1954) , Saturday July 2nd 1932, page 8. Newcastle Sun (NSW : 1918 - 1954), Friday June 24th 1932, page 2 - Alberta Ellks

Source: healthdirect.gov.au - postnatal-depression

CHAPTER 6 - TEMPORARILY MENTALLY DERANGED

Source: Tasmanian (Launceston, Tas. : 1871 - 1879), Saturday 13 December 1873, page 9 – Opening Quote.

Source: Labor Daily (Sydney, NSW : 1924 - 1938), Wednesday 27 July 1932, page 6 – Gabriel Jenkins

Sources: - West Australian (Perth, WA : 1879 - 1954), Wednesday 27 July 1932, page 13. Sun (Sydney, NSW : 1910 - 1954), Tuesday 26 July 1932, page 8 – Gabriel Jenkins

Source: NAA Contents range 1914 – 1920 Series number B2455 Control symbol JENKINS GABRIEL Access status Open Item ID 7361516 – War Record Gabriel Jenkins

Source: Daily Telegraph (Sydney, NSW : 1931 - 1954), Tuesday 23 August 1932, page 8 – Gabriel's Will

Source: Sun (Sydney, NSW : 1910 - 1954), Friday 22 July 1932, page 10 – four men and Immer. Sydney Morning Herald (NSW : 1842 - 1954), Saturday 23 July 1932, page 14 – Hedley Hearne

Source: Sun (Sydney, NSW : 1910 - 1954), Friday 22 July 1932, page 10 – Friday is an unlucky day.

Source: https://lowellcorp.com/evolution-of-the-lineman/ - Lineman

Source: Sun (Sydney, NSW : 1910 - 1954), Tuesday 26 July 1932. -William Chandler

Sources: Sun (Sydney, NSW : 1910 - 1954), Saturday 23 July 1932, page 7 / Labor Daily (Sydney, NSW : 1924 - 1938), Saturday 30 July 1932, page 10 – Bernie Cummins – temporarily mentally deranged

Source: Tasmanian (Launceston, Tas. : 1871 - 1879), Saturday 13 December 1873, page 9 – Insanity of a temporary nature.

Source: Truth (Sydney, NSW : 1894 - 1954), Sunday 24 July 1932, page 14 – Crime Wave

CHAPTER 7 - SUICIDE ETIQUETTE & FENCING

Source: Mirror (Perth, WA : 1921 - 1956), Saturday 9 July 1932, page 1- Opening Quote

Source: Mirror (Perth, WA : 1921 - 1956), Saturday 9 July 1932, page 1- irresponsibles, Stepping-off point for Eternity

Source: Australian Women's Weekly (1933 - 1982), Saturday 25 November 1933, page 4 – 1930 fencing delegation

Source: Northern Star (Lismore, NSW : 1876 - 1954), Thursday 4 August 1932, page 7 – Gold cufflink

Source: Sun (Sydney, NSW : 1910 - 1954), Tuesday 23 August 1932, page 12 – William Bray Note – come back you'll fall

Source: Daily Telegraph (Sydney, NSW : 1931 - 1954), Thursday 4 August 1932, page 7 – William Bray address

Source: Daily Herald (Adelaide, SA : 1910 - 1924), Monday 16 December 1912, page 4 -'Etiquette of Suicide'

Source: Lithgow Mercury (NSW: 1898 - 1954), Wednesday 13 July 1932, page 2. Sound Arbitrator

Source: Coroners Report – William Bray

Source: Advertiser (Adelaide, SA : 1931 - 1954), Saturday 13 August 1932, page 17- Murial Walsh, Ferry Suicide

Source: Daily Telegraph (Sydney, NSW : 1931 - 1954), Thursday 4 August 1932, page 7 – Daily Telegraph - time for action

Source: Daily Telegraph (Sydney, NSW : 1931 - 1954), Thursday 4 August 1932, page 7 – Daily Telegraph - time for action

Source: Daily Telegraph (Sydney, NSW : 1931 - 1954), Friday 5 August 1932, page 7 – Mr May

Source: Daily Telegraph (Sydney, NSW : 1931 - 1954), Thursday 4 August 1932, page 7 – Daily Telegraph - time for action

Source: Daily Telegraph (Sydney, NSW: 1931 - 1954), Thursday 4 August 1932, page 7 – Raise the wall Macquarie Street, Doctor

Source: Sun (Sydney, NSW : 1910 - 1954), Friday 12 August 1932, page 13 – Mr B D Sweetland

Source: Sydney Morning Herald (NSW: 1842 - 1954), Monday 31 October 1932, page 3 - F. S. Burnell Cremorne

Source: Daily Telegraph (Sydney, NSW : 1931 - 1954), Thursday 4 August 1932, page 7 – Salvation Army notice

Source: Sun (Sydney, NSW : 1910 - 1954), Tuesday 20 September 1932, page 6 Rev Reece, Rev Mc Gowen

Source: Daily Telegraph (Sydney, NSW : 1931 - 1954), Thursday 4 August 1932, page 7 - Officialdom

Source: Sun (Sydney, NSW : 1910 - 1954), Tuesday 20 September 1932, page 6 – Mayor of North Sydney

Sources: Examiner (Launceston, Tas. : 1900 - 1954), Wednesday 31 August 1932, page 7. Daily Telegraph (Sydney, NSW : 1931 - 1954), Saturday 18 March 1933, page 5. Constable killed on Bridge – poor lighting

CHAPTER 8 - SINISTER SPELL OF THE BRIDGE

Source: Daily Telegraph (Sydney, NSW : 1931 - 1954), Wednesday 13 September 1933, page 8. – Opening quote

Source: Truth (Sydney, NSW : 1894 - 1954), Sunday 8 October 1933, page 1 – Grim Lure

Source: Sun (Sydney, NSW : 1910 - 1954), Sunday 26 February 1933, page 1 – Downtrodden all my life

Sources: Advocate (Burnie, Tas. : 1890 - 1954), Tuesday 27 September 1932, page 7. Daily Telegraph (Sydney, NSW : 1931 - 1954), Tuesday 27 September 1932, page 1 – Suicide attempts

Source: Sun (Sydney, NSW : 1910 - 1954), Friday 7 October 1932, page 12. – Lunatic Reception House - attempt 22-year-old woman

Source: Sun (Sydney, NSW : 1910 - 1954), Thursday 8 September 1932, page 15 – Jean Susie Boulton

Source: - Truth (Sydney, NSW : 1894 - 1954), Sunday 8 October 1933, page 1. - sinister spell of the bridge

Sources: Daily Telegraph (Sydney, NSW : 1931 - 1954), Friday 9 September 1932, page 1. Labor Daily (Sydney, NSW : 1924 - 1938), Friday 9 September 1932, page 1 – Susie Boulton

Source: Truth (Sydney, NSW : 1894 - 1954), Sunday 8 October 1933, page 1.- Susie Boulton quote.

Source: Labor Daily (Sydney, NSW : 1924 - 1938), Tuesday 29 August 1933, page 7. – Took life in second attempt

CHAPTER 9 - THE WRONG MAN

Source: Arrow (Sydney, NSW : 1916 - 1933), Friday 30 September 1932, page 6 – Opening Quote

Source: Weekly Times (Melbourne, Vic. : 1869 - 1954), Saturday 23 January 1932, page 5 – Albert Jacka VC Funeral

Source: Sun (Sydney, NSW : 1910 - 1954), Monday 19 September 1932, page 7 – William Connoley

Sources: Labor Daily (Sydney, NSW : 1924 - 1938), Wednesday 21 September 1932, page 1, Newcastle Morning Herald and Miners' Advocate (NSW : 1876 - 1954), Tuesday 27 September 1932, page 6 -William Connoley

Source: Arrow (Sydney, NSW : 1916 - 1933), Friday 30 September 1932, page 6 –Fashions in Suicide

Source - Sun (Sydney, NSW : 1910 - 1954), Monday 19 September 1932, page 7 – 'Sun' declares bridge 'Suicide Menace'

Source: Sun (Sydney, NSW : 1910 - 1954), Tuesday 20 September 1932, page 6 – The Bridge to Eternity

Sources: Sun (Sydney, NSW : 1910 - 1954), Tuesday 20 September 1932, page 6 – Bruxner consensus of opinion. Source: Canberra Times (ACT : 1926 - 1995), Wednesday 28 September 1932, page 1

Sources: Daily Telegraph (Sydney, NSW : 1931 - 1954), Monday 26 September 1932, page 7. Daily Telegraph (Sydney, NSW : 1931 - 1954), Thursday 19 October 1933, page 6. Warwick Daily News (Qld. : 1919 -1954), Monday 26 September 1932 – George Williams and Leslie Lionel Dunlop

Source: Barrier Miner (Broken Hill, NSW : 1888 - 1954), Saturday 1 October 1932, page 1 – George Williams

Source: Labor Daily (Sydney, NSW : 1924 - 1938), Wednesday 18 October 1933, page7 – William Lehane quote

Source: Herald (Melbourne, Vic. : 1861 - 1954), Thursday 14 December 1933, page 10 – William Lehane - Judge Sir John Harvey

CHAPTER 10 - DOWN, BUT NOT OUT

Source: Kyogle Examiner (NSW : 1912; 1914 - 1915; 1917 - 1954), Tuesday 9 October 1934, page 6 – Opening Quote

Source: Kyogle Examiner (NSW : 1912; 1914 - 1915; 1917 - 1954), Tuesday 9 October 1934, page 6 – Women Heroines

Source: https://sydneylivingmuseums.com.au/stories/skint-making-do-great-depression Annie Stevens – author

Source: Woman's Distress - Police to the Rescue - Sydney Morning Herald (NSW : 1842 - 1954), Tuesday 15 November 1932, page 9

Source: Sun (Sydney, NSW : 1910 - 1954), Friday 22 July 1932, page 11- Defiant - Woman in Bag Humpy

Source: Barrier Miner (Broken Hill, NSW : 1888 - 1954), Tuesday 23 February 1932, page 3 - Buried Sovereigns in Backyard

Source: Sydney Morning Herald (NSW : 1842 - 1954), Monday 3 October 1932, page 8 – Ethel Hull

Source: Dubbo Liberal and Macquarie Advocate (NSW : 1894 - 1954), Tuesday 11 October 1932, page 1 – Mother and 10 month old child

Source: Voice (Hobart, Tas. : 1931 - 1953), Saturday 1 September 1934, page 3 – poison and 1.5 million

Source: Northern Star (Lismore, NSW : 1876 - 1954), Monday October 17th 1932, page 5 - Ethel Lee

Source: Sun (Sydney, NSW : 1910 - 1954), Sunday 16 October 1932, page 1 – Ethel Lee

Source: Sydney Morning Herald (NSW : 1842 - 1954), Friday October 21st 1932, page 9 – Jessie Marie Couch

Source: Daily Telegraph (Sydney, NSW : 1931 - 1954), Friday October 21st 1932, page 11- Jessie Couch

Source: Daily Telegraph (Sydney, NSW : 1931 - 1954), Thursday October 27th 1932, page 5 – Jessie Couch specialist

Source: Truth (Sydney, NSW : 1894 - 1954), Sunday 16 October 1932, page 22 – Agnes Murphy

CHAPTER 11 - SPRINGBOARD TO DEATH

Source: Mercury - Hobart, Tasmania, Thursday 8 December 1932, page 8.- Opening Quote

Source: - Daily Telegraph (Sydney, NSW : 1931 - 1954), Friday 21 October 1932, page 11- mathematical expectation fatal leap every 16 days

Source: Daily Telegraph (Sydney, NSW : 1931 - 1954), Wednesday 26 October 1932, page 6 – Hubert Primrose

Source: Sydney Morning Herald (NSW : 1842 - 1954), Wednesday 26 October 1932, page 12 – Springboard quote – Ald. David Hunter

Sources: Newcastle Morning Herald and Miners' Advocate (NSW : 1876 - 1954), Monday 31 October 1932, page 8. Labor Daily (Sydney, NSW : 1924 - 1938), Monday 31 October 1932, page 8 Townsville Daily Bulletin (Qld. : 1907 - 1954), Monday 31 October 1932, page 4 – Alfred Stannard

Source: Daily Telegraph (Sydney, NSW : 1931 - 1954), Monday 31 October 1932, page 8 – Bruxner unofficial approach

Source: Sydney Morning Herald (NSW : 1842 - 1954), Wednesday 23 November 1932, page 18 – Buckham's proposal

Source: Sydney Morning Herald (NSW : 1842 - 1954), Wednesday 23 November 1932, page 18 – Ald. F Hardy, Engineer Buckham.

Sources: Labor Daily (Sydney, NSW : 1924 - 1938), Monday 28 November 1932, page 6. Source: Barrier Miner (Broken Hill, NSW : 1888 - 1954), Monday 28 November 1932, page 3 – Daniel Hogan

CHAPTER 12 - A HELL OF A YEAR

Source: Daily Telegraph (Sydney, NSW: 1931 - 1954), Thursday 29 December 1932.- Opening Quote

Source: Bone, James (13 October 2008). "The Times" (ECE). New York. Retrieved 23 October 2008. List of suicide sites – Wikiwand

Sources: Daily Telegraph (Sydney, NSW : 1931 - 1954), Saturday 19 March 1932, page 19 http://nla.gov.au/nla.news-article246557885 - Dr Bradfield - Leap Year. The Observer Adelaide Saturday May 8 1926 page 11 - Bradfield Big-Brained

Source: 1932 – A Hell of a Year – Gerald Stone

Source: National Museum Australia -https://www.nma.gov.au/defining-moments/resources/edith-cowan

Source: National Advocate (Bathurst, NSW : 1889 - 1954), Saturday 3 December 1932, page 4 – Penelope Cameron- mud mystery

Source: National Advocate (Bathurst, NSW : 1889 - 1954), Saturday 3 December 1932, page 4 – Penelope Cameron- mud mystery

Source: Sun (Sydney, NSW : 1910 - 1954), Tuesday 6 December 1932, page 11- Augustus Gallen – brother in law Mr A Over

Source: Labor Daily (Sydney, NSW : 1924 - 1938), Monday 12 December 1932, page 5 – Bridge of Death

Source: Sun (Sydney, NSW : 1910 - 1954), Saturday 10 December 1932, page 5 – Bruxner – Sun Editor – Less publicity

Source: Sun (Sydney, NSW : 1910 - 1954), Saturday 10 December 1932, page 5 – Bruxner – Sun Editor Delamore McCay

Sources: Sun (Sydney, NSW : 1910 - 1954), Wednesday 14 December 1932, page 13. Singleton Argus (NSW : 1880 - 1954), Friday 16 December 1932, page 7. – Norman Gair.

Source: Daily Telegraph (Sydney, NSW: 1931 - 1954), Thursday 29 December 1932.- Charles Diamond

Source: Workers' Weekly (Sydney, NSW: 1923 - 1939), Friday 16 December 1932. – Communist Party - capitalism to blame

Source: Daily Telegraph (Sydney, NSW: 1931 - 1954), Friday 16 December 1932 – Salvation Army -Sign and inclined barrier

Source: North Western Courier (Narrabri, NSW: 1913 - 1955), Thursday 15 December 1932, page 1 – Coroner – December evidence of other suicides

CHAPTER 13 - 1933, A NEW START

Source: Labor Daily (Sydney, NSW : 1924 - 1938), Saturday January 7th 1933, page 1- Opening Quote

Source: Gundagai Independent (NSW : 1928 - 1939), Thursday January 19th 1933, page 2 – Mary Mee Hing

Source: Labor Daily (Sydney, NSW : 1924 - 1938), Saturday January 7th 1933, page 1- Mary Mee Hing - Life's Wheel

Sources: Evening News (Rockhampton, Qld. : 1924 - 1941), Monday 16 January 1933, page 1. National Advocate (Bathurst, NSW : 1889 - 1954), Monday 16 January 1933, page 2. Mail (Adelaide, SA : 1912 - 1954), Saturday 14 January 1933, page 2. – Horace Lock

Source: Labor Daily (Sydney, NSW : 1924 - 1938), Thursday 19 January 1933, page 6 – Senator Arthur Rae

Sources: Daily Telegraph (Sydney, NSW : 1931 - 1954), Saturday 28 January 1933, page 7. Labor Daily (Sydney, NSW : 1924 - 1938), Friday 27 January 1933, page 7. – George Bailey

CHAPTER 14 - BRIDGE ENVY

Source: Daily Telegraph (Sydney, NSW : 1931 - 1954), Saturday 18 March 1933, page 5 – Opening Quote

Source: Daily Telegraph (Sydney, NSW : 1931 - 1954), Friday 10 February 1933 – Carl Phillips Diving prank.

Sources: Sydney Morning Herald (NSW : 1842 - 1954), Saturday 18 March 1933, page 14, Daily Telegraph (Sydney, NSW : 1931 - 1954), Saturday 18 March 1933, page 1 – Thomas Francis McDonald.

Source: Sun (Sydney, NSW : 1910 - 1954), Saturday 18 March 1933, page 4 – Bridge 1st Birthday

Source: Daily Telegraph (Sydney, NSW : 1931 - 1954), Saturday 18 March 1933, page 5 – Our Bridge - 1st Birthday – F.V Coleman

Source: Evening News (Rockhampton, Qld. : 1924 - 1941), Saturday 19 March 1932, page 6 – Sydney people get what they want.

Source: News (Adelaide, SA : 1923 - 1954), Friday 23 June 1933, page 6 – Adelaide criticism

Source: Deirdre Hill – 'A Bridge of Dreams' – a new beginning

Source: Sunday Times (Perth, WA : 1902 - 1954), Sunday 17 September 1933. – Bridge of Sighs

Source: page 13 "Australia - The Making of a Nation"- John Foster Fraser

Source: Sydney Morning Herald (NSW : 1842 - 1954), Saturday 19 March 1932, page 9 – Minnie Filson Poem

CHAPTER 15 – WAR VETERANS, TRAVELLERS & POLICEMEN

Source: Kyogle Examiner (NSW : 1912; 1914 - 1915; 1917 - 1954), Tuesday 16 September 1930, page 2 – Opening Quote

Source: Referee (Sydney, NSW : 1886 - 1939), Wednesday 13 October 1915, page 16 – Lewis Dyson Gallipoli

Source: Newcastle Morning Herald and Miners' Advocate (NSW : 1876 - 1954), Monday 3 April 1933, page 4 – Sydney Festival

Source: Manilla Express (NSW : 1899 - 1954), Friday 31 March 1933, page 1 – Festival description

Sources: Muswellbrook Chronicle (NSW : 1898 - 1955), Tuesday 4 April 1933, page 4. - All Fools Day. Albany Advertiser (WA : 1897 - 1954), Monday 3 April 1933, page 1 – All Fools Day

Source: Sydney Morning Herald (NSW : 1842 - 1954), Wednesday 3 May 1933, page 18. – Gladstone Eyre

Source: Kyogle Examiner (NSW : 1912; 1914 - 1915; 1917 - 1954), Tuesday 16 September 1930, page 2 - 'as dead as Julius Caesar'.

Sources: Evening News (Rockhampton, Qld. : 1924 - 1941), Monday 22 May 1933, page 2. Labor Daily (Sydney, NSW : 1924 - 1938), Thursday 18 May 1933, page 7 – Alon Ison

Sources: Murrumbidgee Irrigator (Leeton, NSW : 1915 - 1954), Tuesday 23 May 1933, page 2, Newcastle Morning Herald and Miners' Advocate (NSW : 1876 - 1954), Saturday 20 May 1933, page 6 – Bridge Hanging

Source: Cessnock Eagle and South Maitland Recorder (NSW : 1913 - 1954), Friday 2 June 1933, page 7- Nude orator

Source: National Advocate (Bathurst, NSW : 1889 - 1954), Tuesday 20 June 1933, page 2, Inverell Times (NSW : 1899 - 1907, 1909 - 1954), Monday 19 June 1933, page 1, Evening News (Rockhampton, Qld. : 1924 - 1941), Friday 23 June 1933, page 3 – Peter McVerry

Source: Labor Daily (Sydney, NSW : 1924 - 1938), Friday 23 June 1933, page 8 - Wallet

Source: Balonne Beacon (St. George, Qld. : 1909 - 1954), Thursday 27 July 1933, page 5 – Bruxner reveals Bridge losing money

CHAPTER 16 - BRIDGE MAYHEM

Source: National Advocate (Bathurst, NSW : 1889 - 1954), Tuesday 8 August 1933, page 2. – Opening Quote

Sources: Sydney Morning Herald (NSW : 1842 - 1954), Thursday 10 August 1933, page 9. Gundagai Independent (NSW : 1928 - 1939), Monday 7 August 1933, page 3. http://thedreadnoughtboys.blogspot.com/. The Dreadnought trust scheme: 'Independent.co.uk' article by Stephen Kelly 2011 – 'Australia's Lost Boys'.

Source: Wagga Wagga Express (NSW : 1930 - 1939), Saturday 12 August 1933, page 10. Dubbo Liberal and Macquarie Advocate (NSW : 1894 - 1954), Saturday 5 August 1933, page 1 – Eric Clements

Sources: Sun (Sydney, NSW : 1910 - 1954), Monday 7 August 1933, page 7. National Advocate (Bathurst, NSW : 1889 - 1954), Tuesday 8 August 1933, page 2. – 'Young Girls Sensational Suicide'. Lithgow Mercury (NSW : 1898 - 1954), Monday 7 August 1933, page 1. Sun

(Sydney, NSW : 1910 - 1954), Monday 14 August 1933, page 9. - Marjorie Cummins.

Source: Sun (Sydney, NSW : 1910 - 1954), Tuesday 8 August 1933, page 9. – 'Let me go' - Attempt

Source: Labor Daily (Sydney, NSW : 1924 - 1938), Friday 11 August 1933, page 1 – Arthur Grayson

Sources: Daily Telegraph (Sydney, NSW : 1931 - 1954), Thursday 31 August 1933, page 9. Sun (Sydney, NSW : 1910 - 1954), Wednesday 30 August 1933, page 11 (1,2) – Unknown man's description

Sources: Sun (Sydney, NSW : 1910 - 1954), Wednesday 30 August 1933, page 11. – 'She sank like a stone'. Goulburn Evening Penny Post (NSW : 1881 - 1940), Thursday 31 August 1933, page 5. – Jessie Daly

Source: Sun (Sydney, NSW : 1910 - 1954), Tuesday 19 September 1933, page 15 – Fred Brady

Source: Sun (Sydney, NSW : 1910 - 1954), Wednesday 30 August 1933, page 11 (1,2) – Suicide roll greater – four men

CHAPTER 17 - WIDOWS OVER THE BRIDGE

Source: Truth (Sydney, NSW : 1894 - 1954), Sunday 8 October 1933, page 1 – Truth – Opening Quote

Source: Truth (Sydney, NSW : 1894 - 1954), Sunday 8 October 1933, page 1 – Truth - uncanny, sinister, menacing spell.

Source: Labor Daily (Sydney, NSW : 1924 - 1938), Wednesday 13 September 1933, page 8 – Widows over the Bridge

Source: Weekly Times (Melbourne, Vic. : 1869 - 1954), Saturday 9 September 1933, page 7- Millicent Dymock, Walter Kinross

Source: Evening News (Rockhampton, Qld. : 1924 - 1941), Friday 8 September 1933, page – Smothered infant

Sources: Daily Telegraph (Sydney, NSW : 1931 - 1954), Friday 8 September 1933, page 9. Braidwood Dispatch and Mining Journal (NSW : 1888 - 1954), Friday 8 September 1933, page 2. - Susan Davis

Source: Labor Daily (Sydney, NSW : 1924 - 1938), Tuesday 26 September 1933, page 6. – Arthur Madden

248 | CHAPTER NOTES

Source: Daily Telegraph (Sydney, NSW : 1931 - 1954), Monday 11 September 1933, page 1 – Allan Ashwin Scott

Source: Northern Star (Lismore, NSW : 1876 - 1954), Thursday 7 September 1933, page 5 – Premier Stevens considering proposal

Source: Australian Women's Weekly (1933 - 1982), Saturday 9 September 1933, page 10 – Editorial - count our blessings

Source: Wagga Wagga Express (NSW : 1930 - 1939), Saturday 16 September 1933, page 13 – Coroner Farrington's displeasure

Newcastle Sun (NSW : 1918 - 1954), Tuesday 12 September 1933, page 7 – Police Commissioner

Daily Telegraph (Sydney, NSW : 1931 - 1954), Wednesday 13 September 1933, page 8. – The Editor of the Daily Telegraph

Source: Truth (Sydney, NSW : 1894 - 1954), Sunday 8 October 1933, page 1 – John Fraser Cocks

Source: Sydney Morning Herald (NSW : 1842 - 1954), Wednesday 11 October 1933, page 16. Singleton Argus (NSW : 1880 - 1954), Friday 20 October 1933, page 3. Labor Daily (Sydney, NSW : 1924 - 1938), Thursday 19 October 1933, page 7. - Desmond Cleary

Sources: Albury Banner and Wodonga Express (NSW : 1896 - 1938), Friday 3 November 1933, page 18. Labor Daily (Sydney, NSW : 1924 - 1938), Tuesday 7 November 1933, page 6. Singleton Argus (NSW : 1880 - 1954), Wednesday 25 October 1933, page 2. – Lucina Moye

CHAPTER 18 - UNREQUITED LOVE

Source: Sun (Sydney, NSW : 1910 - 1954), Monday 30 May 1921, page 5 – Opening Quote

Sources: Labor Daily (Sydney, NSW : 1924 - 1938), Wednesday 15 November 1933, page 8. – Reference - Ashley Ekins, Head, Military History Section - Australian War Memorial – Jessie Stunt

Source: Maitland Daily Mercury (NSW : 1894 - 1939), Wednesday 8 November 1933, page 1. – Madge Hope, Hurtling like a great stone

Source: Wellington Times (NSW : 1899 - 1954), Thursday 9 November 1933, page 1- Late night attempt.

Sources: Maitland Daily Mercury (NSW : 1894 - 1939), Wednesday 8 November 1933, page 1. Truth (Sydney, NSW : 1894 - 1954), Sunday 12 November 1933, page 1 – Francis Madge Hope

Sources: Muswellbrook Chronicle (NSW : 1898 - 1955), Tuesday 14 November 1933, page 5. Evening News (Rockhampton, Qld. : 1924 - 1941), Friday 17 November 1933, page 7 – Gwendoline Cummins

Source: Canberra Times (ACT : 1926 - 1995), Monday 20 November 1933, page 2 – Gwen Cummins

Source: Sun (Sydney, NSW : 1910 - 1954), Tuesday 28 November 1933, page 13 – doped wine

Source: Truth (Sydney, NSW: 1894-1954) Sunday 3 December 1933, page 13 – Gwen's Letter

Sources: Dr. Elise P. Garrison, e-garrison@tamu.edu. Texas A&M University. www.stoa.org/diotima/essays/garrison_catalogue.shtml - contemporary philosophy on unrequited love.

Sources: Truth (Sydney, NSW : 1894 - 1954), Sunday 5 June 1921, page 12. Truth (Sydney, NSW : 1894 - 1954), Sunday 19 November 1933, page 16 – Charles Payne

Source: The Labor Daily, Sydney Tue 21 Nov 1933 – Sgt Bebb -visibly affected

Sources: Australian Worker (Sydney, NSW : 1913 - 1950), Wednesday 6 December 1933, page 14. Newcastle Sun (NSW : 1918 - 1954), Tuesday 21 November 1933, page 8 – Dr Homer on Branford Angell

CHAPTER 19 - BARRIER TO SUICIDE

Source: Daily Telegraph (Sydney, NSW : 1931 - 1954), Friday 24 November 1933, page 10 – Opening Quote

Source: Daily Telegraph (Sydney, NSW : 1931 - 1954), Wednesday 22 November 1933, page 1 (2) – North Sydney Council – Mayor Hodgson

Source: Sydney Morning Herald (NSW : 1842 - 1954), Monday 27 November 1933, page 9 - Commissioner for Main Roads

Source: Daily Telegraph (Sydney, NSW : 1931 - 1954), Thursday 23 November 1933, page 9 – Reported attempts

Source: Sydney Morning Herald (NSW : 1842 - 1954), Wednesday 6 December 1933, page 9 – Richard Oliver Hickey

Source: Daily Telegraph (Sydney, NSW : 1931 - 1954), Friday 24 November 1933, page 10 – Mr Stevens – Speed up construction

Sources: Warwick Daily News (Qld. : 1919 -1954), Monday 18 December 1933, page 5. Examiner (Launceston, Tas. : 1900 - 1954), Monday 18 December 1933, page 5 – Sarah Semlitzky

CHAPTER 20 - WILD RUSH

Source: South Coast Times and Wollongong Argus (NSW : 1900 - 1954), Friday 12 January 1934, page 4 – Opening Quote

Source: Labor Daily (Sydney, NSW : 1924 - 1938), Monday 23 July 1934, page 4 - Petit Journal

Source: Henty Observer and Culcairn Shire Register (NSW : 1914 - 1950), Friday 2 February 1934, page 4. -Wild Rush

Source: Daily Standard (Brisbane, Qld. : 1912 - 1936), Monday 1 January 1934, page 5 -'A tough nut to crack'

Source: Sun (Sydney, NSW : 1910 - 1954), Wednesday 3 January 1934, page 11 – Charles Gallagher Singing Soldier

Source: Sun (Sydney, NSW : 1910 - 1954), Wednesday 3 January 1934, page 11 – Singing Soldier

Source: Sun (Sydney, NSW : 1910 - 1954), Sunday 28 January 1934, page 1. – Charles Gallagher

Source: Labor Daily (Sydney, NSW : 1924 - 1938), Friday 26 January 1934, page . Charles Gallagher

Source: Sun (Sydney, NSW : 1910 - 1954), Sunday 28 January 1934, page 1- Gallagher the horrors of the Harbour Bridge rail.

Source: Australian Town and Country Journal (Sydney, NSW : 1870 - 1919), Saturday 28 January 1899, page 37 – People's Palace – Bootman

Source: Evening News (Rockhampton, Qld. : 1924 - 1941), Saturday 6 January 1934, page 5 – Miss Watson and Miss Leonarder

Source: Sun (Sydney, NSW : 1910 - 1954), Wednesday 3 January 1934, page 14 – Bruxner-Fencing

Source: Daily Telegraph (Sydney, NSW : 1931 - 1954), Friday 5 January 1934, page 1 – Wrestler Frank Graham

Source: Labor Daily (Sydney, NSW : 1924 - 1938), Tuesday 23 January 1934, page 8 – Sidney Stephenson Inquest

Source: News (Adelaide, SA : 1923 - 1954), Friday 5 January 1934, page 3 – Start to Fencing

Source: Newcastle Sun (NSW : 1918 - 1954), Friday 5 January 1934, page 1 – Fencing suicide prediction

Source: Barrier Miner (Broken Hill, NSW : 1888 - 1954), Tuesday 9 January 1934, page 1

Source: South Coast Times and Wollongong Argus (NSW : 1900 - 1954), Friday 12 January 1934, page 4 – suicide season full swing

CHAPTER 21 - A LIFE WELL LIVED

Sources: Sun (Sydney, NSW : 1910 - 1954), Friday 12 January 1934. - Opening Quote

Source: Voice (Hobart, Tas. : 1931 - 1953), Saturday 1 July 1933, page 8 – Outcast Orater, Kempster cowardly death.

Source: Queensland Times (Ipswich, Qld. : 1909 - 1954), Monday 13 March 1933, page 7 – Bravery suicide

Sources: Truth (Sydney, NSW : 1894 - 1954), Sunday 28 January 1934, page 19. Herald (Melbourne, Vic. : 1861 - 1954), Tuesday 23 January 1934, page 5 – Mary Coasby

Source: Goulburn Evening Penny Post (NSW : 1881 - 1940), Friday 12 January 1934, page 3 – Constable Arthur Costello

Sources: Sun (Sydney, NSW : 1910 - 1954), Friday 12 January 1934. Source: Sun (Sydney, NSW : 1910 - 1954), Saturday 13 January 1934. Sun (Sydney, NSW : 1910 - 1954), Friday 19 January 1934 – Jeremiah Sullivan

Source: Newcastle Sun (NSW : 1918 - 1954), Thursday 18 January 1934, page 1 – John McGrath

Source: Daily Telegraph (Sydney, NSW : 1931 - 1954), Saturday 10 March 1934, page 6. – Dr Scott Reid - Schopenhauer

CHAPTER 22 - BEATING THE NET

Source: Daily Telegraph (Sydney, NSW : 1931 - 1954), Monday 22 January 1934, page 1. – Opening Quote

Source: Herald (Melbourne, Vic. : 1861 - 1954), Tuesday 30 January 1934, page 8. – appointment with death

Source: Sun (Sydney, NSW : 1910 - 1954), Monday 15 January 1934, page 7. – John Caves, Beating the Net

Source: Labor Daily (Sydney, NSW : 1924 - 1938), Tuesday 16 January 1934, page 1. – John Caves – Thus Brothers

Source: Daily Telegraph (Sydney, NSW : 1931 - 1954), Monday 22 January 1934, page 1. – Ethel Francis, patrolman evaded

Source: Herald (Melbourne, Vic. : 1861 - 1954), Tuesday 30 January 1934, page 8. – Dr A H Martin

Sources: Sun (Sydney, NSW : 1910 - 1954), Thursday 25 January 1934, page 11- Joseph Baxter Bryson. Courier-Mail (Brisbane, Qld. : 1933 - 1954), Friday 26 January 1934, page 5. Labor Daily (Sydney, NSW : 1924 - 1938), Friday 26 January 1934, page 1 (2). - William Sibbons

Source: Newcastle Sun (NSW : 1918 - 1954), Saturday 27 January 1934, page 2. - Joseph Baxter Bryson.

Source: Newcastle Sun (NSW : 1918 - 1954), Saturday 27 January 1934, page 2. – Bryson/Jack Holland – lottery ticket

Source: Coroners report 1934 – Joseph 'John' Baxter Bryson

Sources: Sydney Morning Herald (NSW : 1842 - 1954), Thursday 1 February 1934, page 11. Canberra Times (ACT : 1926 - 1995), Thursday 1 February 1934, page 3. Mulville – squabble - 16-year-old girl.

Source: Daily Telegraph (Sydney, NSW : 1931 - 1954), Wednesday 7 February 1934, page 7. – woman three attempts

Source: Herald (Melbourne, Vic. : 1861 - 1954), Tuesday 30 January 1934, page 8. – Sinister Arch

CHAPTER 23 - CLOSED FOR BUSINESS

Source: Pinnaroo and Border Times (SA : 1911 - 1954), Friday 2 March 1934, page 2 – Opening Quote

Source: Tweed Daily (Murwillumbah, NSW : 1914 - 1949), Wednesday 21 February 1934, page 3. - fence completion date.

Source: Northern Times (Carnarvon, WA : 1905 - 1954), Wednesday 28 February 1934, page 3. - symmetrical lines.

Sources: Newcastle Morning Herald and Miners' Advocate (NSW : 1876 - 1954), Wednesday 18 April 1934, page 8. Labor Daily (Sydney, NSW : 1924 - 1938), Wednesday 18 April 1934, page 5. – Poison scones - Lina Craig

Source: Coffs Harbour Advocate (NSW : 1907 - 1942; 1946 - 1954), Friday 8 November 1935, page 3 – Live Wire – Archer Whitford

Source: Pinnaroo and Border Times (SA : 1911 - 1954), Friday 2 March 1934, page 2.-Archer Whitford quote

Source: Herald (Melbourne, Vic. : 1861 - 1954), Friday 23 March 1934, page 12. Archer Whitford post office

Source: Labor Daily (Sydney, NSW : 1924 - 1938), Tuesday 12 June 1934, page 7. – Thomas Peers

Source: - Albany Advertiser (WA : 1897 - 1950), Monday 25 June 1934, page 2. The Tramp.

Source: Sunday Times (Sydney, NSW : 1895 - 1930), Sunday 19 November 1922, page 13 – Francis Greenway quote

CHAPTER 24 – A NEW LIFE

Source: 'Australia Through Time' - published by Random House – Opening Quote

Sources: Labor Daily (Sydney, NSW : 1924 - 1938), Monday 23 July 1934, page 4 – Change and Hope. Voice (Hobart, Tas. : 1931 - 1953), Saturday 1 September 1934, page 3 – Montaigne quote

Source: St George Call (Kogarah, NSW : 1904 - 1957), Friday 26 October 1934, page 2 – Charles Bebb

Source: https://www.parliament.nsw.gov.au/members/Pages/member-details.aspx?pk=1371 – Michael Bruxner career biography

Source: Inverell Times (NSW : 1899 - 1954), Monday 24 March 1952, page 1- 1000 bridges and dustless roads – Michael Bruxner

Source: The Australian Bar Gazette 1964 Obituaries page 23. - Obituary Ald David Hunter

REFERENCES

REFERENCES

National Library of Australia

State Library of New South Wales

Sydney Living Museums

Australian National University – Australian Dictionary of Biography

'Australia's Yesterdays' - published by Reader's Digest Services P/L. Cyril Pearl Text

'Australia Through Time' - published by Random House

Australian Government Department of Health - www.healthdirect.gov.au

'Shattered Anzacs' – Author, Marina Larsson

'Australian Battlers Remember' – Author, Keith Smith

Bi-monthly magazine of the presbyterian church in the state of New South Wales and the Australian Capital Territory - https://pcnsw.org.au

Ancestry.com

Australian War Memorial

New South Wales, Australia, Registers of Coroners' Inquests, 1796-1942

National Archives of Australia

Births Death Marriages NSW

State Records of NSW

Victorian State Archives

www.ingramcontent.com/pod-product-compliance
Lightning Source LLC
Chambersburg PA
CBHW050307010526
44107CB00055B/2133